Wales at War

*Critical Essays on
Literature and Art*

Wales at War

Critical Essays on Literature and Art

Edited by Tony Curtis

seren

Seren is the book imprint of
Poetry Wales Press Ltd,
57 Nolton Street, Bridgend,
CF31 1AE, Wales
www.seren-books.com

A CIP record for this title is available
from the British Library CIP Office

ISBN 978-1-85411-460-0

*The publisher acknowledges the financial support of the
Arts Council of Wales*

Cover painting Augustus John: *Fraternity*, (1917, oil on
canvas, 237.5 x 114.7 cm, Imperial War Museum, London)

Printed in Plantin by Creative Print & Design Ltd, Wales

Contents

List of Illustrations

'Entry of the Welsh Troops into Jerusalem' – Frank Brangwyn

'Engineers' – Goscombe John

'Man with Morphine' – John Petts

'Ruby Loftus Screwing a Breech Nut' – Laura Knight

Illustration Acknowledgements

Thanks are due to the Imperial War Museum. for permission to reproduce the painting by Laura Knight and the cover image by August John; the National Museum and Gallery of Wales for permission to reproduce the painting by Frank Brangwyn; Anna Petts for permisison to reproduce the etching by John Petts. Eric Rowan kindly supllied the reproduction of the statuary by Goscombe John.

Introduction

Tony Curtis

This is the companion volume to *After the First Death: An Anthology of Wales and War in the Twentieth Century*. Many of the works of fiction, prose extracts and poems included in that anthology are referred to in the present book. Each volume supports the other. Indeed, some of the editorial decisions determining the contents of the anthology were informed by academic colleagues' work in the field. For example, I was persuaded by Jeremy Hooker's work to include poems by Wilfred Owen; Owen was the outstanding poet of the Great War and perhaps the greatest poet of any war. He recognised his Welsh ancestry, as did the London Welshman Edward Thomas. Robert Graves and Siegfried Sassoon are included as they were commissioned in Welsh regiments and Professor Hooker talks of the "self-protective" strategies in Graves' writing, in contrast to the "extreme vulnerability of Owen's pity". Other colleagues made the case for the inclusion of writers and works, but the final selection of the anthology and the constitution of this collection of essays is solely my responsibility.

The two world wars challenged, broke and shaped political borders, traditions, societies, individuals and their beliefs more profoundly than the wars of previous centuries. While few of us now living have had direct experience of war, in uniform or as civilians, it is likely that the wars our families fought or suffered in, and more recently the fear of nuclear war or terrorism, will have been a signif-icant factor in our lives.

Professor M. Wynn Thomas argues persuasively that R.S. Thomas may be only fully appreciated when his experiences of German bombing – "the lurid nightscape of burning Merseyside" – visible in Manafon, are taken into account. Of course R.S. Thomas, like Dylan, grew up in a country traumatised by the Great War; conflict haunts his writing from *The Stones of the Field* to *The Echoes Return Slow*.

Eric Rowan describes the work of artists such as Augustus and

Gwen John, Goscombe John, Christopher Williams and Frank Brangwyn in the context of that first conflict. Caught between the impulse for public commemoration and the need to reflect continuing personal visions *entre deux guerres*, each of these artists was shaken and challenged by the German threat to Belgium and France.

In my own chapter on art in Wales in the Second World War I draw attention to the common concerns of Dylan Thomas and Ceri Richards and to the astonishing 1950s work of R.S. Thomas' wife Mildred Eldridge. The nuclear threats to which both Eldridge and R.S. Thomas reacted with deep alarm and protest were also informing the later writing of Dylan Thomas, as James A. Davies shows in his essay. Dylan's proposed collaboration with Stravinsky, just before his last, fateful trip to America, was to have been "about the discovery of our planet following an atomic misadventure". Indeed, the original concept for *Under Milk Wood* had the village of Llareggyb excluded from the outside world by a barbed wire fence and sentries.

War has shaped Wales more than any other force through the last century and each of us will at some point in our lives acknowledge that. Wales had enlisted men for the Crimea and the Boer War, but in 1914 Wales, in common with the rest of Britain, was caught up in a wave of patriotic fervour: as many men served in that conflict as worked in the essential mining industry which fuelled the fleet and the factories. From the Somme, at Mametz Wood and through Paschendale, up to the armistice in November, 1918, Welsh regiments and divisions served widely and suffered greatly on the Western Front. It is surely part of most of our families' histories. My Pembrokeshire grandmother's cousin, James Charles Thomas had been a member of the Pembrokeshire Yeomanry and served in the Middle East before being transferred to the Machine Gun Corps on the Western Front; he was killed in the German counter-offensive at Cambrai in December 1917. His body was not recovered until the following January. Some corner of the village of Caudry is forever Tallyhoo Farm, Llangwm.

The Luftwaffe overflew Llangwm and the Haven in 1940 to bomb the huge petrol tanks at Pembroke Dock to produce what was then the largest fire this country had ever seen. In the Second World War Wales, particularly the south Wales docks, was heavily bombed by the Luftwaffe. When Dylan Thomas made his 'Return Journey' to Swansea he found ghosts and insecure memories in the rubble. In 1942 my mother came back to the land of her father and generations of Williams to serve as a Land Army girl; there she met my father who had served on coastal defences around Milford Haven. I memorialised that in a poem 'Land Army Photographs', which conflates events and coincidences to make its point. Now, after further questioning, I know that they met at the end of the war and could never have both looked up, she at her flax gathering and he at the gun emplacement, and seen "the white belly of that flying boat / cut into the Haven". Writing about war, as writing about most things, will be subject to the vagaries of memory and the indulgences of the imagination.

Dannie Abse grew up in the shadow of the rise of fascism and survived the war. As a Jew he became acutely aware of the fate from which he'd been saved: "I often think of not going to Belsen". As a doctor his practice underlined the dilemmas of the humane imperative: "When I palpitated his liver / I felt the soft liver of Goering; / when I lifted my stethoscope / I heard the heartbeats of Himmler". In my chapter on this outstanding writer I attempt to trace the centrality of war in his long and expansive writing career. "Will there always be / a jackboot on the stair / a refugee to roam?"

Arguably the greatest book written about war in the twentieth century is David Jones' *In Parenthesis*. What the London Welshman experienced in the "heavy Picardy mud" would essentially inform his spiritual life and his life as a poet and artist. Duncan Campbell shows this remarkable man to be a "sole inhabitant of a tract of country where matter marches with spirit"; but Campbell does not shirk from confronting Jones' confused and disturbing writings during the Second World War, nor the claim that his work is in danger of sinking beneath its own weight of reference.

In the wars of the century the greatest loss to the literature of Wales were the deaths on active service of Edward Thomas, Wilfred Owen and Alun Lewis. Cary Archard shows how the young officer Lewis reluctantly carried into war a sensibility which would eventually prove his undoing: "violence as a perversion of the natural order of things". Alun Lewis had read the poets of the Great War and felt a particular empathy with Edward Thomas. Thomas had died in shell-fire in 1917 in the Arras sector. Alun Lewis' early death in Burma was a tragedy of a different order.

Until recently I believed that the only casualty from my family of the Second World War was my mother's cousin David White from Vancouver whose mother Leah Williams had emigrated to Canada from Bangor at the turn of the century; he is buried beneath Monte Cassino where he died on 23rd May, 1944. He was a Lance Sergeant in the Seaforth Highlanders of Canada. But last year I learnt that two women related by marriage to my Williams family in Bangor were victims of German bombs jettisoned over the Bethesda area on a raid on Liverpool in 1941: Ellen Davies and Nancy Pritchard are listed on the Bethesda war memorial underneath the names of the soldiers. They died as a consequence of those "lurid nightscapes" of which R.S. Thomas wrote. The experiences of women in war are foregrounded in significant writing from Wales, as Dr Katie Gramich outlines in her chapter. From the ninth century poems *Canu Heledd*, through to Lynette Roberts, Joyce Herbert, Menna Elfyn and Gillian Clarke, women poets from Wales have responded to the war experiences that have affected them on the Home Front. Kate Roberts, Hilda Vaughan and Siân James are among the novelists who explore the ways in which men's military service impacts upon the lives of women.

At the core of Lily Tobias' 1933 novel *Eunice Fleet* is the fate of a First World War Conscientious Objector. Eunice's husband Vincent is jailed and because he believes that "To me 'alternative service' seems a kind of industrial conscription"; he is persecuted to the point of death. Tobias' fiction and her activism as a pacifist run parallel to the boyhood years of her nephew Dannie Abse. The strength of pacifist feelings, the determination of many artists and writers to hold to their position as COs, is sketched in my Appendix. John Elwyn, Waldo Williams, Gwenallt, Glyn Jones, Emyr Humphreys, Arthur Giardelli and others deserve particular mention and my footnotes indicate further important work in both languages relating to pacifism and civil disobedience in the struggle for the survival of Wales' national identity in the twentieth century.

The two world wars and subsequent conflicts shaped us whether or not we know about or remember our losses. The town where I live, Barry, has just renovated its King's Square; there in 1917 the first American 'Dough Boys' lined up before going off to the Western Front; across from my house was the camp of the Lancashire Fusiliers. The inhabitants of Lydstep and Manorbier are currently protesting against the MOD's night firing of missiles from Skrinkle Point: they need to practice. The artist Arthur Giardelli, who came to Merthyr in the war as a CO, lives on the edge of the Castlemartin artillery range. NATO tanks pound that Pembrokeshire peninsula from the other side of his thorn hedge. 'The Men from Hereford' and others tramp at night over Pen-y-Fan; Ghurkhas and their families live as neighbours to Chris Meredith in Brecon. RAF Tornadoes scream over Snowdonia and Powys on low level practice sorties. In the Vale of Glamorgan we are to host the largest MOD centre in the UK. My wife taught Anthony

Keeble, a young Welsh Guards soldier from Cowbridge killed in 1982 in the Falklands on the *Sir Galahad*. Our local papers profile the personnel and casualties in Iraq and Afghanistan. But most of us have lived through decades of peace: wars happen to other people in other places. This book, together with its companion volume, *After the First Death*, serves to remind us that the wars still come back to Wales and affect us all.

Tony Curtis

Haunted Landscapes: War in the Writings of Llewelyn Wyn Griffith, Robert Graves, Wilfred Owen and Edward Thomas

Jeremy Hooker

Not all of the writers discussed in this chapter were Welsh, but all had associations with Wales that affected their experience of the First World War and influenced their writing. Llewelyn Wyn Griffith came from a Welsh-speaking family in north Wales, and served as a captain with the Royal Welch Fusiliers. Robert Graves, a captain in the same regiment, was of mixed Anglo-Irish and German parentage, but was strongly attached to the landscape of north Wales, and had 'Celtic' interests that helped to shape his poetry. Edward Thomas was Welsh on both sides of his family, but was born in Lambeth and lived in the south of England. The landscape of his poetry, however, was strongly influenced by his sense of exile from Wales and his knowledge of Welsh myths and legends. Wilfred Owen was born in Oswestry, a border location which, together with his father's stories about his possible descent from Baron Lewis Owen, a Tudor Sheriff of Merionethshire, helped to make him sensitive to Welsh poetic tradition. An idea can be as potent as an ascertainable fact of ancestry, as we see in Owen in battle "remembering my own duty, and remembering also my forefathers the agile Welshmen of the mountains".[1] In the case of each writer, Wales was an imaginative idea that combined with other factors to shape a particular response to the war.

Griffith and Graves both wrote poetry in response to their experience of the war, but their principal contributions to war literature were prose memoirs. Another difference between their work and that of the poets, Edward Thomas and Wilfred Owen, is that the memoirs were written some years after the end of the war, which Thomas and Owen did not survive. Robert Graves' *Goodbye to All That* was published in 1929, Wyn Griffith's *Up to Mametz* in 1931.

As far as the war is concerned, Griffith and Graves deal with some of the same events. Their accounts of them, however, differ substantially. Graves' book is an autobiography which begins with his birth and effectively ends in 1926; it is his "bitter leave-taking of England",[2] and is very much about Robert Graves, taking liberties with facts in ways that offended his friends Siegfried Sassoon and Edmund Blunden and other fellow soldiers. Griffith's book begins with embarkation for France in December 1915 and concludes with the attack on Mametz Wood in July 1916. Greg Hill fairly remarks that if Griffith's account of the attack "lacks the urbane irreverence of Robert Graves' account in *Goodbye to All That*, it makes up for this with a committed idealism which is determined to give an accurate picture of what happened".[3]

Up to Mametz is closer in spirit to David Jones' *In Parenthesis* (on which it had some influence) than to *Goodbye to All That*. It describes "an initiation into the great mystery of the trench world",[4] and reflects on the discontinuity between the war landscape "unmade" by man and the buildings made by "many generations of peasants".[5] Colin Hughes speaks of Griffith's "understanding of the tragedy of war".[6] This understanding is due not only to his knowledge of "our crucifixion of youth",[7] which included that of his younger brother, whom Griffith sent on the mission that led to his death. It owes something important also to the contrast he draws between life in a long-settled Welsh rural society and "this mad cruelty". Thus, having described a scene of horrible mutilations in Mametz Wood, he continues:

> A message was now on its way to some quiet village in Wales, to a grey farmhouse on the slope of a hill running down to Cardigan Bay, or to a miner's cottage in a South Wales valley, a word of death, incapable, in this late century of the Christian Era, of association with this manner of killing. That the sun could shine on this mad cruelty and on the quiet peace of an upland tarn near Snowdon, at what we call the same instant of Time, threw a doubt upon all meaning in words.[8]

Such doubt could stimulate the renewal of poetry to fit the war experience, as it did in Wilfred Owen. In Griffith's case, it produced a fine prose memoir, but not major poetry. The curious thing about Griffith's poetry about the war, collected in *The Barren Tree*, is that it fails to be fully articulate. The strength of feeling is obvious, feeling above all for "this company of ghosts about my heart",[9] and for the lost joy and gladness of youth, but the language, though occasionally gesturing towards modernist harshness, tends to a vague poeticism, as in this passage from 'The Song is Theirs':

> This servitude of mud
> this sly recumbency beneath a threat
> lurking in rat-disputed dyke,
> this endless struggle with a mastery
> of seeping water, husbandry of filth
> and rank decay, this toil to build a grave
> where once the plough made furrow. ...
> Gave I my freedom thus to spend?[10]

It is as if Griffith wants to abstract the meaning from the experience without once more looking closely at the facts, as he has in his prose.

Griffith's scrupulous concern for accuracy in his illumination of the trench experience contrasts with what Paul Fussell has well described as the 'staginess' of *Goodbye to All That*.[11] This is a conscious feature of Graves' style, as he shows in remarking on his 'caricature scenes', of which the following is an example:

> Myself in faultless khaki with highly polished buttons and belt, revolver at hip, whistle on cord, delicate moustache on upper lip, and stern endeavour a-glint in either eye, pretending to be a Regular Army captain; but crushed into that inky desk-bench like an over-grown school-boy.[12]

His fellow soldiers' indignation with Graves for taking liberties with the facts of their shared experiences is understandable. We should reflect, however, that Graves went from school to the war, and was reported 'died of wounds' in 1916, and suffered from neurasthenia for some years after the war. We should consider also that *Goodbye to All That*, as his autobiography, is a story to tell as he chooses, and a book that expresses the defiance that enabled him to survive the war, as well as his literary persona generally. It is not a book that one reads for its factual accuracy, as one does *Up to Mametz*, but rather for the vivid expression of the author's combative personality. What it gives us is not the war, but Robert Graves' war, rendered with the aid of satire and caricature, and some poetic licence.

Graves' advice to Wilfred Owen to "cheer up and write more optimistically ... a poet should have a spirit above wars"[13] suggests the reason why his own war poems are relatively weak, as he later recognised by omitting all of them from his *Collected Poems* in 1938. As John A. Johnston says, Graves in his war poems "usually fails to communicate any deep sense of involvement or spiritual stress".[14] It would be wrong, though, to assume that Graves did not feel these things. His poems reveal experiences similar to those described in the poetry of Sassoon and Owen. 'Not Dead' is a poignant elegy for his friend David Thomas. 'Two Fusiliers' is a succinct expression of sentiments reminiscent of Owen's in 'Apologia Pro Poemata Meo', which probably alludes to it:

> Show me the two so closely bound
> As we, by the wet bond of blood,
> By friendship blossoming from mud,
> By Death: we faced him, and we found
> Beauty in Death,
> In dead men, breath.[15]

'A Dead Boche', with its graphic description of the corpse ("clothes and face a sodden green, / Big-bellied, spectacled, crop-haired, / Dribbling black blood from nose and beard"),[16] prefigures the realism of Sassoon's trench poems.

But what Graves' war poems reveal also is a resolute "spirit above wars", which generally takes the form of a refusal to dwell on horror, as Sassoon does, and protects him from the extreme vulnerability of Owen's pity and "The eternal reciprocity of tears".[17] As in *Goodbye to All That*, Graves' strategies in his war poems are, indeed, self-protective. In 'Escape', for example, written in response to his experience of being reported 'died of wounds', he makes a seemingly light-hearted use of mythology:

> 'Life! Life! I can't be dead! I won't be dead!
> Damned if I'll die for anyone!' I said ...
> Cerberus stands and grins above me now,
> Wearing three heads – lion, and lynx, and sow.[18]

His playfulness is a form of defiance, and his formal variety and control and use of mythology afford detachment from the extreme experiences that are his subject. "Fear never dies, much as we laugh at fear / For pride's sake and for other cowards' sakes", he says in 'Trench Life',[19] acknowledging fear, and saving face with laughter. His pride is personal, but it is a military virtue, too, as we see in his pride in Royal Welch battle-honours. Writing of *Goodbye to All That*, Bernard Bergonzi says: "the attitudes that governed his literary persona and which were expressed in his stylistic devices were undoubtedly part of a technique for psychological survival."[20] This is equally true of Graves' war poetry, in which he takes the advice he gives in 'Hate Not, Fear Not':

> Fever and fear distract the world,
>   But calm be you though madmen shout,
> Through blazing fires of battle hurled,
>   Hate not, strike, fear not, stare Death out![21]

Having a "spirit above wars" was undoubtedly helped by his ability to escape, when on leave and in his poetry, into the landscape of north Wales, in which, he says in *Goodbye to All That*, he found, from boyhood, "a personal peace independent of history or geography".[22] He looks back to climbing in the Welsh mountains, which helped him to overcome a fear of heights: "winning confidence in those quiet days / Of peace, poised sickly on the precipice side / Of Lliwedd crag by Snowdon."[23] In 'Familiar Letter to Siegfried Sassoon' he looks forward: "Well, when it's over, first we'll meet / At Gweithdy Bach, my country seat / In Wales". This is a place with "[t]he sort of view that makes you shout / For want of any better way / Of praising God".[24] Graves counters war experience with his longing for a world outside the war, which he frequently associates with a poet's life among the Welsh mountains. In his wartime verse he was associated with the Georgians, and it is fair to say that at this time he showed only hints of the poet he was to become. The hints may be detected in his formal control and in his use of myth. He was haunted by the war; "old friends of mine", he abjures in the poem called 'Haunted', "lay ghost hands on everything". "But," he continues, "leave the noonday's warm sunshine / To living lads for mirth and wine".[25] His use of myth and biblical story, as in 'Goliath and David', is rather to control emotion than to express the 'uncanny' experience of war,[26] as Owen does in the underworld vision of 'Strange Meeting'. Graves' detached, ironic persona, which was a strategy for psychological survival, prevented the poems themselves from being haunting. When he came later to his belief in "the supernatural power in poetry: a poem being the magic circle in which poets by their savage dealings with familiar things enclose a living power",[27] he drew upon Irish and Welsh poetic tradition. As a very young man, however, he could not afford to deal savagely with the familiar things of war.

The case was quite different with Wilfred Owen, who was in some ways no less a Georgian than Graves. Towards the end of 1917, Owen wrote to his mother: "I am held peer by the Georgians; I am a poet's poet."[28] It is worth remembering these words when thinking of the famous draft preface he wrote to a book of war poems, which he did not live to see:

> This book is not about heroes. English poetry is not yet fit to speak of them.
>
> Nor is it about deeds, or lands, nor anything about glory, honour, might, majesty, dominion, or power, except War.
>
> Above all I am not concerned with Poetry.
>
> My subject is War, and the pity of War.
>
> The Poetry is in the Pity.
>
> Yet these elegies are to this generation in no sense consolatory. They may be to the next. All a poet can do today is warn. That is why the true Poets must be truthful.[29]

'Poetry' with a capital P may designate what he dismisses in 'Insensibility' as "poets' tearful fooling",[30] a kind of versifying not fit to speak about war, but Owen was one who had been serious about poetry since boyhood, when he discovered Wordsworth. His later feeling for Keats can only be described as hero-worship and love. It was his adaptation of the Romantic heritage to the reality of war experience that made him the iconic British poet of the First World War.

Owen's early poem 'Uriconium: An Ode' reflects his fascination with the archaeological site of the Roman city at Wroxeter, which he knew to be associated with the great Welsh elegy 'Eryr Pengwern'. Had he lived, he might have given the title 'English Elegies' to his war poems. Dominic Hibberd, however, sees 'Uriconium' as a foreshadowing of his war poems: "The Welsh tradition in poetry was musical and elegiac, as much of Wilfred's poetry was to be. He would write as a prophet, conscious of his Celtic blood, warning the earth of wider ways unknown, a task that might well involve uncovering the secrets of the underworld."[31]

Of Uriconium the young poet wrote: "cities such as these one time would breed / Apocalyptic visions of world-wrecks."[32] In 1916, three years after writing the poem, Second-Lieutenant Owen of the Manchesters would be in the midst of a "world-wreck". There, he did not seek a spirit above the war, or not in the same way, the way of detachment, Graves chose. Owen exposed himself fully to the experience of war, for the sake of his men, and in a humanistic form of the evangelical spirit he had inherited from his mother. His stance as a prophetic poet depended equally upon full participation in the tragedy. His meeting with Sassoon at Craiglockhart War Hospital in August 1917 inspired him to write angrily and realistically about the war. But the poems influenced by Sassoon are a relatively small part of his achievement. In his most powerful war poems Owen does not cease to be a participant, but he simultaneously establishes a cosmic perspective and conducts a profound questioning of the meaning of human life in the context of the war's violent affront to nature and humanity. Drawing upon the Welsh elegiac tradition and upon his biblical inheritance, he writes also in the realist spirit of English Romantic poetry – the spirit of suffering and healing – and in effect modernises it. His sensuousness is Keatsian, but so also is his capacity to face terrible realities, though in the context of modern mechanised warfare.

Owen's sensuousness, moreover, is that of a love poet, as we see in both the erotic imagery of a poem such as 'Greater Love' and the poignant tenderness of 'Futility':

> Move him into the sun –
> Gently its touch awoke him once ...
>
> Are limbs, so dear achieved, are sides
> Full-nerved, still warm, too hard to stir?
> Was it for this the clay grew tall?[33]

It is the gentleness of the poet's touch combined with the imagery of biblical and cosmic creation, called into question by the young man's death, that makes this one of the most moving lyrical poems of the First World War. With his sensuous and compassionate appreciation of male youth and male beauty, Owen the war poet is a major love poet in all but name. Guilt and religious feeling, too, are equally elements that go to the making of his poetry. The evangelical Christianity of his youth reappears in the war poems and letters, but in a ferociously chastened form. In a letter of May 1917 he tells his mother: "I am more and more Christian as I walk the unchristian ways of Christendom. Already I have comprehended a light which never will filter into the dogma of any national church: namely that one of Christ's essential commands was; Passivity at any price!" In the same letter, he says: "Am I not myself a conscientious objector with a very seared conscience?"[34]

His "seared conscience" strongly affects the part Owen plays in the drama of his war poems. In 'Dulce et Decorum Est', for example, his guilt as an officer explains why the gassed man, "in all my dreams ... plunges at me".[35] It accounts, too, for the hands of the victims in 'Mental Cases', "Snatching after us who smote them, brother, / Pawing us who dealt them war and madness".[36] Before he became a soldier Owen's intense idealism had taken the form of wanting to teach, to lead, to be at the forefront of civilisation. The price he later had to pay for his ambitions and aspirations was the painful recognition that he too had a share in guilt for the very war against which he protested.

But the stance of Owen in his war poems is not confined to guilt, any more than it is to anger. If there is one key line in his poetry it is: "I am the enemy you killed, my friend."[37] The perception of fellowship twisted into murderous enmity has a profound moral force. But this is made even stronger by the concern of 'Strange Meeting' with poetry:

> Courage was mine, and I had mystery,
> Wisdom was mine, and I had mastery:
> To miss the march of this retreating world
> Into vain citadels that are not walled.
> Then, when much blood had clogged their chariot-wheels,
>
> I would go up and wash them from sweet wells,
> Even with truths that lie too deep for taint.
> I would have poured my spirit without stint
> But not through wounds; not on the cess of war.
> Foreheads of men have bled where no wounds were.[38]

These lines are about the poet's gifts: his courage and mystery, his mastery and idealism, above all his capacity as healer and truth-teller. In killing his "enemy" the poet-dreamer has destroyed a fellow poet, and perhaps himself as well. But it is the war that has wasted their gifts. The dreamer is foreseeing his own death also; he is a victim as well as killer; it is the war that murders the spirit of poetry. Yet if this is what 'Strange Meeting' says, we may reflect that it was having a spirit both in and above war that enabled Owen to write a poetry fit to speak about war, and therefore to survive the war.

Writing to his cousin in November 1917, Owen said of walking over the Winchester Downs: "I could almost see the dead lying about in the hollows of the downs."[39] The words are strangely reminiscent of another poet with whom Owen may have come into contact, Edward Thomas.[40] In 'Roads' Thomas wrote:

> Now all roads lead to France
> And heavy is the tread
> Of the living; but the dead
> Returning lightly dance:[41]

Thomas was a poet much afoot in the English countryside during the earlier years of the war, before, having enlisted in the Artists' Rifles in July 1915, he embarked for France in January 1917. Thomas, in fact, wrote all his poems in wartime England, and is a war poet in the sense that he records the effect of the war on the home country.

'Home', in this context, is potentially an ambiguous word. For Thomas, from boyhood, was conscious of his Welshness, referring to Wales, parts of which he knew well from visits, as "my soul's native land".[42] This sense of having his 'home' elsewhere affected his experience of the English 'South Country', as he called it, where he actually lived. Thus he wrote of the South Country: "Yet is this country, though I am mainly Welsh, a kind of home, as I think it is more than any other to those modern people who belong nowhere."[43] Acutely conscious of his modernity, Thomas felt it as a kind of spiritual displacement. It was this, perhaps, together with his Welshness that enabled him to adopt a detached, critical view of nation and patriotism:

> I seem to see that England, that swan's nest, that island which a man's heart was not too big to love utterly. But now what with Great Britain, the British Empire, Britons, Britishers, and the English-speaking world, the choice offered to whomsoever would be patriotic is embarrassing, and he is fortunate who can find an ideal England of the past, the present, and the future to worship, and embody it in his native fields and waters or his garden, as in a graven image.[44]

These words first appeared in a book published in 1909. The war concentrated his feelings, and overcame his embarrassment; in an essay written in the early months of the war, he said: "the whole land is suddenly home."[45] The essay is called 'England', but there are good reasons for supposing that, while Thomas' quintessential landscape is the South Country, "the whole land" meant to him a more continuous tradition than that of England alone, and a more mysterious domain. In simpler terms, it meant the English language, too, which in 'Words' he identified with border country (Herefordshire) and Wales, as well as Wiltshire and Kent.

Edward Thomas' imaginative country, the country of his poetry, has no strict geographical bounds. It is, however, primarily country, in the sense that he is a poet of the earth, the land. Ultimately his idea of myth relates to this, as a story about the proper relation of the human to the non-human world, or, as he wrote, "the fact that the earth does not belong to man, but man to the earth".[46] It is significant that when he thinks of men killed in the war or soldiers generally he thinks of countrymen (the ploughman of 'A Private' and the ploughman's mate in 'As the team's head-brass', the "young English countrymen" in 'Tears', the dead flower-gatherers in 'In

Memoriam [Easter 1915]').

"The great mystery of the trench world", in Wyn Griffith's phrase, well describes the strangeness of the Front as other writers, such as David Jones and Wilfred Owen and Isaac Rosenberg, render it, both the weird configurations of a shattered natural and manmade world and the numinous borderland between life and death. Thomas' homeland, in wartime, is also a haunted place. It is where the dead returning from France "lightly dance" on the roads; and like Owen's vision on the Winchester Downs, it is full of haunted "hollows".

The latter owes a significant debt to Thomas' fascination with myth, including *The Mabinogion* and other world tales.[47] In 'The Gypsy' the Romany boy

> peopled for me the hollow wooded land,
> More dark and wild than stormiest heavens, that I searched
> and scanned
> Like a ghost new-arrived. The gradations of the dark
> Were like an underworld of death ...[48]

Similar imagery appears in 'Wind and Mist' ("A hollow land as vast as heaven") and 'Health' ("the dark hollow land"), imagery born in part from actual southern landscapes, wooded combes and chalk downs that are ancient burial grounds. This is a landscape "far more ancient and dark" since the destruction of the badger, "That most ancient Briton of English beasts".[49] But if Thomas' South Country was always dark and hollow, it is the present war that has helped to activate his mythopoetic imagination, stimulating him to depict in his poetry a haunted landscape of "dark echoes" where "the hollow past / Half yields the dead that never / More than half hidden lie"[50] and making him face a highly uncertain future.

Robert Graves found insincerity in Thomas' reaction to the war in 'This is no case of petty right or wrong'.[51] Certainly the poem has a rhetoric that is uncharacteristic of Thomas, but what it also shows is both how personal his response to the war was, and how he tended to see it as a natural phenomenon: "Two witches' cauldrons roar. / From one the weather shall rise clear and gay; / Out of the other an England beautiful / And like her mother that died yesterday."[52] In 'February Afternoon', "Time swims before me, making as a day / A thousand years, while the broad ploughland oak / Roars mill-like and men strike and bear the stroke / Of war as ever."[53] The harshness of the image in 'Blenheim Oranges', "when the war began / To turn young men to dung",[54] may be offset by the implication that the dead become part of the natural cycle. In any event, the equation of

human with natural continuity shows a strong psychological need in
Edward Thomas. But it is not the whole truth of his poetry. His
different uses of a Shakespearian allusion in two poems show rather
the complexity of his responses to the war. In 'Lob' the eponymous
hero, "One of the lords of No Man's Land", who "seen dying at
Waterloo, / Hastings, Agincourt, and Sedgemoor, too, – / Lives yet",
is, in one of his incarnations, "tall Tom that bore / The logs in, and
with Shakespeare in the hall / Once talked".[55] The allusion to the
song, 'Winter' ("When icicles hang by the wall"), from *Love's
Labours Lost*, exemplifies Lob's continuity, and therefore the survival
of a tradition at once literary and historical, in effect, the life of a
people belonging to the land. An allusion to the same song in 'The
Owl', describing "An owl's cry, a most melancholy cry" as "No
merry note, nor cause of merriment", affects the poet differently:

> And salted was my food, and my repose,
> Salted and sobered, too, by the bird's voice
> Speaking for all who lay under the stars,
> Soldiers and poor, unable to rejoice.[56]

One response of Edward Thomas to the war is to assimilate it to
human continuity in relation to the land, and thus to see it as a storm
which causes damage that nature will restore, rather than a fatal
breach in a social or civilisational order. This may be vulnerable to
Raymond Williams' criticism of 'Lob' as projecting "a version of
history which succeeds in cancelling history".[57] But it may be inter-
preted also as the psychological need of a man who shares a common
predicament with the men actually exposed to the war, as he would
eventually be. That is to say the war is his personal crisis also, and one
that makes him aware of the utter loneliness of those outcast or otherwise exposed, the soldiers and the poor. In 'Lights Out' Thomas
characteristically deployed a metaphor drawn from the depths of
European mythology to describe the 'darkness' with which he was
faced, and in which all the writers discussed in this chapter ventured:
"The unfathomable deep / Forest, where all must lose / Their way."[58]

Notes

1. Letter to Susan Owen, 8th October 1918 in: Wilfred Owen, *Selected
   Letters* (ed. John Bell). Oxford: Oxford University Press, 1985, p.352.
2. 'Prologue' in Robert Graves, *Goodbye to All That*. Harmondsworth:
   Penguin, 1960, revised edition.

3. Greg Hill, *Llewelyn Wyn Griffith*. Cardiff: University of Wales Press, 1984, p.3.
4. Llewelyn Wyn Griffith, *Up to Mametz*. Norwich: Gliddon Books, 1988, p.37.
5. *Ibid.*, p.97.
6. 'Introduction' in *Up to Mametz*, p.26.
7. *Up to Mametz*, p.232.
8. *Ibid.*, pp.232-233.
9. Wyn Griffith, *The Barren Tree*. Cardiff: Penmark Press, 1947, p.9.
10. *Ibid.*, p.15.
11. For Fussell's discussion of 'The Caricature Scenes of Robert Graves' in *Goodbye to All That* see: Paul Fussell, *The Great War and Modern Memory*. New York and London: Oxford University Press, 1975, pp.203-220.
12. *Goodbye to All That*, p.150.
13. Quoted in *The Poems of Wilfred Owen* (ed. Jon Stallworthy). London: Chatto & Windus, 1990, p.102.
14. John A. Johnston, *English Poetry of the First World War*. London: Oxford University Press, 1964, p.76.
15. Robert Graves, *Poems About War*. London: Cassell, 1988, p.35.
16. *Ibid.*, p.30.
17. *The Poems of Wilfred Owen*, p.123.
18. *Poems About War*, p.31.
19. *Ibid.*, p.53.
20. Bernard Bergonzi, *Heroes' Twilight*. Manchester: Carcanet, 1996, third edition, p.147. Bergonzi also observes: "During the Great War his devotion to regimental tradition may well have been a device for the preservation of psychic equilibrium." *Ibid.*, p.147.
21. *Poems About War*, p.62.
22. *Goodbye to All That*, p.35.
23. *Poems About War*, p.21.
24. *Ibid.*, p.40.
25. *Ibid.*, p.54.
26. Jay Winter observes the recreation in war literature of "the uncanny world of the soldiers". "If the war created 'modern memory' as Paul Fussell has claimed, it was a traditional, even archaic, kind of memory that came out of the conflict". This bears directly on the use of myth in poetry of the First World War. Jay Winter, *Sites of Memory, Sites of Mourning*. Cambridge: Cambridge University Press, 1995, p.73.
27. Letter to Alan Hodge, 31st July 1942 in: Robert Graves, *In Broken Images: Selected Correspondence* (ed. Paul O'Prey). Mt. Kisco, New York: Moyer Bell, 1988, p.313.
28. Letter to Susan Owen, 31st December 1917 in *Selected Letters*, p.306.
29. *The Poems of Wilfred Owen*, p.192.
30. *Ibid.*, p.122.
31. Dominic Hibberd, *Wilfred Owen: A New Biography*. London: Weidenfeld & Nicolson, 2002, p.106.
32. *The Poems of Wilfred Owen*, p.44.
33. *Ibid.*, p.135.

34. Letter to Susan Owen, [?16th] May 1917 in *Selected Letters*, pp.246-247.

35. *The Poems of Wilfred Owen*, p.117.

36. *Ibid.*, p.146.

37. *Ibid.*, p.126.

38. *Ibid.*, pp.125-126.

39. Letter to Leslie Gunston, 16th November 1917 in *Selected Letters*, p.291.

40. According to Dominic Hibberd, Owen "may well have been taught" by Edward Thomas (Lance-Corporal P.E. Thomas, map instructor) at army camp, "either on Hampstead Heath in October or at Romford during the winter" of 1915 (*Wilfred Owen: A New Biography*, pp.173-174). Owen bought Thomas' book on Keats published the following year.

41. Edward Thomas, *The Collected Poems of Edward Thomas* (ed. R. George Thomas). Oxford: Oxford University Press, 1981, p.90.

42. In a notebook, 31st August 1899. Quoted in: R. George Thomas, *Edward Thomas: A Portrait*. Oxford: Oxford University Press, 1985, p.80.

43. Edward Thomas, *The South Country*. London: J.M. Dent & Sons, 1932 [1909], p.7.

44. *Ibid.*, p.75.

45. 'England' in: Edward Thomas, *The Last Sheaf*. London: Jonathan Cape, 1928, p.108.

46. Edward Thomas, *In Pursuit of Spring*. London: Nelson, 1914, p.150.

47. His interest in myth appears in his writing as early as *Oxford* (1903). His retelling of Irish tales and stories from *The Mabinogion, Celtic Stories*, was published in 1911.

48. *The Collected Poems of Edward Thomas*, p.33.

49. 'The Combe'. *Ibid.*, p.21.

50. 'Two Houses'. *Ibid.*, p.81.

51. Robert Graves, *The Common Asphodel*. London: Hamish Hamilton, 1949, p.130.

52. *The Collected Poems of Edward Thomas*, p.86.

53. *Ibid.*, p.91.

54. *Ibid.*, p.118.

55. *Ibid.*, pp.55-56.

56. *Ibid.*, p.40.

57. Raymond Williams, *The Country and the City*. London: Chatto & Windus, 1973, p.257.

58. *Ibid.*, p.121

David Jones:
"No End to these Wars, No End, No End / At All"[1]

Duncan Campbell

I

To say that the Great War left its mark on David Jones would be an understatement. 22579 Jones, Private Walter David, enlisted in the Royal Welch Fusiliers in 1915 (the same regiment as Siegfried Sassoon, Robert Graves, Llywelyn Wyn Griffith and Frank Richards), took part in the Battle of the Somme in 1916, where he was injured in the assault on Mametz Wood, and was discharged in 1919. He was to carry the war with him for the rest of his life. On meeting Siegfried Sassoon in 1964 – nearly fifty years on from their experiences in France – Jones was to write: "he [Sassoon] said that however much he tried he could never get that 1st War business out of his system, which is exactly the case with me."[2] Jones also noted in an 'Autobiographical Talk' that "the particular Waste Land that was the forward area of the West Front had a permanent effect on me and has affected my work in all sorts of ways – so much that it is impossible now for me to imagine myself without that period in the *ffosydd* in Gallia Belgica."[3]

Certainly, the effects of the war on Jones' health, both physical and mental, are undeniable. Despite René Hague's assertions to the contrary, shellshock (neurasthenia) played a major part in the "old Rosy" that was to leave him in "in a state of pretty near continuous psychic disorder [...] intermittently until he died".[4] Described as "quite unfit for routine service" when he registered for war-time industrial service, in later life he was prescribed a cocktail of drugs in combinations so complex he needed a colour-coded chart to remind him of his daily regimen.[5]

The war was a crucial influence on the development of Jones' system of thought, as the third of the over-riding obsessions that comprised his personal mythology, in addition to Catholicism and

Welshness. This can be most clearly seen in the quasi-military structure of his 'Map of Themes in the Artist's Mind' (1943) (Malory
outflanked by Wagner and Tennyson; reinforcements on-hand from
the early English tradition). That singular inflection of Welshness
Jones was to make his own was inspired by his wartime experience,
embodied in the heritages of his fellow soldiers: "nothing could be
more representative. These came from London. Those from Wales.
Together they bore in their bodies the genuine tradition of the Island
of Britain."[6] Jones' first sight of a Catholic Mass also took place
during the war, in late 1916 or early 1917, "somewhere in the neighbourhood of Ypres".[7] While out gathering firewood, he saw a mass
taking place in an outhouse; even as "an uninitiated bloke prying on
the Mysteries of a Cult", he regarded it as a "great marvel".[8] This
myth of origin is revisited many times in Jones' work, in the watercolour 'A Latere Dextro' (1943–9), as well as the 'Mass poems' of
the late 1930s, out of which *The Anathemata* was to emerge, and,
indeed, in the Mass that opens *The Anathemata* itself.

War therefore figures in Jones' work on many different levels: as
a historical and biographical experience, as a symptom of cultural
and personal crisis, and as a source of poetic (and ultimately
religious) sign-making potential. We also should not forget the other
'great marvel' of Jones' formative years, the primal scene of his "first
memory – of seeing armed men on horseback", the mounted City
Imperial Volunteers recruiting for the Boer War.[9] Replayed in *The
Anathemata* through the prism of both Catholicism and Welsh myth,
the infant Jones asking his mother, "what were those men on those
beautiful horses?", is recast as a Christ-like version of Peredur: "he
has seen the / questing *milites*, he would be a *miles* too".[10] It is
Peredur, of course, who "frees and restores the Waste Land".[11]

II

Written in the main between 1928 and 1932, although not
published until 1937, *In Parenthesis* won the Hawthornden Prize in
1938, and earned now-legendary praise from the blue-shirted Yeats
("I salute the author of *In Parenthesis*").[12] Talking to William Blissett
in 1974, Jones commented: "it's funny that practically the whole of
the actual experience of life I have been able to use in my writing
comes from the Western Front, 1915–16, and from the few weeks in
Jerusalem in the mid-1930s."[13] The concrete factuality of *In
Parenthesis* as biographical event is immediately apparent; it is
specifically a record of a *historical event*, or more precisely, a record
of "some things" that David Jones "saw, felt & was part of" between

December 1915 and July 1916.[14] Colin Hughes has shown how "in writing *In Parenthesis* David Jones used a strictly accurate account of the capture of Mametz Wood and of events leading up to it as a frame on which to weave his poetry, using as raw material his own observations and experiences".[15] Yet, despite this, and despite its formal similarity to many other war books, particularly in its trajectory from bewildered initiation towards the carnage of (in this case) the assault on Mametz Wood, what is remarkable about *In Parenthesis* is the manner in which it moves away from the purely biographical in order to make sense of that concrete eventuality, much of which, as Jones wrote later, "at the time of suffering, the flesh was too weak to appraise".[16] War as experienced in *In Parenthesis* is an event after which nothing remains the same, shattering language, landscape, bodies. In many ways, Jones' work, beginning with *In Parenthesis*, is an attempt to make sense of that event, of the wasteland of the Forward Zone, where "[y]ou feel exposed and apprehensive in this new world".[17]

The price of personal understanding that was to serve Jones so well in writing about the experience of war – "[w]e can guess, better than our immediate forebears, something of what a paid foot-soldier at Crécy felt about a damp bow-string and the heavy Picardy mud" – is, as Neil Corcoran puts it, a poem "in which the First World War dreams itself newly, terrifyingly and pitifully awake as a personal and historical nightmare".[18] *In Parenthesis* connects the modernist fragmentation of representation – the flux of language experienced in the art-work – to the literal fragmentation and disorientation of military experience in the Forward Zone:

> Under earth shorn-up, seeled and propt. Substantial matter guttered and dissolved, sprawled to a glaucous insecurity. All sureness metamorphosed, all slippery a place for the children of men [...][19]

This can also be seen in John Ball's experience coming up to the line – the bomb falls, "a consummation of all burstings out; all sudden up-rendings and rivings-through – all taking-out of vents – all barrier-breaking – all unmaking [...] the dissolving and splitting of solid things".[20]

And yet, at the same time, as Jones writes in the 'Preface' to *In Parenthesis*, "at no time did one so much live with a consciousness of the past, the very remote, and the more immediate and trivial past."[21] In his otherwise unflattering assessment of *In Parenthesis*, Paul Fussell writes that it "poses for itself the problem of re-attaching

traditional meaning to the unprecedented actualities of the war",
that is, to understanding the war in terms of the past, a view shared
by René Hague, who writes that "one might attempt to define *In
Parenthesis* as a poetic transmutation of personal experience into a
memorial to, and a lament for, the ancient unity of this island of
Britain."[22] As Jones writes in 'Past and Present', "the poet is a
'rememberer'", whose task is to "show forth, recall, discover and represent those things that have belonged to man from the
beginning", to "keep open the lines of communication" between
past and present.[23] Jones' genetic method aims to uncover, to reveal,
to re-present those "foundational things" which have been forgotten
and covered over in our "megalopolitan technocracy"; it is a "recalling of certain things which I myself had received, things which
are part of the complex deposits of this Island".[24]

Similarly, Tom Dilworth has argued that *In Parenthesis* moves
outwards from a realist narrative ground to encompass the whole
range of secular and sacred mythos appropriate to "a Londoner, of
Welsh and English parentage, of Protestant upbringing, of Catholic
subscription".[25] In other words, for Jones, history is always "historia
intermeddled with potent and light-giving, life-giving, cult-making
myths", which explains why, despite his insistence on historical
particularity and accuracy, he claims in the Preface to *In Parenthesis*
that "none of the characters in this writing are real persons, nor is
any sequence of events historically accurate".[26] The Forward Zone
of *In Parenthesis* is a zone of palimpsests, of meanings superimposed
on each other, of sedimentations, associations and recessions that
link the present to the past. Similarly, the actual literary search for
that past is represented as traversing the Zone: as Jones describes it,
"in considering the tradition of a folk and a locality, we must be
prepared for a tortuous journey. The zone we search is traversed and
troia'd, we stumble from sections of well-revetted entrenchment,
upon old workings fallen-in and shapeless, bombarded by the creep-
ing barrage of successive traditions"; it is "a place of deep recession
and superimposition, of booby-trap and trip-wire".[27] Here, the past
has not been erased by the violence of the present; it remains as
"visible and tangible survivals" in the waste land of contemporary
culture. An example of this is the billet John Ball and his platoon are
shown to in some farm buildings:

> You bunch together before a tarred door. Chalk scrawls on its
> planking – initials, numbers, monograms, signs, hasty, half-
> erased, of many regiments. Scratched out dates measuring
> the distance back to antique beginnings.[28]

So too, with John Ball's dream, where "his night phantasm mazes a pre-war, more idiosyncratic skein, weaves with stored-up very other tangled threads" and ends with his "[s]tepping over Miss Weston's thrown about belongings".[29] The dream in fact suggests itself as an analogue for the representational strategies of *In Parenthesis* itself, the weaving-together of the past and the present, the historical and the archetypal, the metaphorical and the literal. Such a weaving together is reminiscent of Jones' essays, in which he describes man as a "borderer, the sole inhabitant of a tract of country where matter marches with spirit", or writes of humankind's "rightful *imperium*, its native *Raum*, its double homeland along all the frontiers and uncertain borders of matter and spirit".[30]

This movement from historical particularity to the mythical and archetypal can also be seen in the presentation of one of the central figures of *In Parenthesis*, Dai Greatcoat (a figure who, along with Private John Ball, in many ways represents Jones himself). Dai's 'Boast' derives from a historical event (Jones' conversation with an 'Evan Evans' at Ypres about "a shit-house for Artaxerxes"), and, as Tom Dilworth has noted, is "a catalogue of military service extending back through history and quasi-historical legend to mythological time immemorial".[31] Beginning with the tradition of Welsh military service – "my fathers were with the Black Prinse of Wales [...] it is in the histories you can read it" – the boast runs through the whole gamut of myth and legend back to Judaeo-Christian and Arthurian traditions: "I was with Abel when his brother found him [...] I was the spear in Balin's hand / that made waste King Pellam's land".[32] Wounded and then blown to pieces while on a stretcher (nothing left but "clots and a twisted clout"), Dai is, like all soldiers, one of the "appointed scape-beasts come to the waste-lands".[33]

III

According to Jones, *The Anathemata* "had its beginnings in experiments made from time to time between 1938 and 1945", most notably *The Book of Balaam's Ass*, which he "abandoned [...] as it would not come together", and the overlapping manuscripts later published as *The Sleeping Lord* and *The Roman Quarry*.[34] He wrote that, unlike *In Parenthesis*, which "was chained to a sequence of events which made it always a straightforward affair [...] this effort is, I fear, about 'ideas'".[35] After leaving Sidmouth, where he had been staying, in 1940, Jones spent the rest of the war in London, where he endured the continual irritation of air-raids ("that low whine and dull thud away in the distance reminded me of my first shell in Xmas 1915"), complaining how *"bloody* annoying" it was "when these fucking sirens go just when you want to get somewhere".[36] However, the two 'wedding poems', written in late 1940 "at the time of the dooms [...] toward / The time of the ultimate uncovering", reveal a far more apocalyptic view of the Blitz, with their vision of "flame-lap and split masonry, / where the high fires leap [...] when the glass towers / shiver and the shrouds of a plutocracy look / very far from fine".[37]

The Second World War exacerbated Jones' sense of cultural and spiritual crisis, of living in the "failing / (Finished?) West"; as he wrote in 1942-43, we "are experiencing the infliction of another and larger war upon that same civilization grown a little more complex, far more disillusioned, more highly organised, more megalopolitan, more neurotic".[38] However, his political analysis of the war's happening "directly because of the merchants' rule" chimes rather uncomfortably with the fascist opposition to commerce and Pound's obsessive economic vision.[39] Despite Jones' recognition that it was 'hate' that lay at the root of Nazi ideology, he still – as a result of his own experiences of war, his "natural sympathy [...] with the vanquished" and "the enemy front-fighters who shared our pains against whom we found ourselves by misadventure" – supported appeasement, and was also deeply impressed by *Mein Kampf*:

> There is much in both Fascist and Nazi revolutions that demand our understanding and sympathy. They represent, for all their alarming characteristics, an heroic attempt to cope with certain admitted corruptions in our civilization.[40]

Without going into too much detail here, the most striking thing about Jones' politics is its naivety, as in 'The Brenner', an 'occasional poem', also from 1940, where his desire to see Britannia and Germania embracing leads to wishful mis-reading of the political situation (Jones had even sent a copy of *In Parenthesis* to Chamberlain in 1939, with a letter thanking him for attempting to "mend things in Europe & to save us from the worst").[41] His relationship to the far-right Chelsea group has also been well-documented, as has what Tony Conran rather uncharitably describes as his "addiction to empires, Papism or Mussolini".[42]

Just as *In Parenthesis* is as much an intervention (however naïve) in the political situation of the 1930s, so too *The Anathemata*. Although not published until 1952, it can be read as a commentary on the 1930s, whether in the literal identification of figures such as Tiberius Gracchus with Giacomo Matteotti, or Sejanus ("co-ordinator of groupings: / civil, military / security, secret") with Ernst

Roehm, or in a more general Spenglerian vision of the pre-war cultural climate as analogous to Rome in the first century BC: once more, we see "Peace in Our Time / the whole world expectant of war"; once again, we experience "the beginnings of the end and the waxing of the megalopolis and the acute coarsening of the forms".[43] Jones' most direct comment on the Second World War in *The Anathemata* comes at the end of the 'Angle-Land' section, which deals specifically with the cultural and linguistic chaos of post-Roman Britain; again, it compresses the multiple strands of his personal mythology:

> (O Balin O Balan!
>   how blood you both
>   the Brudersee
>   toward the last pháse
> of our dear West.)[44]

War in *The Anathemata* is always linked to cultural chaos and instability, and a sense of civilisational crisis and change, whether the sack of Troy or the Dorian jarls and "transmontane storm-groups [who] fractured the archaic pattern".[45] Even an interlude of relative peace, such as 'Arthurian' Britain is insecure: "Elbe-men blacken with red fire the east wheat-belt, and nothing through from Loidis, and elsewhere the situation is obscure."[46]

However, despite this, the metaleptic reference to Jones' own war experiences ("when I was a young man in France") and the Christmas ceasefire, held "BECAUSE OF THE CHILD", holds out the possibility of redemption.[47] Similarly, 'Prothalamion', Jones' only lyric poem, written in 1940, celebrated Harman and Margaret Grisewood's marriage as "mock[ing] the unmaking" of the war, with a glance backwards to Jones' wartime experiences in the Great War:

> So have I heard bird-song, beneath the
> trajectory zone, at Passchendaele, or seen
> flowers lean toward each other, under the sun
> that shined to delineate the hate and mutilation
> of the Forward Area.[48]

Writing slightly later, in 1942-3, Jones argued that "the artist, however, in whatever age, and whatever the determined destiny, has both to believe and to tremble and somehow or other, to affirm delight", that is, to assert the power of *poesis*, of making, as a response to the 'unmaking' of war, especially "because the Land is Waste".[49]

Similarly, the opening of *The Anathemata* explicitly foregrounds the creative, sign-making act of "the cult-man [who] stands alone in Pellam's land".[50] Even "at the sagging end and chapter's close [...] so late in time", *The Anathemata* asserts the power of *poesis* to overcome the 'unmaking' of war through the fundamentally religious impulse of "making this thing other".[51] As Jones wrote to Saunders Lewis, "the action of the Mass was meant to be the central theme of the work for as you once said to me 'The Mass *makes sense* of everything'."[52] Just as the Mass is itself a "showing again", because for Jones, "man is unavoidably a sacramentalist and [...] his works are sacramental in character", art also involves "a recalling, a re-presenting again, anaphora, anamnesis".[53] Jones' 'commemorative *intention*' in writing *The Anathemata* is therefore analogous to (although not in the same order as) what happened in the Upper Room, an act of remembrance, of *anamnesis*, that attempts to make the past present, to oppose "the purely utile, [...] what functions", with an act of *poesis* that is necessarily extra-utile and gratuitous, "of necessity the sign [...] of something other".[54]

IV

In an April 1971 letter to Saunders Lewis, Jones recalled his trip with Eric Gill to Palestine in 1934, which he took while recovering from his first breakdown. Jones' letter is worth quoting extensively:

> I caught sight of a figure who carried me back a couple of decades or thereabouts [...] it might have been a rain-soaked Givenchy duck-board trackway instead of a sweltering Hierosolyma back street [...] in their full parade rig [they] evoked not the familiar things of less than two decades back, but rather of two millennia close on [...] so they were a section from the Antonia, up for duties in Hierosolyma after all![55]

This interweaving of past and present recalls Jones' own immediately post-war drawings, such as 1919's 'Crucifixion', showing British tommies at the foot of the Cross, and directly inspired many of the poems collected in *The Sleeping Lord* and *The Roman Quarry*. These poems deal broadly with what could be called 'the fact of empire', and the experiences of the 'ordinary soldier' at the edges of empire, whether anticipating the invasion of Britain ('The Narrows'), "furnish[ing] / That Fatigue" which is the Crucifixion ('The Fatigue'), or resisting an attack against Hadrian's Wall, a situation that could have come directly from *In Parenthesis*: "[t]he Onager is jammed. / The Commandant is dead. / The Senior Centurion takes over."[56]

Set in primarily in Palestine, Britain and the Welsh Marches, the poems take place in sites of resistance to empire, where, against a background of continual war, the Celtic world and Palestine at the time of the Passion offer the potential for resistance against the Imperial centre, whether the 'past' of the Roman empire in decline, or the 'present' of the British empire in withdrawal: the 'fact-man' (in this case Pilate) could be from either epoch: "it is the empty time / after tiffin / and before his first stiff peg. / The fact-man [...] within the conditioned room / sleeps on".[57] The aim of empire is, as the Tribune suggests, "to discipline the world-floor / to a common level / till everything presuming difference / and all the sweet remembered demarcations / wither".[58] And yet, even in defeat, there is potential for resistance in the figure of the 'maimed king', whether Christ or an unknown Celtic chieftain:

> They crane their civvy necks half out of their civvy suits to bait the maimed king in his tinctured vesture, the dying *tegernos* of the wasted *landa* [...] bitched and bewildered and far from his dappled patria.[59]

Hector, Troy's 'decorous leader' also fulfils the function of the scapebeast, dragged "widdershins / without the wall" of Troy, "his beauties made squalid, his combed gilt / a matted mop".[60]

Despite its total destruction, Troy remains the 'mother of forts' and, both in terms of literature and myths of origin, becomes the 'matrix' of Western culture, including Britain and – of course – "*Terra Walliae*! [...] Enclosure of the Children of Troy".[61] Even after the death of Llywelyn, in a Wales whose Marches are controlled by the 'Eingl-Francwyr', "in the broken / *tir y blaenau* / these broken dregs of Troea / yet again muster".[62] Whether or not Jones' vision of Wales has anything at all to do with contemporary Wales, in his work, Wales stands in for the act of *poesis* itself, as a way of *thinking* about (and in) contemporary culture that has been forgotten. As Jonathan Miles suggests, Wales becomes "an imagined receptacle for his anti-imperial and non-industrial Catholic vision which embodies and expresses the very manner of poetic activity itself".[63]

The figure of the 'dying Gaul' always held particular significance for Jones and his sense of national and cultural identity. In a 1959 BBC broadcast he described how "one of my first recollections of the Antique happens to have been a plaster cast of a Roman marble copy of a Greek bronze, which was labelled 'The Dying Gaul'. That was in

1909".[64] The "prostrate form of this Galatic *uchelwr* or 'high-man'"
also occurs in *The Anathemata*, here as another indicator of the time
of the Passion: "two centuries / since Rhine-progeny / become dying
Galatae / in Pergamon bronze."[65] The indignities Hector suffers link
him to all analogues of the Dying Gaul, whether Arthur, Christ, Dai
Greatcoat, as a symbol of victory in defeat. In Jones' sacramental
aesthetics, the image of the dying Gaul – and by extension of Arthur
– is in the last instance an analogue of Christ: "from the inevitable
failure the splendour of the extra-utile will shine out".[66] For Jones, the
dying Gaul represents a "a kind of defeat tradition" that resonates
through Celtic and Welsh poetry: "the birth-poetry of Wales makes
continuous anamnesis of the Dying Gaul".[67] Yet, while "[t]he Gaul
dies daily" in his encounters with imperialism (in whatever form –
military, cultural, linguistic), the Celtic still remains as other: "the
Dying Gaul is not dead yet".

V

And yet, what if the transformation of defeat into artistic or poetic
victory is not enough? What if the sense of chaos and cultural crisis
that Jones' *poesis* is meant to stand against is too strong to be
overcome through the art-work? In particular, paintings such as
'Aphrodite in Aulis' (1940) and 'The Four Queens' (1941), both
typical of his later style, demonstrate this problem. Here, the
feminine form represents the renewal of fertility, the restoration of
the Waste Land, and the assertion of beauty and form against the
unmaking of war and civilisational crisis. However, in attempting to
give new life to the "dead symbols" that "litter to the base of the
cult-stone", what happens instead is the return of the historical,
whether cultural or biographical, as a disruptive force; in these two
images, the pathological compression of cultural anxiety with sexual
disquiet, the implied maimed King and aggressive female sexuality.[69]
Figures dissolve into the ground they spring from, falling back into
the cultural wasteland out of which they are formed. This is also the
case with later works such as 'Vexilla Regis' (1947–8) and especially
'The Paschal Lamb' (1951), which is intended as celebratory, as the
sacramental or incarnational absorption of the concrete and particular into the whole, but instead "the overall effect is that of stress and
ruin [...] a crazed itemising of each detail to fulfil the obsessive
conception".[70] In this one painting, the lamb, *agnus triumphalis*,
ultimately merges into the very fragments it emerges against: the
standard of the Roman Legion XX Victrix; an *authentic* view of
Rome; a megalithic circle; the "storm-tossed bark [...] suggestive of

all sorts of things"; mermaids; sirens; wild hills, "no doubt with Wales in mind!"[71]

Jones' "feeling of wanting to include 'everything'; 'the whole' in such works as I've tried to make" means that while the Mass remains the central node of all his writing, because anything and everything can be related to it, as Hague notes, "at any particular point in his writing the number of alternatives open to him was so great that he had difficulty [...] organizing the work".[72] Hence Jones' feelings of writer's block, characterized by his continual complaints: "I can't work [...] the whole thing's a monumental bollux, a first-class buggeration"; hence also the obsessive reiteration, or continual reinscription, which can be seen in the 'busy style' of the later paintings, in his letter-writing and in the extraordinary amount of annotation to *The Anathemata*.[73] The elements that make up Jones' poetry and painting are loaded with meaning they cannot hold; the historical tends to the mythological and archetypal: every man is Arthur, is Christ, every woman Gwenhwyfar, Mary. The particular is raised to the level of the universal, given weight and significance it ultimately cannot bear, finally collapsing into fragments, shards of a culture.

The contrast between the formal innovations of modernist poetics and its ideological conservatism are well known. As Terry Eagleton has argued, "it is a paradox of modernism that its exhilarated sense of fresh technological possibilities finds itself constantly displaced into some static, cyclical world in which all dynamic process seems permanently arrested."[74] This can be seen quite clearly in Eliot's review of *Ulysses*, in which he praises Joyce's use of myth as "a way of controlling, of ordering, of giving a shape and significance to the immense panorama of futility and anarchy which is contemporary history".[75] In effect, the timelessness of myth compensates for the chaos and waste of history. Yet, in the work of David Jones, the origin is already a catastrophe, the disaster has already happened, we are writing after the Fall from the Word into words, from myth into history, and every act of recovery, of gathering together, perhaps of 'making' itself, is doomed to failure in advance. As Theodor Adorno notes, "antagonisms that are unsolved in reality cannot be solved imaginatively either; they work their way into the imagination and are reproduced in imagination's own inconsistency".[76] In other words, the land has already become waste, and, no matter how hard we may try, history never remains in parenthesis.

Notes

In the light of Jones' typographical inventiveness, ellipses inserted by the essayist have been enclosed in square brackets to indicate they are not those of Jones.

1. David Jones, 'The Narrows' in *The Roman Quarry and Other Sequences* (eds. Harman Grisewood and René Hague). London: Agenda Editions, 1981, pp.59-63 (p.59).

2. David Jones, *Dai Greatcoat: A Self-Portrait of David Jones in his Letters* (ed. René Hague). London: Faber and Faber, 1980s , p.210.

3. David Jones, 'Autobiographical Talk' in *Epoch and Artist* (ed. Harman Grisewood). London: Faber and Faber, 1959, pp.25-31 (p.28).

4. Jonathan Miles and Derek Shiel, *David Jones: The Maker Unmade*. Bridgend: Seren, 1995, p.252. Hague comments that "It has often been said that David's breakdown in 1933 was caused by his war experiences. For my own part, I believe this to be completely untrue" (*Dai Greatcoat*, p.58).

5. *Dai Greatcoat*, p.113.

6. David Jones, *In Parenthesis*. London: Faber and Faber, 1937; 1978 impression, p.x.

7. 'Autobiographical Talk', p.28.

8. *Dai Greatcoat*, p.249.

9. William Blissett, *The Long Conversation: A Memoir of David Jones*. Oxford: Oxford University Press, 1981, p.121.

10. David Jones, 'In Illo Tempore' in *The Dying Gaul and Other Writings* (ed. Harman Grisewood). London: Faber and Faber, 1978, pp.19-29 (p.19); David Jones, *The Anathemata*. London: Faber and Faber, 1952, p.225.

11. *The Anathemata*, p.225.

12. On the reception of *In Parenthesis*, see for example, Thomas Dilworth, *The Shape of Meaning in the Poetry of David Jones*. Toronto: University of Toronto Press, 1988, p.3.

13. *The Long Conversation*, p.136.

14. *In Parenthesis*, p.ix.

15. Colin Hughes, 'David Jones: The Man Who was on the Field: *In Parenthesis* as Straight Reporting' in John Matthias (ed.), *David Jones: Man and Poet*. Orono, ME: The National Poetry Foundation, [n.d. (1989)], pp.163-192 (p.179).

16. *In Parenthesis*, p.x.

17. *Ibid.*, p.9.

18. David Jones, 'Art in Relation to War' in *The Dying Gaul*, pp.123-166 (p.128); Neil Corcoran, 'Spilled Bitterness: *In Parenthesis* in History' in *David Jones: Man and Poet*, pp.209-225 (p.225).

19. *In Parenthesis*, p.76.

20. *Ibid.*, p.24.

21. *Ibid.*, p.xi.

22. Paul Fussell, *The Great War and Modern Memory*. London: Oxford University Press, 1975, p.146; René Hague, *David Jones*. Cardiff: University of Wales Press, 1975, p.38.

23. David Jones, 'Past and Present' in *Epoch and Artist*, pp.138-142 (p.141, p.140, p.141).

24. David Jones, 'Preface' in *Epoch and Artist*, pp.11-18 (p.16); 'Autobiographical Talk', p.30.

25. See *The Shape of Meaning in the Poetry of David Jones*, pp.62ff.; *The Anathemata*, p.11.

26. David Jones, 'The Kensington Mass' in *The Roman Quarry*, pp.87-96 (p.92); *In Parenthesis*, p.ix.

27. David Jones, 'The Myth of Arthur' in *Epoch and Artist*, pp.212-259 (p.232, p.233).

28. 'Autobiographical Talk', p.27; *In Parenthesis*, p.22.

29. *In Parenthesis*, p. 32, p.33.

30. David Jones, 'Art and Democracy' in *Epoch and Artist*, pp.85-96 (p.86); 'Art in Relation to War', p.165.

31. *In Parenthesis*, p.79; *The Shape of Meaning in the Poetry of David Jones*, p.108.

32. *In Parenthesis*, p.79.

33. *Ibid.*, p.177, p.70.

34. *The Anathemata*, p.14; *Dai Greatcoat*, p.250.

35. *Dai Greatcoat*, p.86.

36. *Ibid.*, p.101, p.104.

37. David Jones, 'Prothalamion', in *The Wedding Poems* (ed. Thomas Dilworth). London: Enitharmon, 2002, pp.32-33 (p.32).

38. *The Anathemata*, p.231; 'Art in Relation to War', p.127.

39. 'Prothalamion', p.32.

40. *Dai Greatcoat*, p.93; Harman Grisewood quoted in Thomas Dilworth, 'David Jones and Fascism' in *David Jones: Man and Poet*, pp.143-159 (p.154); *In Parenthesis*, p.xvii; David Jones, unpublished typescript essay, 11th May 1939, quoted in 'David Jones and Fascism', p.149.

41. David Jones, 'The Brenner', in *The Wedding Poems*, p. 79; 'David Jones and Fascism', p.146.

42. Tony Conran, *Frontiers in Anglo-Welsh Poetry*. Cardiff: University of Wales Press, 1997, p.202. On Jones' politics, particularly in the 1930s, see also Corcoran, 'Spilled Bitterness' and Gareth Joseph Downes, "'2 Alleluias and a Heil": David Jones' *In Parenthesis* and the Civilisational Crisis of the Thirties' in *Welsh Writing in English: A Yearbook of Critical Essays*, 6 (2000), pp.1-20.

43. *The Anathemata*, p.186, p.90.

44. *Ibid.*, p.115.

45. *Ibid.*, p.90.

46. *Ibid.*, p.204.

47. *Ibid.*, p.216.

48. 'Prothalamion', p.33.

49. 'Art in Relation to War', p129.

50. *The Anathemata*, p.50.

51. *Ibid.*, pp.49-50, p.49.

52. David Jones, letter to Saunders Lewis, April 1971 in *Agenda* (Vol.11 No.4 / Vol.12 No.1, 1973-4), pp.18-25 (p.20).

53.   *Dai Greatcoat*, p.190; David Jones, 'Art and Sacrament' in *Epoch and Artist*, pp.143-179 (p.155, p.167).
54.   'Autobiographical Talk', p.31; David Jones, 'Notes on the 1930s' in *The Dying Gaul*, pp.41-49 (p.44); 'Art and Sacrament', p.150.
55.   Letter to Saunders Lewis, April 1971, p.23.
56.   David Jones, 'The Tribune's Visitation' in *The Sleeping Lord and Other Fragments*. London: Faber and Faber, 1974, pp.45-58 (p.51); 'The Fatigue' in *The Sleeping Lord*, pp.24-41 (p.41); 'Under Arcturus' in *The Roman Quarry*, pp.64-83 (p.79).
57.   *The Anathemata*, p.239.
58.   'The Tribune's Visitation', p.50.
59.   'The Wall' in *The Sleeping Lord*, pp.10-14 (p.11).
60.   *The Anathemata*, p.84.
61.   *Ibid.*, p.56, p.57, p.55.
62.   'The Sleeping Lord' in *The Sleeping Lord*, pp.70-96 (p.94, p.95).
63.   Jonathan Miles, *Backgrounds to David Jones: A Study in Sources and Drafts*. Cardiff: University of Wales Press, 1990, p.154.
64.   David Jones, 'The Dying Gaul' in *The Dying Gaul*, pp.50-58 (p.50).
65.   'The Dying Gaul', p.50; *The Anathemata*, p.185.
66.   'Under Arcturus', p.70.
67.   'The Dying Gaul', p.53.
68.   'The Dying Gaul', p.53, p.58.
69.   *The Anathemata*, p.50.
70.   *David Jones: The Maker Unmade*, p.238.
71.   David Jones, letter to Nicolete Grey, 15th March 1964, quoted in *David Jones: The Maker Unmade*, p.238.
72.   David Jones, *Letters to a Friend* (ed. Aneirin Talfan Davies). Swansea: Triskele, 1980, pp.80-81; *The Roman Quarry*, p.217.
73.   *Dai Greatcoat*, p.55.
74.   Terry Eagleton, *The Ideology of the Aesthetic*. Oxford: Blackwell, 1990, p.317.
75.   T.S. Eliot, 'Ulysses, Order and Myth' in *Selected Prose* (ed. Frank Kermode). London: Faber and Faber, 1975, pp.175-178 (p.177).
76.   Theodor Adorno, *Aesthetic Theory* (eds. Gretel Adorno and Rolf Tiedemann, tr. Robert Hullot-Kentor). London: Continuum, 2002, p.169.

From Mametz Wood to the Jaffa Gate: The Great War in Welsh Art

Eric Rowan

To an outsider, one of the remarkable features of the British attitude to the outbreak of war, in August 1914, was the response of the Welsh people. Considered for centuries past as a peaceable, cultured nation, and just beginning to enjoy a 'national revival', there was a surprising reaction – both patriotic and bellicose – to the looming conflict. The most eminent Welshman, David Lloyd George, then Chancellor of the Exchequer, soon to become Secretary for War and Prime Minister, was immediately converted from doubt and scepticism to active and fervent support for hostilities. About six weeks into the war, he gave a rousing speech to the Welshmen of London at the Queen's Hall, calling on their patriotism and courage, while vilifying the 'Prussian caste'.[1] Charles F.G. Masterman, a fellow Liberal, ex-MP and Chancellor of the Duchy of Lancaster, in a fit of hyperbole, called it the "finest speech in the history of England". Lloyd George, however, was depressed about it and said "the audience made him sick ... they were far too stodgy and 'comfortable' ... you had to talk your way through layers of fat."[2] After the speech, a special recruiting station in the hall was inundated with volunteers. Lloyd George's rhetoric was clearly effective – he soon changed his own opinion of it – for of all the nations of the British Isles, Wales had the highest per capita rate of volunteers for the armed forces; greater than England and Scotland and nearly four times that of Ireland.[3]

The Irish, of course, were absorbed in their divisive struggle for Home Rule, with religious sectarianism and a prominent, often violent nationalism complicating their response to the war. Wales was not so divided, and the generosity of spirit, combined with a loathing for the German invasion of Belgium, prompted a largely unanimous support for Britain's coming struggle. This whole-hearted acceptance of the war was reflected in Welsh art, most

dramatically in two paintings by Christopher Williams (1873-1934).
A strong supporter of nationalist aspirations and a pacifist, three
years before the outbreak of war he had depicted the cultural, social
and presumably political aspirations of the Welsh people in his
allegorical '*Deffroad Cymru*' ('The Awakening of Wales'). This
showed a draped, comely woman, gazing ecstatically upwards and
soaring heavenwards away from the jaws of a fearsome dragon. In
1916 he produced – at Lloyd George's command – the propaganda
histrionics of a now legendary episode from the Somme campaign,
'The Charge of the Welsh Division at Mametz Wood, 11 July 1916'.

Although a remarkable painting, it was curiously out of character with most of the official art of the Great War. Williams was given
permission – a rare privilege at the time – to visit and sketch at the
Somme battlefield in November 1916 but, although he had recently
turned to landscape painting, there is little topographical detail,
none of it specific. Instead, there is a dramatic heaving of bodies
picked out in a strong, theatrical chiaroscuro. With this emphasis on
action, the painting is more in tune with the art of the Boer War,
when photography was less developed, newsreels rare, and graphic
artists employed by the illustrated magazines were expected to
produce thrilling scenes of fighting. Williams was lent a soldier by
the War Office, to serve as a model, and he used the studies in the
painting, but it was also his custom to work in his studio using lay
figures highlighted by a powerful electric lamp.

Williams was fortunate in his contacts; Lloyd George was by
then the newly appointed Secretary for War, and Williams painted
three portraits of him at various times. Other would-be patrons of
real location war pictures – social luminaries such as Lady Emerald
Cunard and Lord Northcliffe – were thwarted by the intransigence
of the War Office. This official resistance was reinforced by the
awesome slaughter of the Somme battlefield, where 57,470 soldiers
died on the first day, 1ˢᵗ July 1916. Yet, despite his unique Mametz
commission and his exalted connexion, Williams was never
appointed as an official war artist; he was probably considered too
outmoded in style with an insufficient reputation outside Wales.

The responsibility for selecting artists for war propaganda rested
in a secretive intelligence department known simply as 'Wellington
House', from its location at Buckingham Gate in London. Set up in
late August 1914, it was run by Charles Masterman, a close friend
of Lloyd George, and Chairman of the National Health Insurance
Commission, which had been created by Lloyd George in 1911 and
was also based at Wellington House. Dedicated to promulgating

'comment' – i.e. propaganda – the intelligence department was first concerned exclusively with written material. It was only as the war progressed that films and photographs were deemed useful, indeed, more effective, with world-wide audiences.

But film and photography had their limits; imagination and invention were needed to make the flat, drab, battered landscapes of Flanders and the dreary, deadly monotony of trench warfare exciting – as Christopher Williams discovered. By 1916, Masterman was convinced of the need for visual artists to contribute to Wellington House's propaganda. Fortunately, he was advised by leading figures from the literary and art communities and decided not to use illustrators of the Boer War type but to enlist leading artists of the day.[4] The first artist officially 'embedded' in a military unit in France was the Scottish etcher Muirhead Bone, who was attached to the Intelligence Branch, and arrived at the front in mid-August 1916, at the height of the Somme campaign. Later, on 27th November, Bone drew a portrait of Christopher Williams, who was then on location researching his 'Mametz' painting.

In January 1917, a month after becoming Prime Minister, Lloyd George reorganised the various propaganda departments as the Department of Information (DoI), with the novelist John Buchan as Director. The Wellington House unit now had its own independent funding and was to recruit an impressive list of leading British artists – only one of them Welsh. A year later, in January 1918, Lloyd George elevated the DoI into a full Ministry, with an old friend and supporter, the Canadian Lord Beaverbrook, as its first Minister.[5] Beaverbrook quickly established a new organisation, the British War Memorials Committee (BWMC), based on his charitable, London-based body, the Canadian War Record Office. The BWMC was not concerned with the subsequent post-war memorials; it was dedicated to compiling a pictorial record of the war, and recruiting artists for that purpose. An influential member of the committee was the novelist Amold Bennett, who prided himself on his appreciation of modern art and who denigrated "the reactionary mess of RA and ARA muck".[6] Unfortunately, Bennett's strictures eliminated two of the most eminent Welsh artists of the period: the sculptor Sir William Goscombe John, RA and the painter Frank Brangwyn, ARA (RA in 1919, knighted in 1941). On 4th April 1918, Bennett wrote to Thomas Bodkin:

> The object of the [British War Memorials] committee is to procure a complete record of the whole blooming war in paint, ink and sculpture. I have succeeded in turning down *all*

R.A. painters, except Clausen. Some feat, believe me! Yes, I
have turned down even the inevitable Brangwyn.

This was, indeed, presumptuous, for Brangwyn (1867-1956) was
one of the most internationally esteemed British painters of his time
and could, with some reservation, be called a giant of Welsh art. The
reservation applies not to his international stature as an artist, which
was immense and apparently unassailable at the outbreak of war, but
to his Welshness. He was born in Bruges of a Welsh mother, but never
lived in Wales, although he is now accepted by the Welsh as one of
their most successful past masters.[7] He was also too renowned to be
excluded entirely by Bennett's anathema and he contributed largely
to the art of the Great War, either independently, through other
patronage, or for the BWMC through secondary commissions.

Brangwyn was prodigiously productive; he had many commissions, both public and private, and employed about fourteen
assistants during his years of success. Although immensely inventive, the sheer scale of his output meant that his work became
somewhat formulaic. Brangwyn's war art simply perpetuated this
propensity. At the beginning of hostilities, he was busy with at least
three commissions for mural decorations in Horsham and San
Francisco, and church mosaics in Leeds. In 1915, he was commissioned to decorate the state capitol in Jefferson City, Missouri.
During 1916 he was working in stained glass, although his output
dwindled during 1917 (his fiftieth year) due to illness – he had
overworked himself and had to endure several operations. But he
was active again early in 1918 on a lunette for the Manitoba
Legislative Building and designing an art gallery for Kobe in Japan.[8]

Consequently, Brangwyn was too busy to visit the war zones –
although it is likely that, with his exalted reputation, he could have
secured permission – so he relied on stock images from his reper-
toire of human labour and endeavour, which had always been a
favourite theme of his. He was a rapid sketcher and adept both at
etching and lithography, although lithography was more suited to
the immediacy of propaganda, and to Brangwyn's fluent, graphic
technique. He had already designed pre-war posters, and his war art
continued to use this medium and this form. Many of his figure
studies were taken from newspaper photographs and official propaganda, as well as specifically posed photographs taken by himself
and others. He was a competent photographer and had used photographs as early as 1895 for his mural at the Paris gallery, 'L'Art
Nouveau'. In his war posters, Brangwyn adapted his earlier studies
of workers, put them into uniform, flavoured them with a reference

to historical battle paintings, and produced variations on several major themes: prisoners, refugees, wounded soldiers, as well as scenes from trench life and the Home Front.

One example is the poster 'Zeppelin Raid', with a typical Brangwyn figure raising a clenched fist defiantly towards the sky. Another unsubtle propaganda poster, equally melodramatic but with a note of added sadism, shows a British soldier bayoneting a German, with the caption: 'Put Strength in the Final Blow'. A series of six lithographs commissioned by the Canadian War Record Office, *The Ruins of War*, showed battle locations where Canadian forces had fought, and the destruction wrought by the German shelling.[9] More domestic, but still dramatic images appeared on his posters for the Belgian Red Cross, his 'Buy War Bonds' poster and the stamps he designed for the British Red Cross. One lithograph / poster, 'National Fund for Welsh Troops', depicts the back view of a massive solitary soldier, with a pencilled inscription on the reverse: "National Funds for the Welsh Troops: Poster designed to advertise a Grand Matinee St David's Day March 1st at the Alhambra". A large painting of 1915, 'Mater Dolorosa Belgica', shows another typical figure; a seated, half-naked man supported by a tearful, cloaked, female personification of Belgium, with refugees and ruins in the background. Given his antecedents, Brangwyn naturally emphasised the Belgian content in his war art. In 1916 he contributed fifty-two illustrations to the commemorative book *Belgium*, which was dedicated to the King of the Belgians.

Brangwyn also contributed to an ambitious enterprise by the DoI; a series of sixty-six lithographs by eighteen artists under the umbrella title *Britain's Efforts and Ideals in the Great War*. This scheme was unconnected with the practice of sending artists to the Western Front, and was seen simply as a propaganda campaign for the Home Front and friendly nations. Brangwyn and Augustus John were two Welsh artists whose work was included, and Brangwyn was allocated the 'Effort' of 'Training the Navy' because of his known love of the sea, his many sea pictures, and his earlier membership of the Royal Naval Volunteer Reserve.[10] The collection was exhibited in London, and later in Paris, New York and Los Angeles, receiving an enthusiastic reception in the USA, and amply fulfilling the aims of the DoI.

Brangwyn was equally committed on a social level, with particular affection for the country of his birth. When several Belgian refugee artists were exiled in Wales and England, Brangwyn helped them in various ways. In 1914, after the outbreak of war, the painter Pierre Paulus was given sanctuary in Brangwyn's London home, while the painter Edgar Gaevart in Wrexham and the sculptor George Minne in Llanidloes were sent art materials by Brangwyn.[11]

Although the BWMC had "charge of the task of having the war recorded in paint and marble" (Bennett), by the nature of their medium, sculptors did not figure prominently among the artists chosen by the committee. The most distinguished Welsh member of the British art establishment at the outbreak of war was a sculptor, Sir William Goscombe John (1860-1952). Born humble William John in Cardiff,[12] he had been elected a Royal Academician in 1909 and knighted for services to Welsh art at the investiture of the Prince of Wales at Caernarfon in 1911. A loyal Welshman, he was also a tireless illustrator of the British imperial ideal, with many portraits of king-emperors, proconsuls, victorious generals and other worthies distributed across the empire, in such places as Capetown, Calcutta, Cairo, Lucknow, Surabaya, Nairobi, Nagpur and Montreal, as well as in Washington, Geneva and numerous locations in England and Wales.

Goscombe John became well versed in portraying images of wars and warriors, harking back to images from the eighteenth century. A commission of 1904 for a memorial to the King's Regiment for Liverpool, embodied his most popular sculpture, the colossal 'Drummer Boy', an heroic figure of the 1743 Battle of Dettingen in the War of the Austrian Succession.[13] Two years later John moved on to the Crimean War with a commission for a bronze equestrian portrait, now prominent in Cardiff, of Viscount Tredegar, a hero of the Charge of the Light Brigade in 1854. A bronze bust of General Lord Kitchener, exhibited at the R.A. in 1917 (the year after Kitchener's death) and commissioned for the Gordon Memorial College in Khartoum, stood for the colonial wars in the Sudan, South Africa and India, as well as the early campaign on the Western Front in the First World War. Another imperial veteran portrayed by John was Sir Stanley Maude, who served in the Boer War and then in the Dardenelles but made his reputation fighting the Turks in Mesopotamia in 1916-17, a campaign which culminated in the capture of Basra and finally Baghdad. John's bronze equestrian portrait of Maude, a somewhat pedestrian affair, was sent to Baghdad but its present whereabouts are unknown.

In 1916, John produced another memorial to war, again intended for Liverpool but this time in homage to a lower order of civilian heroes. His monumental, architectural 'Engine Room Heroes', carved in granite and located at the Pier Head, shows figures of engineers and stokers on two faces, surmounted by four allegorical figures representing the elements, an obelisk topped by four female personifications of the sea and crowned by a gilded torch, its flames symbolising the ships' furnaces. The monument was funded by international subscriptions and was originally commissioned in 1912, to commemorate the engine room heroes of the *Titanic*, who sacrificed their lives to keep the ship afloat as long as possible. In November 1912, John went to Liverpool and made sketches and notes of the engine room of the *SS Caronia* and the engineers' dress. However, problems with location and the possibility of enlarging the scope of the memorial delayed the project, and John returned to Liverpool in May 1914 to make more notes and sketches aboard the *SS Arabic*. With the outbreak of war, the monument was finally dedicated to all engine room heroes and placed prominently at the river front. It is the most elaborate of the several Pier Head monuments to the merchant marine, and it remains a striking tribute to the unknown, unseen, unremembered heroes of the sea, braving the dangers of the surface and the submarines.

Early in his career, in 1894, John had been hailed as "the youngest of the important sculptors of the new school, the latest of the little band by whom the ninth decade of our century will be famous in the Art history of the future". To the writer, Edmund Gosse, the New Sculpture was defined by "the bold introductions of the picturesque, a close and reverent observation of nature".[14] But the inventiveness of John's early work, often influenced by Rodin, became gradually diluted by the more profitable genres of portraiture and public and private monuments, while his observation of nature became confined to securing the likeness of a sitter, and perhaps his horse. The war seemed to have been a stimulus for John, a compassionate man, and his 'Engine Room Heroes', and subsequent post-war memorials, demonstrated a revival of his inventiveness when freed from the shackles of portraying a likeness.

John's namesake and fellow countryman, the painter Augustus John (1878-1961), was no relation but was equally celebrated and certainly more notorious. The *enfant terrible* of the British art establishment, his social reputation was at a polarity to that of Sir William, and he was also considered far more avant-garde. On 27th November 1917, the art critic of *The Times* hailed John as "the most famous of living English [sic] painters". By then, John had become an ardent Francophile, and the outbreak of war both challenged and intrigued him and left him undecided about his response:

> I can't leave my painting at this stage nor can I leave my family without resources ... I shall be doing better to keep on

> working at my own job. However, I long to see something of
> the fighting ... I feel a view of the havoc in Belgium with the
> fleeing refugees would be inspiring and memorable.[15]

Whatever his bravado, John was not eligible for active service,
having damaged both knees in separate foolhardy accidents, and
anyway, he was thirty-six at the outbreak of war, when there was a
rush of much younger volunteers. However, his reputation as a
fashionable portraitist ensured that he gained several prestigious
commissions: high-ranking officers including Admiral Lord Fisher
and, in the winter of 1915-16, Lloyd George himself. This was
unsatisfactory from the point of view of both parties, and the
expected rapport between two libidinous Welshman did not materi-
alise. Lloyd George, with his manifold responsibilities, was difficult
to pin down, and John, despite his professed admiration for his
fellow countryman, became frustrated, and described Lloyd George
as "a rotten sitter ... a hot-arse who can't keep still and be patient".[16]
His contact with Lloyd George was not propitious and did not lead
to a commission to visit the Western Front:

> I have applied for a temporary commission which I think is
> indispensable to move with any freedom in the British lines
> ... you might suppose that I could do something with Lloyd
> George but I fear that gentleman will never forgive me for
> painting a somewhat unconventional portrait of him.[17]

John still hankered to see and depict the action at the Front. "I very
much want to do a great deal in the way of military drawings and
paintings," he informed the publisher Grant Richards. But John was
thwarted by red tape; in order to be seconded as a war artist, the
applicant had first to enlist, and John was not medically fit to enlist.
However, he did allow the DoI to use a 1917 lithograph, 'The
Dawn', to be included in the series *Britain's Efforts and Ideals in the
Great War*, it was not one of his best and had not been specifically
produced for the project. It shows an anguished, Dorelia-like
woman clutching a skull, with a John-type child at her feet and a
war-torn landscape behind. Finally, Masterman of the DoI was
persuaded to invite John to act as one of its official war artists. But
Masterman was too late; Beaverbrook, who was not yet Minister for
Information but was still chairman of the Canadian War Record
Office, used his influence to recruit John before Masterman could.
John was given the rank of major with full pay and allowances and
expenses of £300 – much more generous than the British would

have been. With an honorary commission in the Canadian Overseas Military Forces, John became the only Welshman to gain official status as a war artist.

Nevertheless, his appointment aroused indignation and some confusion in certain Welsh quarters. In June 1918 *The Welsh Outlook*, 'A Monthly Journal of National Progress', protested indignantly that John should have been attached to a Welsh division, "but owing to ignorance of his work in the Principality he was not approached on the subject", which neatly demonstrated the *Outlook*'s ignorance of the relevant bureaucracy. By January 1918, John was at the Front in France, billeted in a chateau at Aubigny, near the Vimy sector. In addition to his compulsive socialising, there were several enticing art prospects: a commission from the Canadian War Memorials Fund (CWMF) for a vast forty-foot canvas, 'The Pageant of War', as well as 'fighting' sketches of soldiers.

Unfortunately, John's actual Front Line work was minimal, and the most memorable fighting he witnessed was of his own making. He lasted barely three months in France before a drunken brawl at HQ in March 1918, when he knocked out a junior officer, resulted in his hasty recall to London by Beaverbrook. Before John's appointment, Beaverbrook had described him as "the greatest artist of our time and possibly of any time".[18] But disillusionment soon set in: "Do you know I saved [John] at a Court Martial for hitting a man? ... I cannot tell you what benefits I did not bestow on him. And do you know what work I got out of John? – not a damned thing."[19] Back in London, and in disgrace, John was finally commissioned by the BWMC for a canvas, nine by twenty feet (2.74 x 6.09 m), with the title 'The Junction of Our Lines with the French'. This was one of two super-pictures commissioned towards the end of the war; the other was by the American painter John Singer Sargent, and it was Sargent – not John – who was personally recommended by Lloyd George. These pictures were intended to be the dramatic centre-pieces of a planned Hall of Remembrance, to be built after the war. But whereas Sargent's 'Gassed' has become a famous image of war, John's super-picture never materialised – but then neither did the Hall of Remembrance.

John battled on with 'The Pageant of War' (his 'Canadian incubus' he called it) which was shown in cartoon form in the Canadian War Memorial Exhibition at the Royal Academy in January 1919, which also included works by Paul Nash, Wyndham Lewis and C.R.W. Nevinson. John's huge charcoal drawing was lauded by *The Times* for its timeless appeal: "Even Mr Paul Nash may grow old-fashioned with the years, but it is hard to imagine a time when Major John's cartoon (not yet finished) 'The Pageant of War' will not interest by its masterly suggestion of what war means."[20] William Rothenstein described it as 'superb', while to Kenneth Clark it was the 'one masterpiece' of the CWMF collection, "which may eventually prove to be the finest thing he [John] ever did". The cartoon was offered to the Imperial War Museum for £1,000 but the offer was refused, and Clark claimed to have 'discovered' it many years after the war, entitled 'The Kensingtons at La Bassae', "in a cellar in Ottawa".[21]

Now known as 'The Canadians Opposite Lens' (National Gallery, Ottawa) the huge drawing is one of John's more coherent, inventive compositions – a frieze-like panorama of figures, set amongst blasted trees, ruined buildings and a battered, symbolic Calvary. It is a synthesis of events from the campaign, showing refugees, German prisoners and Canadian soldiers, posed before a background of gun emplacements and a barrage balloon, all set against the distant Vimy ridge and the town and spoil heaps of Lens.[22] However, the painting itself, like the art gallery Beaverbrook planned for Ottawa to house the Canadian war pictures, never came to fruition and the canvas remained in a permanent state of "not yet finished", rolled up in John's studio until his death.[23]

From his time at the Front, John did produce some simple, effective, half-length portraits of low-ranking, young and earnest Canadian soldiers. These are probably his most enduring and endearing images of the war. A more ambitious painting was a large, tall canvas entitled 'Fraternity', which shows a close-knit group of three battle-weary soldiers, standing among ruined buildings and sharing a light from a cigarette. A touching scene, it became a minor icon of the camaraderie of war. However, it later transpired that the painting was not sketched from life, but was an almost exact copy of a postcard photograph from a popular series issued by the *Daily Mail* and entitled 'A "Fag" after a Fight'.[24] The figures in the painting are identical to the postcard, although John has transformed the background from a dreary muddy road into a rudimentary ruined building with an iconic blasted tree, a setting that seems to have been borrowed from his 'Pageant of War'.

Augustus John's sister Gwen (1876-1939), who continued to live in Paris throughout the war, also made copies from war photographs. These were portrait drawings of generals and diplomatic luminaries, taken from newspapers and magazines, which she copied in 1915-16, and sent to her American patron John Quinn to be exhibited in New York. Unusually, perhaps uniquely, she pressured Quinn to buy or sell the folios of drawings and was reluctant to accept his low evaluation of them. For the project was, she informed Quinn on 15th February 1916, "an idea of Monsieur le Curé!", the priest at Meudon, an injunction which overcame her normal diffidence about selling her work. Even so, the usually irresistible Quinn found it difficult to move them, for they could not be ranked among her best drawings. Surprisingly, Gwen John does not seem to have been inspired by the harrowing scenes of wounded soldiers that she witnessed in Paris, evocative of Sargent's 'Gassed':

> It is dreadful to see the maimed in the streets it is even more heart-rending to see a body of blind men ... a man goes before and cries *Faites place! Faites place!* and the poor men follow holding on to one another.[25]

Around this time, Gwen John was recommended to the BWMC by Muirhead Bone as a potential war artist. In a sudden fit of egalitarianism, the committee had decided to recruit women artists, and Bone suggested Gwen John, Dora Carrington, Dorothy Brett and Gwen Raverat. But the committee, usually so enterprising, opted for three lesser-known, more traditional women artists, none of them Welsh, and then never actually acquired any work from any of them.[26]

After the armistice, there was another spate of war art, mainly in the form of war memorial monuments, which appeared in many shapes and sizes in many places across Britain. Those with Welsh connections have been thoroughly documented in a separate study,[27] but it is worth commending Goscombe John's contribution to the genre in other parts of Britain, particularly the monumental memorial at Port Sunlight. Meanwhile, Augustus John's contentious reputation was still robust enough for him to be given a prestigious commission. The great Peace Conference, which opened in Paris on 12th January 1919 and lasted for over a year, was attended by the leaders of thirty-two sovereign states representing about three quarters of the world's population. Lloyd George demanded "some suitable and permanent memento of these gatherings" and so Augustus John and Sir William Orpen – "two of the most famous British artists"[28] – were each commissioned by the MoI to produce a large painting (£3,000 apiece plus £3 a day expenses) showing the main players. Orpen, an Irishman, had been an accredited – and also a reliable and prolific – war artist, while for John this was a commission that could have restored his reputation and his status as one of the leading portrait painters of Europe. Despite Orpen's

disdain for the leaders of men ("very small personalities in comparison with the fighting men") he renegotiated his contract and did at
least turn out the three paintings (at £2,000 apiece) now required of
him. John, however, although in desperate need of the money, was
again seduced by social distractions – this time of post-war Paris and
his enhanced status as an artist, an officer and (presumably) a
gentleman. He made many revealing drawings of leading statesmen
– some verging on caricature – but failed to produce the required
conference painting. Instead, he donated eight drawings to the
Imperial War Museum, and sold 'Fraternity' to the museum for the
bargain price of £140.

Brangwyn suffered from a condition contrary to John's; he was
incapable of abandoning a project. Unfortunately, his epic war
memorial commission – a vast mural scheme for the House of Lords
– had a troubled destiny. The fateful 'Empire Panels', originally
commissioned in 1924 as a memorial to those peers or relations of
peers who had died in the war, went through three versions. The
final version – Brangwyn's potential *magnum opus* – was rejected by
the Royal Fine Art Commission but can be seen today in Swansea's
Guildhall.[29] Brangwyn was devastated by the rejection of "the work
of seven years of a life the sands of which are running low". As some
consolation, in 1931, Brangwyn was offered a commission by the
War Memorial Committee of the National Museum of Wales for a
war painting with a specific Welsh theme. Brangwyn offered two
works from his abandoned first House of Lords design – 'Tanks' and
'Gun' – but the committee insisted on an original subject, and so
Brangwyn dolefully donated the two works to the museum and
began a new painting. The outcome was 'The Entry of the Welsh
Division into Jerusalem', a picture which did not satisfy the artist,
perhaps because of doubts about the historical accuracy of the
painting's subject.[30]

Brangwyn was not, of course, present at the surrender of
Jerusalem in December 1917 (a year of persistent ill-health for him)
although he must have been aware of contemporaneous visual
records. One official war artist, James McBey, a Scot, who had been
'embedded' with Allenby's campaign from its beginning in Cairo,
painted at least two versions of Allenby's formal entry on 11th
December from life [IWM], which correspond to photographs and
newsreels of the event. In his inimitable style, Brangwyn dramatised
his version to resemble a tableau from grand opera. He kept the
architectural setting of the Jaffa Gate and the viewpoint of one of the
photographs but introduced a more numerous and more colourful

crowd of spectators. The victorious General Allenby and his entourage of British, French and Italian commanders dressed in staff uniform (who respectfully entered on foot, having dismounted outside the gate) were replaced by Welsh soldiers in battle dress, with the leader carrying a drawn sword. Brangwyn's bravura, melodramatic version of the event makes McBey's reportage look very prosaic, but once again, as with Christopher Williams' 'Mametz Wood', it is a victory of aesthetics over facts.[31]

Williams made a final statement on the monumental folly, the useless slaughter, the horror and heroics of the war, that would never have been sanctioned by the DoI. Around 1920, he reverted to his pacifist sentiments and his preference for allegory with two studies for a painting, 'The Spirit of the Unknown Soldier Rising from his Grave Against the Futility of War'.[32] This was designed using classic Resurrection iconography, with a writhing, half-naked figure rising from a sepulchre, but like the eternal peace envisioned after the Great War itself – "the war to end all wars" – the intended painting was never realised.

One factor common to all these war artists was a considerable measure of detachment; they were often compassionate observers – but always observers. The outstanding exception was David Jones, the one Welsh artist who served and suffered in the hellish Somme campaign. For him, the response was personal, profound and traumatic. And it was not until ten years after the war that he began to formulate those harrowing experiences into his epic poem *In Parenthesis*;[33] that artistic search for the "formal goodness in a life singularly inimical, hateful, to us".

Notes

1. *The Times*, 21st September 1914.
2. Frances Stevenson, *Lloyd George: A Diary*, 21st September 1914 (ed. A.J.P. Taylor). London: Hutchinson, 1971.
3. Recruitment figures: Wales: 13.82% of population (2,025,198 at 1911 census); England: 13.30%; Scotland: 13.02%; Ireland: 3.87%. From Ivor Nicholson and Lloyd Williams, *Wales its Part in the War*. London: 1919, p.26.
4. Masterman's visual advisers included a future director of the V & A Museum (Eric Maclagan), the Keeper of Prints and Drawings at the British Museum (Campbell Dodgson), a former editor of the *Art Journal* (Alfred Yockney) and a teacher at the Royal College of Art (Thomas Derrick). His literary advisers included Arthur Conan Doyle, John Buchan, Ford Madox Ford, Hilaire Belloc and Arnold Bennett.

5. To ensure full newspaper support, Lloyd George appointed Beaverbrook's rival newspaper magnate, Lord Northcliffe, as Director of Propaganda for European Countries.

6. Arnold Bennett to Hugh Walpole, 12th December 1919. Bennett was referring to an exhibition of BWMC pictures, which had opened that day at the Royal Academy. He credited the non-academic nature of the collection to "Beaverbrook having the wit to leave the commissioning of pictures for the M of I to Masterman and me". In 1918 Bennett bought two pieces by a "new war artist", William Roberts, as well as etchings by Picasso, Rops and Sickert.

7. Brangwyn's father, William Curtis Brangwyn, had some Welsh blood; his mother, Eleanor Griffiths, hailed from Brecon. Brangwyn was baptised a Catholic, as Guillaume François.

8. In 1916 the collector Kojiro Matsukata appointed Brangwyn and Léonce Bénédite (Director of the Luxemburg Museum in Paris) as advisers to the new Kyoraku Museum in Kobe. Brangwyn was also asked to design the museum but his plans were rejected in 1919, and the project was completed by Le Corbusier.

9. *The Ruins of War:* 'Vimy', 'Dixmude', 'Cambrai', 'Arras', 'The Church of St Martin at Ypres' and 'The Entry of the Canadians at Cambrai'. With his economical working methods, Brangwyn adapted his drawings of the Messina earthquake, made on location in 1909, to illustrate some of the subjects of *Ruins of War*.

10. The other sixteen artists included George Clausen, William Nicholson, William Rothenstein, Muirhead Bone, Eric Kennington, Charles Shannon and Charles Ricketts. Most of the records of this scheme were destroyed by fire at the HMSO in the 1960s.

11. For a full account of the Belgian artists' exile in Wales during WWI see: Oliver Fairclough, Robert Hoozee and Caterina Verdickt (eds.), *Art in Exile: Flanders, Wales and the First World War*. Ghent / Heino-Wijhe / Cardiff, 2002. Eric Rowan and Carolyn Stewart, *An Elusive Tradition: Art and Society in Wales 1870-1950*. Cardiff: University of Wales Press, 2002.

12. At the beginning of his career, John adopted the name Goscombe from a village near his mother's birthplace in Gloucestershire.

13. The complete monument can now be seen in St John's Gardens, Liverpool, behind St George's Hall. A cast of the 'Drummer Boy' is in the National Museum in Cardiff.

14. From four essays by Edmund Gosse on New Sculpture in *The Art Journal* for 1894, pp.138, pp.199, pp.277, pp.306.

15. Augustus John to John Quinn, 10th October 1914.

16. Augustus John to John Quinn, 16th February 1916. Lloyd George was also suspicious of John's interest in his mistress Frances Stevenson. Lloyd George forbad her to sit for a portrait by John and also from going to the painter's notorious parties.

17. Augustus John to William Rothenstein, 26th April 1916.

18. Lord Beaverbrook to F.E. Smith, 28th November 1917. He was referring to John's current exhibition at the Alpine Club in London.

19. Lord Beaverbrook to Sir Walter Monckton, 30th April 1941.
20. 'War Story in Pictures. Canadian Exhibition at the Royal Academy', *The Times*, 4th January 1919. According to Cynthia Asquith (*Diary*, 19th July 1918), John's canvas was "all sketched in, but without any painting yet".
21. Foreword by Sir Kenneth Clark to Alan Ross, *The Colours of War*. London: Jonathan Cape, 1983, p.7. Clark gives an erroneous date of 1916 for the original R.A. exhibition. Clark's memory – or disdain – caused him to fall into further error; the cartoon was restored at the National Gallery of Canada in 1947-8 and always preserved above ground.
22. The large cartoon (3.7 x 12.3 metres) is now in the National Gallery of Canada in Ottawa, and has been separated into eight sections and mounted on canvas. It was noticed in John's studio in 1938 by Vincent Massey, the Canadian High Commissioner, when he sat to John for his portrait. Massey bought the cartoon, and in 1972 it was donated to the National Gallery of Canada.
23. The unfinished painting was part of the sale of John's studio contents by Christie, Manson & Woods Ltd. on 20th July 1962 (lot 184). It was bought by Paul Channon MP and destined for his house in Cheyne Walk, Chelsea.
24. The title 'Fraternity' was chosen by Alfred Yockney, a member of Masterman's committee. The postcard was part of the *Daily Mail Official War Pictures, Series 2 No.11*. The connexion between postcard and painting was first noticed by a sharp-eyed member of the Art Department of the Imperial War Museum.
25. Gwen John to John Quinn, 17th March 1916.
26. The three women artists appointed by the BMWC were Anna Airy, Dorothy Coke and Flora Lion. Airy had a painting of an army cook house in the 1919 Canadian exhibition, where Laura Knight was represented with the unusual subject, for her, of a boxing match.
27. Angela Gaffney, *Aftermath: Remembering the Great War in Wales*. Cardiff: University of Wales Press, 2000.
28. Lloyd George's private secretary to Sir Alfred Mond, February 1919.
29. For a detailed account see: David Bell, *The British Empire Panels*. Swansea, 1958.
30. According to one account, the actual surrender of Jerusalem on 9th December was not particularly heroic. The first British troops to enter the holy city were Welsh and Home Counties units. Before that, the surrender was reputed to have been willingly offered by the mayor of Jerusalem to two passing Cockney privates from the 60th (London) Division – who were out scouting for water. See: Lawrence James, *Imperial Warrior: The Life and Times of Field-Marshal Viscount Allenby 1861-1936*. London: Weidenfeld & Nicolson, 1993, p.140.
31. The Welsh troops certainly distinguished themselves in the capture of the city. Writing to his wife, Lieutenant-General Sir Philip Chetwode, commander of the 20th Corps, commented: "Tell Wales that my division fought magnificently and stood up to superior numbers for three days and nights and guarded my right flank while we broke the Turkish

centre. I am intensely proud of my troops, who fairly carried the Turk off his legs with their impetuosity." The 1917 photograph, which bears a striking similarity to Brangwyn's painting, is 'General Allenby's Entry into Jerusalem, 11 December 1917' by George Westmoreland. British Official Photograph commissioned by the War Office. Imperial War Museum [neg.Q12616].

32.   The two studies, in chalk and charcoal on one sheet of green paper, are in the collection of NMGW under the title 'Figure Study for a War Memorial'. It was exhibited in the Christopher Williams centenary exhibition (NMGW, 1973, no.76) under the title given in the text.

33.   "It was in 1927 or 28 [at his parents' rented house at Portslade] from the balcony of which I used to make paintings of the sea, I began to write down some sentences which turned out to be the initial passages of *In Parenthesis* published some ten years later." David Jones, 'Autobiographical Talk' in *Epoch and Artist: Selected Writings* (ed. Harman Grisewood). London: Faber and Faber, 1959.

Art in Wales during and from
the Second World War

Tony Curtis

At the outbreak of the Second World War many of the artists who would make significant contributions to the visual identity of Wales were elsewhere. The war would bring some artists, British and European, both new and established, back to Wales and take others away; it would focus the energies and visions of many in profound ways; the personal and creative lives of all would be changed.

The first casualty of the war was Gwen John (1876-1939). She had lived in Paris since before the outbreak of the 1914-18 war. In that conflict she had escaped the very real threat of a German advance on Paris by spending periods in Brittany; in September 1939, two weeks after the declaration of war on Germany, seriously, probably terminally ill, she left her house and studio in the city's suburb of Meudon and travelled to the coast. Perhaps she was trying to reach the comparative safety of her brother's house in Fordingbridge. She collapsed in Dieppe and in the confusion of the imminent conflict, the inevitable German invasion, unrecognised, she died and was buried in an unmarked grave in that town. At the end of September her nephew and principle heir and executor, Edwin, was able to cross the Channel and go to the converted hut in which she'd spent her last months. From the work he retrieved an exhibition was held at the Wildenstein Gallery in London the follow-ing year. This work greatly moved Augustus, "I am flummoxed by their beauty," emphatically underlining the loss both the family and British art had suffered by her decline and death.[1]

Augustus John (1878-1961) had also been in France that September, summering in Provence with Dorelia and a selection of his children. At the last moment, Augustus acknowledged the inevitable and fled by car to Le Havre. The rich and famous painter secured safe passage for his company and his two cars on one of the last ships out. That was eleven days before his sister's death in Dieppe.

John had been the pre-eminent Welsh, pre-eminent British painter of his generation but his work during the Second World War was no more significant than that in the 1914-18 conflict. Remarkably, he had been commissioned by the Canadians as one of their war artists on the Western Front. Chauffeured from chateau to chateau, he was strikingly deferred to by the columns of marching Tommies, the only bearded man in the Allied armies other than the King himself. Unlike his contemporary William Orpen, Augustus John avoided the horrors of the fighting and represented the greatest European conflict by one painting of two Tommies sharing a cigarette on a bare road. His wartime responses were as ignominious as his Versailles peace paintings were grandiloquent.

In 1939 he was, of course, in his sixties, and with many years of hard living under his belt. The war and Gwen's death was a double blow: "I don't see what I can do but go on painting," he said.[2] And, in fact, his life during the war was little changed. He frequented the usual, even less-well-lit haunts of Fitzrovia and met other ex-pat Welsh exiles such as Dylan Thomas and Nina Hamnett. This was the time of Dylan's *Deaths and Entrances*, "When the morning was waking over the war". John, the elder statesman of the Bohemians, continued to exhibit in the Wildenstein, the Redfern and the Leicester galleries and undertook portraits of the rich and famous, including Lord Portal, Marshall of the Royal Air Force and Montgomery, the hero of the Eighth Army. Monty was an uneasy sitter who observed of John that, "He drinks, he's dirty and I know there are women in the background!"

John had been politically active in the Thirties in the sense that he had supported the formation of the Artists' International Association; during the war he donated paintings for war funds and to aid the relief of refugee artists. He felt uneasy seeing his son Edwin in the uniform of the Military Police, but father and son collaborated over the retrieval of Gwen John's work from Meudon before the Germans arrived and exhibitions of her work were held by the Wildenstein Gallery in 1940 and again in 1946.

Augustus John's Tite Street studio remained resolutely open despite the German bombers and John's work was lauded in the *British Painting since Whistler* exhibition held at the vacant National Gallery: vacant because the treasures of the permanent collection had been secretly transported to the safety of Manod Quarry in Blaenau Ffestiniog.[3] Two books were published on his work during the war and in 1942 he was awarded an O.M. He wrote regularly for *Horizon*: pieces of autobiography and opinion which would later form the core of his book *Chiaroscuro*. Dorelia and he gave shelter to evacuated children at Fryern. Michael Holroyd sees the war years as the last colourful manifestation of John the aging bohemian. He supported Bertrand Russell's anti-nuclear campaign in the Fifties, but was ill and lacking real energy. In truth, his best work had largely been produced before the First World War and his significance as a British artist and a famous Welsh painter was based on fame rather than contemporary work between the wars and in his final decade.

Morland Lewis (1903-43), had studied with Sickert and was one of the most accomplished painters between the wars in Wales, bringing a Euston Road sensibility to the Welsh landscape. He was a casualty of the war in north Africa, succumbing to malaria in Tunisia. Lewis had known the Welsh bohemian-manqué set in London before the war; he knew Ceri Richards, Alfred Janes, Merfyn Levy and John Petts. Like Richards, he had taught for a time at Chelsea. In 1939 when he got married Dylan Thomas acted as his best man.

Art continued, of course, despite of and in some cases because of the war. Lieutenant Kyffin Williams, serving in the Royal Welch Fusiliers, was invalided out when it was discovered that he had epilepsy. He took up art as a therapy and was accepted at the Slade School because they had few male students. Staff, including Schwabe, Rutherston, Allan Gwynne-Jones and George Charlton, and students had been moved out of London to Oxford for the duration and Kyffin Williams commanded a Home Guard platoon in which both staff and fellow students served. Ironically, in 1948 the Slade-qualified painter was invited back to his regiment to paint portraits of the soldiers: a fine example, 'Fusilier Dean', of a soldier in wartime battledress, hangs in the regiment's museum in Caernarfon Castle.

That museum also has drawings by Fusilier David Jones from the Western Front trenches. Jones remained in his dugouts in London throughout the Second World War. The most significant poet-painter since William Blake had been essentially formed by his experiences in the trenches, his conversion to the Catholic faith and his resolution of the trench horrors and the positive virtues of comradeship and shared hardship were celebrated in his epic prose-poem *In Parenthesis*, published under the editorship of T.S. Eliot at Faber and Faber in 1937.

David Jones (1895-1974) was the only Welsh artist to have seen active service in the 1914-18 war still producing work in the Second World War. In 1939 he was living in Sidmouth, recovering from an appendix operation, but for most of the war he lived in London, in the Chelsea and Kensington homes of friends. *In Parenthesis* had brought him serious critical attention as a writer and had, to a large extent, resolved some of the issues and experiences of his three years on the Western Front. There were further complexities, personal and intellectual, which were perhaps never resolved. Jones had read *Mein Kampf* and, in common with others, and though he was disturbed by the 'hate thing', had found much to applaud in the sweeping rhetoric against capitalist exploitation, the lack of direction in the post-war European societies, the need for a radical fresh start. Hitler, like Jones, had served in the Mametz sector and the argument that British and German soldiers shared common experiences as cogs in a massive killing machine was central to Jones' ability to make sense of the horrors of that conflict. Both sides were brothers in arms, tragically hung on the same wire.

In 1938 David Jones began work on a large watercolour 'Aphrodite in Aulis'. This work uses the story of Agamemnon offering his daughter as a sacrifice in order to raise the necessary winds for his expedition. In Jones' version the buxom girl is pedestalled at the centre of a chaotic circus of conflict from the classics to the twentieth century. She is modestly clothed in birds and flowers and flanked on each side by one Tommy and one German soldier; each is naked from the waist and partly dressed in contemporary uniform and Roman armour. At the base of Aphrodite's column there is a sacrificial lamb. In the sky there is a sickle moon, messenger birds and a barrage balloon. Again, David Jones is working to resolve the current conflict by creating a vision of ancient conflicts and their interconnectedness. European brother fights brother; they are flesh that bleeds, but also pawns, players in a continuing military dance.

During the war years Jones also worked on 'Guenever' and 'The Four Queens', an incident from Malory's *Morte d'Arthur*, both were bought by the Tate Gallery. Also, 'Britannia and Germania Embracing', subtitled 'Epiphany 1941', which specifically responds to the German bombing of Coventry that year. The destruction of much of that city shocked Jones profoundly and he included at the bottom of this work the words from the Coventry carol "O sisters two what may we do".

In the Malory works the figure of Lancelot wears what could be a German helmet, while the two feminised figures in 'Britannia and Germania Embracing' have helmets derived from the classical and pagan. They grasp phallic, penetrative weapons and again the background has messenger birds, a heavenly body, howling dogs, a church in ruins and ships sunk at sea. The two figures are caught at the instant of an awkward, ambiguous embrace. Jones' art work at this time is often held between poles of war and sexuality. Other drawings, 'Woman', 'Schoolboy & Soldier on Tube' (1940) and 'Woman Warden During the Blitz' (1941)[4] in which women are juxtaposed with phallic rifle and torch, are cruder examples of sexualised wartime scenes. The air-raid warden is bare-breasted, with her bare thigh caressed by a cat – more lady of the night than Aphrodite.

When in 1941 David Jones was examined as part of the process to register for Industrial Service it was declared that he was "quite unfit for routine service". There were long-term effects from the Western Front and his sexual apprenticeship in the perverted world of Eric Gill's community would continue for the rest of his life. In 1946, in fact, he again had a serious depression and was treated in hospital.

Nevertheless, the war years were a period of success for Jones. He was championed by Kenneth Clark and was included in the National Gallery's *British Painting since Whistler*, as well as his solo shows at the Redfern and having a painting purchased by the Queen. Work began on the introduction to his work in the *Penguin Modern Painters* series, written by Robin Ironside; that monograph was eventually published in 1949. His success continued throughout the war and as V.E. Day approached Jones had work included in the re-opened St George's Gallery in the West End. He had lost his mentor Eric Gill, but had enjoyed a positive relationship with T.S. Eliot, who was to continue to support Jones and publish his *Anathemata* in 1951. He had written and painted steadily through the war, though whether he had truly resolved his sadness and confusion over the conflict with Germany is debatable.

Of course, several writers and artists were confirmed in their pacifist stance by the war. That principle would bring Arthur Giardelli (1911) to Wales to work as a teacher in the Rhondda. Arthur Giardelli had lived in Wales when his family moved from London to Amroth in Carmarthenshire in 1928. After Oxford and the Ruskin he had been appointed a teacher of English and French at Folkestone Grammar School, and in 1940 the school moved to Merthyr Tydfil for the duration of the War. When he registered as a conscientious objector he lost his job. He was supported by local Quakers and served as a part-time fireman. He also taught Music at Cyfarthfa Grammar School and lectured on the History of European Art for the Workers' Educational Association. He was involved immediately after the war in tracing art works for the London dealer Estorick and settled in Wales in 1947, teaching in the extra-mural department for UC Aberystwyth, painting and creating three-dimensional works, inspired by the Pembrokeshire coast. He became a friend and correspondent of David Jones to whom he'd been introduced by Ray Howard Jones.

Two women were engaged in work in Wales as commissioned war artists: Ray Howard Jones and Laura Knight. Jones (1903-96) drew and painted the preparations for D-Day, particularly around the Bristol Channel. Born in Berkshire, she had been brought up in Penarth and spent much of her later life in Pembrokeshire which became one of her principal subjects. She trained at the Slade School of Fine Art, London, becoming a Senior Slade Scholar. At the outbreak of the war she had been working for the National Museum of Wales on archeological reconstruction drawings and was involved in Cardiff in organising classical concerts in the city's parks. During this period she and Gomer Llywelyn Jones, the Welsh composer, also directed the East Moors Settlement theatre. In 1943 she was appointed as an Accredited War Artist, and recorded the D-Day preparations, shipping and Coastal Defence around the Bristol Channel. She was thus one of a very small number of women to hold such a position. Ray Howard Jones injured her hand seriously in completing that work and carried that injury through the remainder of her long career as an artist, working with the Pembrokeshire landscape and coastline.

Dame Laura Knight (1877-1970), based in the Cotswolds, travelled to Newport in 1943 and recorded the work of one of the first pre-fabricated munitions factories. This had been erected in a matter of weeks in 1940. Her painting of 'Ruby Loftus Screwing a Breech-Nut' became an iconic image of the role of women on the Home Front and was used on war-effort posters: it was named as the 'Picture of the Year' in 1943 at the Royal Academy Summer Exhibition. Cinema newsreel showed Dame Laura taking Ruby Loftus to see the work in London.

Esther Grainger (1912-90) and Felicity Charlton (b.1913) were also active during the war. Charlton had moved to Cardiff when her husband Evan took charge of the School of Art. It was he who invited Ceri Richards to teach at the beginning of the war. Felicity Charlton drew and painted through the war years in Cardiff, notably scenes on city buses and an oil of a flag seller, now in the Newport City Art Gallery.

Esther Grainger had been working in the Settlement at Pontypridd and with the unemployed in that area. She met Cedric Morris (1889-1982), a descendent of the wealthy Morriston copper family, on his visits to the valleys and became involved with the East Anglian School of Painting at Benton End which he had started with his partner Arthur Lett-Haines. Both Morris and Grainger painted the valleys landscapes during the war and both met Heinz Koppel (1919-80) there. The Berlin-born Koppel had come to England in 1936. His London studio had been bombed and he had moved to a cousin's house in Pontypridd. In 1944, Grainger, "that noble spirit",[5] was responsible, with Morris and Koppel, for setting up the Federation of Welsh Music and Art Clubs, based on the Pontypridd and Dowlais Settlements. Cedric Morris used his influence as a successful, if self-taught, painter to generate the production of and support for art in the south Wales valleys. After his youthful excesses in Chelsea and Paris, he had in the 1930s re-discovered an affinity with "the unearthly and untouchable beauty that is Wales".[6] He determined to make a difference to his country through the art of his country.

John Elwyn (1916-97) as a CO was in 1940 sent to work in the forestry at Pontrhydyfen in the Afan Valley above Swansea. He painted that industrial and post-industrial area and for some years afterwards returned to the subject of those mining and steel communities in a series of genre works. In 1942 he was included in the National Eisteddfod exhibition and in 1944 was commissioned to illustrate stories of Christ and the disciples by Leslie Harris in the children's magazine *Y Twysydd*, as well as a book by Harris. At this time he had returned to Cardiff to work in food production and had joined a Quaker community there. He became very close friends with the writer and fellow CO Glyn Jones. He was also attended classes taught by Ceri Richards at the School of Art.

In common with many artists and writers John Elwyn was deeply affected by the revelations of Belsen and the death camps. In 1946 and 1947 he produced a series of paintings which reflected that collective fall from innocence: 'Tree Roots' (1945) records a bombed, uprooted destruction which 'The Stillness of the Roots' (1946) goes some way to resolve with its bared roots offering some semblance of protection to the dreaming man beneath them. 'The Aftermath' (1945) is a particularly anguished version of the landscape as Golgotha. After the war he returned to study at the Royal College and taught throughout his career in England. His subject matter remained, however, almost exclusively that of Ceredigion, re-visioned as a rural idyll with more positive light; fewer thorns and angled rocks than Sutherland's Pembrokeshire.

Merlyn Evans (1910-73) was born in Cardiff, but grew up in

Scotland and England. He exhibited with the London Group and at the International Surrealist Exhibition in London in 1936. He emigrated to South Africa in 1938 and served in North Africa as a commissioned officer engineer in the South African army. He fought up through Italy and witnessed the execution of Mussolini. The National Museum has 'Refugees' (1946), an angular representation of war-time civilian suffering. He returned to England after the war and amongst notable works was a series of lithographs much influenced by American contemporaries and his war-time experiences.[7]

Will Evans (1888-1957),[8] who had established the lithography department at Swansea School of Art in 1937, painted a series of watercolours and oils recording the 1941 blitz of the city. The Glynn Vivian has a substantial number of these: 'The Ruins of Messrs Ben Evans Store, 1942' and 'Wrecked Fish Shop, Swansea, 1941', among them. More conventional than the work of Piper and Sutherland, they are, nonetheless, a dramatic engagement with the reality of bombing by someone who had lived through it and those works resonate with Dylan Thomas' 'Return Journey', first broadcast in 1947.

Alfred Janes (1911-99) had been taught at Swansea and then the Royal Academy School. He served as a Captain in the Pioneer Corps in North Africa and was not de-mobbed until 1946. Before the war he had been one of the 'Kardomah Boys', the circle of gifted, witty Swansea youths who met with Dylan Thomas. He painted celebrated portraits of Dylan and Vernon Watkins, Dylan in 1934 and Vernon after he and Janes were de-mobbed. He met Dylan and Nina Hamnett in London during army leave "but the war was a different part of one's life and very little to do with art, except for some drawings which I did". He had returned to Swansea on leave after the fire-bombing of the town and in 1947 produced a fine oil, 'Castle Street, Swansea after the Blitz'. "Swansea disappeared overnight and after the bombing I was given compassionate leave. The centre of the town was devastated, including my studio. I had written some of my painting recipes on the wall, thinking that if I lost my notebooks they would be there!"[9]

Leslie Moore (1913-76) was a commissioned officer who served in the Middle East and Italy. After the war he worked as an Art Adviser and HMI and was an important influence on younger artists. A number of his war-time pen and ink drawings have been shown at the Martin Tinney Gallery in Cardiff. Moore discovered and supported through to art school the painter Peter Prendergast who was being taught by Gomer (Terry) Lewis (1921-?). Lewis had suffered badly at the hands of the Japanese in one of their barbarous POW camps. Like Terry Frost, he had begun drawing while a prisoner. Unable to return to his career as a PE teacher, he became an art master at Cwm Amman. Peter Prendergast recalled Lewis working at his memories of that imprisonment at the back of the large hut that was the school's art room. His work was subsequently acquired by CASW and the Welsh Arts Council and he had some success exhibiting at the Boyson Gallery and the Zaydler Gallery in London.[10]

A number of Jews escaping Fascism arrived in Wales. Heinz Koppel (1919-80) arrived in Wales in 1940 and became an influential figure for young Valleys painters such as Charles Burton and Ernest Zobole. The most influential refugee artist to live in Wales at this time was, though, Josef Herman (1911-2000). He had escaped Poland in 1938; his Jewish community had been constantly subjected to pogroms, but could not have imagined the Holocaust that was to obliterate them entirely. Herman arrived in Britain after a formative stay in Belgium and a dramatic journey through France. Deemed unfit for service with the exiled Polish army in Scotland, he had been patronised by the Scottish Jewish community, especially the Isaacs family. He arrived in south Wales in 1944 after an unhappy relationship and was instantly drawn to the mining community of Ystradgynlais where he stayed and worked as an artist for most of the next decade. In 1951 Herman was one of those artists chosen to exhibit at the Festival of Britain where his large works 'Miners Crouching' and 'South Wales' were shown.

His most profound influence was on the de-mobbed Will Roberts (1910-2000) who worked closely alongside Herman after the war, but Herman's expressionist work, developed from his contact with Belgians such as Constant Permeke, and his fresh approach to the subject-matter of working people, including studies of miners working at the coal face, would reverberate through Welsh art for the next fifty years – Will Roberts, Colin Jones, Jack Crabtree, Valerie Ganz, Peter Prendergast and James Donovan among them. After the war Will Roberts returned from RAF duties in Bath and Cambridgeshire where he had worked servicing aeroplanes. He had attended art evening classes during the war, and had visited the 1945 Picasso exhibition in London which had deeply impressed him, but it was his friendship with Herman which both widened and focussed his work: "I did no official war drawing or painting. What I was doing was purely private, but I was, in a small way, recording Britain as it was: country churches, farms, barns, landscape … I like the watercolour of a barn done at Comberton, just outside Cambridge. A beautiful barn – that could have disappeared."[11] That, essentially, is the underlying motive for much art produced at this time of war. Will Roberts also acknowledged the influence of Martin Bloch (1883-1954), who visited Wales both during and directly after the war. Wales needed a fresh stimulus, fresh influences and, ironically, the war and its consequences brought that about.

John Petts (1914-91), who in 1937 had founded the Caseg Press with Brenda Chamberlain (1912-71), was a CO and spent the first two years of the war as an agricultural worker in England. He and the poet Alun Lewis met in 1941 while Lewis was undergoing training and Petts was doing farm work in Surrey. Petts' fine drawing of the writer was used as a frontispiece for Lewis' first collection *Raiders' Dawn*. It was Alun Lewis who had written out of the blue to Petts and Chamberlain to suggest a collaboration and the possibility of broadsheets. The *Caseg Broadsheets*, which were produced from December 1941 to June 1942, represent an idealistic attempt to take Welsh poetry and art to the wider public. Printed on necessarily poor paper and selling by subscription for a modest sum, the broadsheets were a commercial failure, but a noble artistic gesture. Petts' 'Debris Searcher', used with two Lewis poems on the first broadsheet, is one of the more striking modernist images of the period. It takes and distorts to great effect the solidity of Petts' earlier rural images of working life to portray the frantic and desperate effort to rescue victims from the Blitz. Alun Lewis had been shown this wood engraving by Petts and was convinced the scheme could work with art of that quality. "John showed me a new engraving of his, of a man with terrible hands hanging like a sinewy demon against a beam, with searchlights tangled and wildly seeking him below. Air raid, all its horror and height and frenzy."[12]

Broadsheet No.3 'War and Wales' had ink drawings by both Chamberlain and Petts which are influenced by classical images of suffering: the themes that Richards would explore to greater effect in the immediate post-war years. *Broadsheet No.6* has Petts' 'Flower of the Bone', a Neo-Romantic wood engraving that has the skill in execution and the imaginative power of a Richards or Gertrude Hermes.

John Petts, in due course, gave up his CO position, enlisted and joined the Parachute Regiment as an unarmed medic. There he met and worked with another former CO, Jonah Jones. Jones (1919-2004) had also moved from the position of Conscientious Objector to enlisting as a medic. He had admired an engraving by Petts used

Entry of the Welsh Troops into Jerusalem: – Frank Brangwyn (National Museum, Cardiff)

Engineers – William Goscombe John, Liverpool Pier Head

Man with Morphine – John Petts

'*Ruby Loftus Screws a Breech Nut*' – Laura Knight (Imperial War Musuem)

to illustrate a Dylan Thomas story in *The Listener* and with it still folded in his pocket ensured that he was drafted into the same unit. Both men worked on a small press while on active service in Palestine. After the war, Jones trained for a period at Eric Gill's former studio and then joined the Caseg Press which John Petts had started up again in north Wales with his new wife, Kusha. He went on to major a substantial contribution 'to art in Wales, both as an artist and as an administrator.

In 1948 another Petts work was used in the posthumous collection of stories by Alun Lewis, published by Allen & Unwin. 'The Dying Soldier' shows the head of a mortally-wounded soldier with the morphine details of his treatment written on his forehead by the medical orderly, using the man's own blood.[13] Two moths, or butterflies, flutter above the bed; they are the spirit of the man and also perhaps that of the relationship between the artist and the writer who shot himself in India. Gweno, Lewis' widow, wrote to Petts: "I know that Alun was probably foreseeing his own death when he wrote the story and the power of the *face* in the drawing shocks me. I must nerve myself to look at it. I can't bear it, John. The War Graves Commission photograph of his wooden cross doesn't speak so loudly."[14]

Graham Sutherland (1903-1980) visited north Pembrokeshire first in 1934. Although he never resided in the county, Sutherland continued to visit and work in the landscape both before and during the war, and later in the 1970s. These visits and periods of residency were both pivotal and nourishing to the man and his art. He painted war scenes in Cardiff, Swansea and Pembroke. His 'Welsh Sketchbook' was published in *Horizon* in 1942.

Sutherland was possibly the leading British painter of his generation, though his reputation has declined since his death in 1980.[15] Born in London and trained at Goldsmith's as a printer, his early graphic work owed much to Samuel Palmer – Romantic English landscapes celebrating the rural idyll of cottages and hedged lanes. But in 1936 his etchings 'Clegyr-Boia I & II'[16] he began to explore the Pembrokeshire landscape and the forces of rock, hill and sky off which he would feed for decades. His works have their roots in the topographical and the naturalistic structures of landscape, but his best work in Pembrokeshire creates both a spiritual matrix and an emotional geometry of the actual. Sutherland converted to Catholicism in 1926 and it is almost impossible to view his twisting lanes and anguished tree-forms without involving the suggestion of Calvary and the crucifixion. From his 'Estuary with Rocks' (1937/8) to 'Cathedral (Study of Rocks)' (1975), the two periods of his engagement with Pembrokeshire can be seen as a series of encounters with the spiritual in nature, God manifested in the landscape.

In 1940 Graham Sutherland was appointed as an Official War Artist and he later undertook a commission to paint the blitzed buildings of Swansea and Cardiff; also foundry work in Cardiff, Guest, Keen and Baldwin's, which had "a Dantesque kind of atmosphere". The early wartime works 'Ruined Farmhouse, Wales', 'Devastation: House in Wales', 'Devastation: Solicitor's Office, Swansea' and 'Farmhouse on Fire, Wales' from 1940[17] have those concerns with the angularity of buildings in decay and the organic flaming of fire and another sort of growth that may be seen to be a constant preoccupation of his mature work. Sutherland also visited and worked in the Brecon Beacons, Barry, Llantwit Major and the Gower. In 1943 he recorded work at the open cast mine at Pwll Du near Abergavenny. He was changing as an artist: "I had been attempting to paraphrase what I saw, and to make paintings which were parallel to, rather than copy of nature. But now, suddenly, I was a paid official – a sort of reporter – and naturally not only did I feel that I had to give value for money, but to contrive somehow to reflect in an immediate way the subjects set me."[18] Kenneth Clark had worked to set up the War Artists scheme at the beginning of the war; he argued for the worth of art as national work of importance. Of Sutherland he wrote: "Why does he think he is serving his country better by digging potatoes than by painting the few pictures now being produced in Britain which have any chance of survival?"

He and Kathleen settled in a farmhouse near Whitesand Bay and it was their base in Pembrokeshire for some years. In 1944 Sutherland stayed in the Mariner's Arms in Haverfordwest with John Craxton and Lucian Freud (whose almost surreal, playful view of Tenby – Castle Hill and the harbour with a distorted Gosgar Rock becoming a dragon – is in the National Museum of Wales collection.)

Craxton (b.1922) visited Sutherland on several occasions in 1943 and 1944 and he, too, found the Pembrokeshire landscape and the instructive presence of the older artist an important experience. He has written of those visits: "Conditions are very important to the way in which art is made. By 1945, circumstances had changed with the end of the war, and I no longer needed this self-protective imagery [of bucolic calm as a sort of refuge]. But in wartime I went to St David's Head, in Pembrokeshire, with Peter Watson and Graham Sutherland, in 1943. There were cloudless days and the land was reduced to basic elements of life: rocks, fig trees, gorse, the nearness of sea on all sides, essential sources of existence." Craxton was mentored by Sutherland and tutored by Pembrokeshire: "There Craxton sketched alongside the older man and learned from him how to paraphrase an entire landscape in one intensely observed fragment of it, whether a rock, a tree root, or a sprig of gorse."[19] This is evident in works such as 'Tree Root in Welsh Estuary' (1943).

John Minton (1917-57) was another young painter who stayed with and was influenced by Sutherland. He had served in the Pioneer Corps, at Barmouth, for two years before being discharged in 1943. Minton's 'Recollections of Wales'[20], from 1944, poses an androgynous figure – bare-thighed like a David Jones subject of this time – with wind-swept hair under a wind-swept tree gazing at stubborn hedgerows, lanes and promontory that are pure Sutherland. Sutherland's visions of Pembrokeshire, as well as the work of Samuel Palmer, underpinned much of Minton's work. Pembrokeshire too, after the early bombing of Pembroke Dock's oil tanks, was comparatively safe, a base for Sunderland Flying Boat operations over the Atlantic, rather than London or the Welsh cities to the east.

Of course, what Graham Sutherland created from his Pembrokeshire experiences may not necessarily be apprehended by the public as being essentially Pembrokeshire. This is no tourist art, no direct representation of the sweep of coastline. But the rocks forms around St David's Head and the herons, river banks and tree-roots of the Cleddau estuary near Picton Castle are *his* Pembrokeshire and they become essential to the vocabulary of an artist whose bio-morphic and bestial forms in paintings and graphic art resonated so strongly in Britain and Europe in the post-war years.

At the end of the war in 1945 Graham Sutherland was staying with the Philipps family at Picton Castle. The thorns he drew then later greatly influenced his commission for a Crucifixion at St Matthew's Church, Northampton, which in turn led to more Church commissions, culminating in the tapestry at the re-built Coventry Cathedral. As an artist and as a Catholic, he needed to absorb the horrors that had emerged from the war; the rugged roots and thorns of his Pembrokeshire visits took on larger significances. He wrote: "I made some drawings, as I made them, a curious change developed. As the thorns rearranged themselves, they became, while still retaining their own pricking, space-encompassing life, something else – a kind of 'stand-in' for a Crucifixion and a cruci-fied head ..."[21] What he found and returned to constantly in Pembrokeshire was to drive much of his mature work.

Pembrokeshire was so central to so much of Sutherland's work that, until his final moments, he had expressed a wish to be buried in St Ishmael's churchyard. He was a regular visitor again in the last fifteen years of his life, staying in the Lord Nelson in Milford. It is certain that this significant artist continued to have personal and thematic roots in Wales and was particularly formed by the periods he spent here immediately before and during the Second World War.

John Piper (1903-92) was the other artist of considerable repute to work in Wales. John Russell Taylor in conversation with Piper says: "Piper once said to me that he could not imagine quite where Sutherland had found all the twisted, tortured roots which played such a prominent role in his paintings of the period, as Piper had never seen anything similar in Pembrokeshire. Then, after a moment's consideration, he added: 'But of course painters find only what they are already looking for, and paint what is in their heads rather than what they see outside'."[22]

That observation is instructive with regard to the work Piper did as an official War Artist from 1940. Piper had had very close associations with Wales, especially Pembrokeshire; he was married to the writer, critic and librettist Myfanwy, his second wife, and together they spent much time both in Snowdonia and in west Wales. At various times since 1939 they had stayed for periods in Pontrhydfendigaid in Ceredigion where Piper completed paintings and drawings of the Teifi lakes and Strata Florida Abbey. He was particularly drawn to the crumbling magnificence of Hafod. This grand house had been built in the late eighteenth century by Colonel Thomas Johnes the local MP, with some designs added by Nash. It was a doomed house, however, and was largely destroyed on two occasions by fire. Treasures and art were lost on both occasions. But the Pipers were evidently attracted to its faded glory and its ruinous beauty which, no doubt, appealed to the Neo-Romantic sensibility of the time. One senses a resonance with the *Foliate Heads* series and with many of the nearly obliterated stone faces and forms which Piper included in his responses to buildings. Just as Graham Sutherland saw in the roots and rocks of south Pembrokeshire forms elemental and susceptible to his imaginative re-structuring of the world; so Piper sought and found 'some new invention' in buildings and landscape, in Snowdonia and later in west Wales in the lanes which had featured so importantly in Sutherland's work, and later in that of John Elwyn, but also in the faded houses and castles of the rulers of the land, and in the austere chapels of Non-conformity. The artist chosen to record Windsor Castle as the Blitz threatened to destroy it was clearly working to celebrate the British heritage and

British values located in landscapes and buildings. In 1944 he visited Cardiff to paint the docks' activities.

Grongar Hill, with Paxton's Folly in the background, which John Dyer (1699-1757) had memorialised in verse, was the subject of several of Piper's works, as was Dryslwyn Castle nearby. 'Grongar Hill' was included in *English, Scottish and Welsh Verse*, chosen by John Betjeman in 1944. Such publications were clearly a morale-boosting exercise to focus the nation's resistance against the threat of invasion, the destruction of the Luftwaffe's bombing campaign and the very real possibility of the destruction of British traditions and culture.

The roads and lanes leading from and around the Piper's cottage south to St David's and beyond feature in many drawings and mixed media works. This is similar to Sutherland's concern with the twisting progress one makes through this landscape, but Piper's works are more impressionistic, less concerned with the geometry of meaning than with the exuberance of growth; the circles and arabesques of stones, low trees and bushes. His paintings are closer to Miro than Sutherland's blocking of colour and contour. Both artists sought to touch elemental natural forces in their work in west Wales; each was working in an aesthetic that we can now characterise as Neo-Romantic; each was championed by Kenneth Clark as necessary to the nation under threat of invasion.

Ceri Richards (1903-71) was teaching in London when war was declared, but moved to a post in Cardiff School of Art in 1941 where he worked with Evan Charlton. Ceri and Frances Richards lived in Whitchurch and the painter was also engaged in fire-watching duties around Ely racecourse. Richards had been darkly fascinated by Count Ciano's descriptions of Italian bombing in Ethiopia in 1938 and this, together with the experience of the London Blitz led to drawings and paintings: two works, 'Blossoms' (1940) and 'Falling Forms' (1944), are notable and are a development from the more restrained 'Flowers' (1938). Using frottage and other textured applications of the oil paint, Richards works to recreate the violent beauty of explosions. In this period his work conflates the biomorphic buddings and flowerings that sit centrally in the Neo-Romantic aesthetic with more wildly exciting procreative forces, elements of the surrealists, especially Max Ernst. A work from 1941, 'Desolate Landscape' is a radically modernist piece which makes a fascinating comparison with David Jones' work from the same year. The sword, shield shape and standard which might come out of a Jones composition are caught in a maelstrom of dark but organically fertile forms and forces.

In 1942 his first solo exhibition was held at the Leger Gallery; based in Cardiff, Richards was still making his reputation in London. Also that year, he was engaged by the Ministry of Information to document war workers and he completed a series of drawings of tinplate workers at the Gowerton mill where his father had worked. These are dignified, heroic figures portrayed with much sympathy. He continued also to work on the Coster figures of London and had begun to explore the forms and energies located in Delacroix's 'Lion Hunt', as well as some stark and powerful landscapes in Wales. None of this, however, prepares one for the major works of the last two years of the war.

In 1944 Richards produced the most astonishing painting to have been completed in war-time Britain. 'Cycle of Nature' combines the balletic sky swirls of Nash's 'The Battle of Britain' (1941) with the explosive distortions of a Francis Bacon nude. The roots of the work and much of what was to engage this artist in the decade after the war was the poetry of Dylan Thomas. 'The force that through the green fuse drives the flower' in particular had struck Richards and he was inspired by the poem to produce a series of works. Drawings from 1945 were used as a lithograph centre-piece for the 1947 edition of *Poetry London*. In 1943 and 1944 he had worked on 'The Force that Drives the Water Through the Rocks', a large oil which had been included in his exhibition at the Redfern Gallery in 1944. It is a surreal, disturbing piece.

That fascinated, vital engagement with Thomas' imagery would inform and energise much of Richards' mature work. A sense of the deep ambiguity of human existence, the inevitability of violence as part of the nature of things, continued for Richards in the decade following the war. His *Rape of the Sabine Women* series of works immediately after the war are trying to resolve that ambiguity. The Romans abduct and rape the daughters of their guests, but the violation is part of the survival and development of each tribe. Through violence comes change and resolution.

Richards, in 1953, hearing of Dylan Thomas' collapse and coma, bought four copies of the *Collected Poems* and began to re-read the poems, drawing copiously on the pages of the books in the days before Thomas' death.

The poem in Thomas' *Collected Poems* which is illuminated by Richards' 'Black Apple of Gower' is 'I dreamed my genesis', published in *18 Poems* (1934). This is a work of creative violence; it shows a creative spirit born out of destructive forces: the poet from a "sweat of sleep" breaks through a "rotating shell" that is both seashell and artillery shell as the poem proceeds to develop a set of war images:

> I dreamed my genesis and died again, shrapnel
> Rammed in the marching heart, hole
> In the stitched wound and clotted wind, muzzled
> Death on the mouth that ate gas.

Dylan Thomas was born in 1914, the year the world plunged into a blood bath that would stretch from Verdun to Gallipoli, from Palestine to Ypres. One should not forget that the generation who grew up between the wars were haunted by the horrors they had missed but that had traumatised their parents. The artist Charles Burton, one of the 'Rhondda Group' years later worked on a series of First World War paintings and drawings to exorcise the memories of the maimed and shell-shocked survivors he saw daily as a boy in the 1930s in Treherbert.[23] Though it is nowhere recorded, the young Ceri Richards must have had closer, if second-hand, experiences of the Great War as he was a teenager in Dunvant during that period. The 'Black Apple of Gower' painting deals with the Gower-genesis of the poet and artist, as well as the war-nightmares of the poet's dream, re-enacted in 1939. There is an ambiguity of the Gower-mandala's darkness – seed, womb, tunnel, the 'rotating shell' even – and of the presence of the owl, bringer of death and conveyer of souls. This is a work still haunted, as were much of the 1950s, by the war.[24]

In 'Black Apple of Gower' (*'Afal du Brogŵr'*) (1952) on which Richards quoted from 'The force that through the green fuse', the black apple is an invention of Richards himself. A bright sun and striped sky hangs over a perspective view of the peninsular which is dark and sectioned (like a mandala, Jung thought)[25] and which contains both the owl and the written quotation from Thomas' 'The force that through the green fuse drives the flower'. At the foot of the painting is the inscription *"Gwrogaeth I Dylan Thomas"* ("Homage to Dylan Thomas"). It is a key work which draws on the specific links, poetic and geographical, of the two artists. It is also a work of universality, recognised by Jung and Adler as re-presenting an archetypal experience. The Gower is where one is born and where one's roots remain; the encircling sea is the birth-water, the water that receives our ashes: to begin at the beginning, for our end is in our beginning.

The black apple connotes womb and seed, cross-sectioned root and trunk. The fig-form is suggested in the black apple-mandala and this connects this work to the Genesis creation myth and which is the fruiting sex-organ that appears first in the *Sculptor in his Studio* works of the 1930s, in the *Poetry London* lithograph and afterwards in works up to the final screenprint 'Origin of Species'.

The owl at the upper left edge of the mandala is, of course, an important link to Thomas and flies above his corpse in the *Do Not Go Gentle* works of the 1950s and 1960s. Ceri Richards was familiar with the *Mabinogi* myths and could include owls in his work as rich suggestions of both female sexuality and as a harbinger of death.

The 1939-45 war left a legacy in terms of personal and social loss and advancement: nothing would be the same after the bombing of Wales, the disruption of families, institutions and government. Nothing could be the same after the revelations of the death camps and the Japanese atrocities when Welsh service men and women returned; the deaths of Morlais Lewis and Alun Lewis were significant losses. But there had been the invigorating influx of other artists – Giardelli, Herman, Piper, Sutherland and others. The most remarkable work in three dimensions to result from the war was Jacob Epstein's 'Christ in Majesty' (1955) which became the centrepiece of George Pace's restoration of Llandaff Cathedral, badly damaged by German bombing in 1941. But that work resulted from German aggression, not native remembrance. There would be no grand, epic commemorative work. The two decades of re-building that centres such as Cardiff and Swansea underwent were less distinguished; the bombed ruins which Piper and Sutherland had recorded were swept away to be replaced eventually by the modernist architectural adventures and mistakes of the 1960s and 1970s. However, the work of CEMA developed into the Welsh Arts Council; the art schools became more accessible, to students and to the contemporary art of Europe and America.

The most impressive body of work from post-war Wales was Ceri Richards' *La Cathedrale Engloutie* series. This engaged him from 1959 to 1963 and was included in his Venice Biennale exhibition in 1962. Out of the legends of Dunwich in East Anglia and Ys in Britanny, out of the music of Debussy, Richards created paintings and collages in which broken columns, shattered stained glass windows, collapsed roofs, turned over and over by the tides would, in their own time, rise again and compose themselves in music. After the Sabin works – scenes of war and rape which constantly reappear on the walls of his lyrical, Matisse-like music piano rooms – after the creative violence of the Dylan Thomas-inspired works, this majestic series of drowned and risen cathedrals may be the most enduring, convincing redemption from the century of two world wars.

The largest work produced in Wales in this period, though, was by Mildred Eldrige (1909-91), a mural over 100 feet long, for the Jones and Hunt Orthopaedic Hospital at Oswestry. She was the wife of the poet R.S. Thomas and painted the enormous canvas panels in her husband's parish of Manafon, between 1953 and 1956. This linear narrative takes one from scenes of European pastoral to the jet planes and descending parachutists of the Cold War. On a beach figures are trapped in enormous fish traps, unexploded bombs lie on the sand. The post-war euphoria and relief has already been replaced by the nuclear arms race and a new world order which threatened another war, an end-of-the-world war.

Notes

1. Quoted in Michael Holroyd, *Augustus John: The New Biography*. London: Chatto & Windus, 1996.
2. All quotations from *Augustus John: the New Biography*.
3. Also, art works from the Glynn Vivian were stored in the vaults of the sewage pumping station close to Mumbles pier.
4. Both illustrated in Jonathan Miles and Derek Shiel, *David Jones: The Maker Unmade*. Bridgend: Seren, 1995.
5. So described by Cedric Morris in a 1947 radio talk – see Peter Lord, *Industrial Society*. Cardiff: University of Wales Press, 1998.
6. See Chapter 7 of Eric Rowan and Carolyn Stewart, *An Elusive Tradition: Art and Society in Wales 1870-1950*. Cardiff: University of Wales Press, 2002.
7. *Merlyn Evans: A Retrospective Exhibition*. London: The Mayor Gallery and the Redfern Gallery, 1988, notes by Mel Gooding.
8. See *The Story of Swansea during the Second World War*. Swansea: Glynn Vivian Art Gallery study pack, 1997.
9. Quoted in Tony Curtis, *Welsh Artists Talking*. Bridgend: Seren, 2000.
10. Peter Prendergast in conversation with the author in 2005.
11. Quoted in Tony Curtis, *Welsh Painters Talking*. Bridgend: Seren, 1997.
12. Quoted in Brenda Chamberlain, *Alun Lewis and the Making of the Caseg Broadsheets*. London: Enitharmon Press, 1971.
13. Confirmed by Jonah Jones in conversation with the author.
14. Quoted in Alison Smith, *John Petts and the Caseg Press*. Aldershot: Ashgate, 2000.
15. Unfairly, argued William Boyd in 'The Draughtsman's Comeback'. *The Observer Magazine*, 26th September 1993.
16. Tassi 33 & 34 in Roberto Tassi, *Graham Sutherland: Complete Graphic Work*. Barcelona: Ediciones Poligrafa, 1988.
17. Roberto Tassi, *Sutherland: The Wartime Drawings*. Milan: Electra Editrice & London SPB, 1979.
18. Quoted in Roger Bertoud, *Graham Sutherland: A Biography*. London: Faber and Faber, 1982.

19. Malcolm Yorke, *The Spirit of Place: Nine Neo-Romantic Artists*. London: Constable, 1988.
20. Illustrated in David Mellor, *A Paradise Lost*. London: Lund Humphries / Barbican, 1987.
21. Quoted in *Graham Sutherland: A Biography*.
22. In his 'Introduction' to Clare Rendell, *David Tress*. Llandysul: Gomer Press, 2002.
23. 'Ambulance Men on the Somme' was used as the cover of the present author's collection *The Last Candles*. Bridgend: Seren, 1989.
24. See James A. Davies' excellent study of Dylan Thomas and the Great War in '"A Mental Militarist": Dylan Thomas and the Great War' in Tony Brown, Jane Aaron and M. Wynn Thomas (eds.), *Welsh Writing in English: A Yearbook of Critical Essays* (Vol. 2, 1996), pp.62-81. This includes a particularly interesting comment on 'And death shall have no dominion' (p.79).
25. See letter from Richards to Adler in Richard Burns, *Ketys to Transformation – Ceri Richards and Dylan Thomas*, London: Enitharmon, 1981, p 63.

"Some Things You See In Detail, Those You Need": Alun Lewis, Soldier and Poet

Cary Archard

None of us are ourselves now, the Welsh boy sat thinking: neither what we were, nor what we will be."[1] Many of Lewis' stories in *The Last Inspection* (February 1943), from which this comes, are strongly autobiographical – as a glance at his journals confirms. Here, the main character is referred to as 'the soldier' or is called 'Taffy' by the other characters; he is never named. The absence of a name doesn't seem like a writer's universalising device so much as a reinforcement of the character's loss of identity, which was something Lewis himself experienced after signing up in May 1940.[2] This was the effect of the war, of becoming a soldier and of the army training. Of the tedium, the vulgarity of the soldiers' language, the banality and harshness of army talk, and of the boredom of routine. The apparent lack of purpose. But this was not strictly a new feeling or new anxiety for Lewis. In 1937, two postgraduate years at Manchester University[3] had left him feeling unsure about his future. In his journal he speaks of a "time when there was no objective and therefore no volition, no enjoyment, no response to life when the twenty year boy rejected one alternative after another".[4] He had had a tendency to dream throughout his adolescence, which was linked to his ambition to be a poet and to his love of the natural world. His journals are full of very detailed descriptions of the natural scenery he encountered on his walks, which he usually made alone amongst the woods and hills he was drawn to wherever he was staying. Descriptions which, if they now seem gushing and naïve in their language, must be taken seriously as the real feelings of this dreamy, idealistic young man: "This day I am part of Creation ... I hear the cattle pulling at the short October grass, their heavy breathing, their earthiness. I see the harvesters bowed over the green mangold leaves, tugging and with sharp knives cutting ... I see all colours and the sun, alchemist in the woods ...

And my body is pressed against this branch, my cheek against the rough flaked bark. I see and hear and love and am alive." (This closeness to the tree, it will become clear, is more than casual.) Frequently self-critical, he was capable himself of trenchant comments on his dreaminess and romanticism: "Stop judging by absolutes. Don't set beauty or love or goodness as urgent necessities, but interest yourself in everything and get on with your job." He spent 1937-38 teacher training in Aberystwyth, then worked for a while for his home town Cwmaman's local newspaper, the *Aberdare Leader*, before getting a temporary post as a school teacher in Lewis Boys' School, Pengam.[5] During this period of uncertainty about the direction his career should take, he was writing furiously, working on novels, on short stories, and on his poetry, the latter published in the *Western Mail* and *The Observer*.

Lewis came to the role of soldier already bewildered by the question of identity. He was Welsh but his language was English and he had read extraordinarily widely in English and other literatures (among his favourite authors were Goethe, Mann and Rilke). He had spent the first twenty-one years of his life in Wales; some of his deepest feelings, linked to his family and the beauty of the natural world, had been formed during the many summers he had spent on family holidays at Penbryn on the Cardigan coast. So deep were these roots that it is hard to over-estimate the effect on him of being based as a soldier first in Hampshire, then in Morecambe and Suffolk. The 'soldier' in the story hears footsteps behind as he walks from the station to his base and he wonders whether they are the steps of the spirit of Welsh history coming after him, haunting him: "they seemed to come trotting out of the past in him, out of the Welsh mining village, the colliers gambling in the quarry, the county school where he learned of sex and knowledge, and college where he had swotted and slacked in poverty, and boozed, and quarrelled in love. They were the footsteps of the heavy-jawed deacon of Zion, with his white grocer's apron and his hairy nostrils sniffing out corruption."[6] Later Lewis refers to them as "the dark gods wrestling in him in the mining valley" in language straining to express their power. These Welsh forces seem reluctant to let the soldier, or his creator, go. They also suggest influences outside his control.

How did Lewis' experiences as a soldier affect his writing? They affected him as a man and yet, as I have suggested, they were not totally new in their effects. Were their effects on his writing dramatic? Did they bring about new directions in his poetry – new forms, new languages? The claim is often made about war poets, particularly the First World War poets Rosenberg and Owen, that the experience of war changed their writing styles. To what extent, if any, might this also be true of Lewis?

Lewis felt he was most himself when he was being a poet, when he was writing poetry. His identity, his sense of self, largely rested on his belief in himself as a poet. In his first years in the army, throughout 1941 and 1942, in his journals, he struggled to understand the role of the poet in this new situation. To understand his poetry, it is vital to understand how he thought about the poet, and how he viewed writing poetry. Lewis also wrote prose. Did he see himself differently when he thought of himself as a poet from when he thought of himself as a short story writer or novelist? His journals provide a valuable insight into how he thought about these questions.

★ ★ ★ ★ ★

In the summer of 1939, Lewis was dissatisfied with the poetry he was writing; in his journal he speaks of his 'vapourising poems': "There was a time when my poems satisfied me, when I repeated them in my mind with Blake's." Now he mocks them as "velvet shorts with pearly buttons", seeing them as if they are beautiful objects, unrelated to his true nature. Around the same time, Dylan Thomas, Lewis' contemporary in Wales, was writing to Vernon Watkins and praising that aspect of Watkins' poetry which "has a lot more vulgarity in it, breaches of the nostalgic etiquette".[7] Thomas also had had enough of 'pearly buttons'. Despite these feelings, when Lewis speaks at length in his journal of poetry, his language still seems influenced by the 'velvet shorts'. He links poetry to "the quiet hillside" and "the glittering lake": the beautiful natural world rather than the social world. And he speaks of the urge to write poetry in sexual terms or at least in the language of desire: "the ache for a new thought in the poet is like a woman wanting a new necklace, a man a new model car, the desire to say something new is the next desire after the desire to express the emotions, love and the capacity for pain." He trivialises the wish to say something new ('necklace' and 'model car') because it is the old subjects that should dominate the poet, those eternal emotions of love and pain. There is the hint here, soon after Lewis enlisted, of how difficult it could be for his experience of the army to change his view of poetry. Perhaps, faced with the new experience, he deals with it not by changing his view of the poet's role or by changing his style of writing. It could be that instead of Lewis the poet changing his writing styles, as Wilfred

Owen does in the face of devastating experiences, he will respond by strengthening the forms and style he has already developed.

* * * * *

Events helped to hasten Lewis into the army. In April 1940, the British force sent to Norway was evacuated. Early in May, Germany started to overrun Holland and Belgium. On 25th May, the British Expeditionary Force retreated to Dunkirk, from which it was evacuated by 4th June. During this tense, anxious time, on 15th May 1940, Lewis enlisted and joined the Royal Engineers in London, from where he was sent to the No.1 Railway Training Centre at Longmoor in Hampshire. It is significant that he soon felt most himself when he left the camp. He quickly recognised something hostile to poetry in the training centre itself: "The bawdy of the barrack room and the pub, the crude and naïve confessions of the soldier who cannot write but who has guarded the frontiers of multitudes of colonies – the poet fades against the hot breath of such talk." This description tries to convince us that the experience of the army must be resisted. Should the poet attempt to come to terms with these conditions, the danger is that he will "be no more than a clever talker, an *habitué* of salons, practitioner of a tiny declining art".

Poetry always seems to be a 'declining art' according to some poets and readers, but Lewis hadn't been at Longmoor very long before he came across another soldier poet. This soldier was never going to publish his poetry in magazines such as *Life and Letters Today, Horizon* and *Poetry London*[8] where Lewis' poems were appearing but it is worth considering the nature of his work, whatever its quality, for the surprising parallels it shows with Lewis' own view of poetry. Among the many vignettes of his fellow soldiers in the journals (which are full of wonderfully vivid sketches, the basis of so many of the characters in his short stories) is an account of Corporal Hunter:

> Tells everyone of his girl. The number of times they had sexual contact during his 7 days leave. He believes in forbidden fruits. He doesn't want any woman but her. Treat [sic] it as a joke with men, but he is serious about it with women.

This corporal appears as a character in the story 'Lance-Jack' (in *The Last Inspection*), one of the most openly autobiographical of all the stories – it even refers to 'Dick', Lewis' friend Richard Mills, and 'Bill', another friend, and 'Gweno', his wife. The corporal in the story, has no name but he writes poetry:

> One of the corporals saw me reading a book of poetry the other day. He said 'Do you like poetry?' I flushed and looked at him for a moment to see what he was playing at. Then I said 'Yes. Why?'
>
> 'Oh, nothing', he said. Then he looked at me like a little boy confessing a longing for apples. 'I like it, too,' he said. 'I like writing it, at least. I never read any. I write a lot, though. Every letter I write to my girl I put a poem in it. Of course some of them are pretty soft, but now and again they're really good. She was proper nuts about one I wrote last week. Pretty intimate it was – about having a baby. She copies them up into a notebook. In INK. Tell me, can you have verses longer than four lines? Or have they got to be four lines?"[9]

In the journal are more details. Hunter tells Lewis he has written more than one hundred and fifty letters to his girl, which adds up to a lot of poems. "He shows me one – strangely sincere and clumsy, with a naïve and direct appeal. 'My thoughts of you, without them I would die. I think of you when in my bed on dirty ground I lie. My thoughts of you will live when earth has creaked and groaned away, Still fresh and beautiful beloved as today.'" Lewis the published poet warms to the efforts of the amateur. He does not assume superiority. Indeed, he recognises a fellow poet and includes in his journal jottings Hunter's remark that "a verse of poetry is better than a page of prose". For anyone considering Lewis' own view of the poet and poetry, what is interesting is that the corporal turns to poetry when he wants to write about his feelings; for the 'soft', 'intimate' things, he adds poems to his letters and these are the pieces of writing that his girl keeps in a book. Poetry is for love and beauty, the deeper and lasting things. This popular romantic view of poetry is not far away from Alun Lewis' own position. The final words in his journal about Hunter – Hunter's description of himself – do not appear in the story. Significantly, it is a description that draws the corporal and the writer even closer together because it could be a description of Lewis himself: "I'm a lonely chap, I don't smoke or drink. I'm not convivial." This is an extreme version of a romantic view of the artist as the one who tries to remain uncontaminated, the outsider.

* * * * *

In June of 1939, Lewis had been sure he was in love. He and Gweno had shared their first kiss. He was transported: "It's only five days since I kissed you first. They seem like years. Like a traveller who has long wanted to go to Italy, but didn't. Then did

and on the fifth day was in Naples." Engrossed by love, he
expressed his feelings predominantly through a rapturous account
of the natural world in sentences which run into one another, full of
rich visual details:

> It is only the red foxgloves standing proudly above the
> brambles like high ladies waiting their coach. And bees about
> them for the hidden sweetness in their hoods. And insects
> with wings the sun shines through. And a wanton uncertain
> careless butterfly and a harsh magpie in the beech over the
> coombe and the coombe full of water music – unseen for the
> long lush grass and cress and buttercup and dock.

It seems inevitable, as we read this, that he should immediately go
on to compare himself to Keats: "It was you [Keats] were using my
eyes this morning. Watching the linnet spring up from the wet
rushes. And for no reason I could see at all, making the tears come
bubbling down my cheeks." This is a comparison with the Keats of
close observation of the physical world, and Lewis certainly sees
accurately the nature of the foxglove flower; how in June it towers
over the other plants and attracts the bees. But the "high ladies
waiting their coach" and their "hoods" do not seem to be images
taken from Lewis' experience. They are the images of romance and
fairy tale and could come from the Keats of 'Endymion'. It is the
rhythm too which is noticeable, the repeated 'and's – the movement
from thought and observation, into sound and the hint of transcen-
dency in the words 'hidden' and 'unseen'.

Lewis often writes in this way about nature in his journals. He
links nature to poetry and to the themes of beauty and love. When
he writes his vignettes of his fellow soldiers his prose is different. It
has the same acute observation but the rhythms and vocabulary are
different. This is something he is very aware of. In his fiction he has
a different goal. He is trying to achieve a sort of documentary
realism. It is as though when he is not writing about his feelings
everything changes:

> I want to write – to get away from love themes which engross
> me, to write something else – about the poor, to make people
> see what I feel, the waste, the hate. Writing is the game – art
> – of reproducing exactly and making live ordinary life – ...
> My book must be utterly simple, lucid, broad...

He is speaking here of his novel 'Adam'.[10] He was reading Katherine
Mansfield and, influenced by her, decided the aim of his prose

should be "to recreate the nervous progression of people among people and alone with themselves" which is a perceptive comment on the quality of his own short story writing at its best.

Lewis, who had studied history at Aberystwyth and Manchester, was politically educated and leftward leaning. With war coming, he tried to understand what he felt about 'Hitlerism'. He found it difficult to feel very patriotic or feel any real commitment to fighting against the forces that threatened Britain: "his egocentric mind cannot enlarge its scope sufficiently to identify himself with Britain, with the Prime Minister's exhortation." It seems that in the period before he enlisted he spent time imagining what fighting would involve ("the hands that bayonet"). His thoughts constantly turned away from the "cruelties" and he protected himself by choosing "to be no more than the number by which he is known". When in May the following year, he finds himself at Longmoor training, he still rejects the plain fact of his weapon, that it is made for killing. He wishes to see it as something other than it is, perhaps as something beautiful: "The rifle is so silent and passive and smooth, and we abuse the smooth hilt, the oiled and shining breech. It revolts against violence, kicking the shoulder, exhaustedly smoking and burnt and wasted." It is extraordinary the degree to which he sees violence as a perversion of the natural order of things. However, there are times when he does find a cause worth fighting for, a reason linked to a major personal concern, the preservation of the tradition of literature: "the tradition is being suppressed by the Gestapo – all the presses and bookshops, I must fight – for the pen, not with it." This view found general expression in a while in the manifesto 'Why Not War Writers?'[11] which appeared in *Horizon* in 1941 and which Lewis signed along with Arthur Koestler, George Orwell and Stephen Spender: "For every writer, the war is a war for survival. Without victory our art is doomed."

★ ★ ★ ★ ★

As important as the romantic view of the poet to him, was the process by which his poems came. Getting away from the camp and walking around Petersfield and Steep, not that far away, where his friends Bill and Lesley Sykes lived, was very important to the process of writing poetry, which he found difficult during the early days at Longmoor: "I can't get at the poem in me by thinking or waking. I sleep and still it doesn't come." At Steep, he walked in the footsteps of Edward Thomas[12] and began to absorb some of the melancholy loneliness of that wonderful writer who died in 1917.

Above all, he needed the peace of the surrounding countryside, "to walk and recover the peace of the green cornfields". In younger days he had criticised his romanticism; now he grappled with what he believed was poetry's essential romanticism and its problematic relationship with reality: "Reality; the integrity, the quick; poetry spins beautiful metaphors and resemblances across it, hides it or sugars it – or reconciles us to it?" Is poetry then fundamentally dishonest? Or, he wonders, has the gap between realism and romanticism changed and narrowed because of the war? Perhaps they are no longer opposites. He begins to think that there may be no significant difference between them. He discusses these ideas with Howell Davies[13], his friend from Aberystwyth days whom he met at the Red House during a stay over Halloween in 1940.

> Emotions and desires and dreams are half real and realism is only a submission of the will to circumstance. Today the bombed Londoner [the Blitz had begun that autumn] does not accept the realist interpretation – ruin, dust, wounds, loss, misery. It is a noble sacrifice, a quiet endurance, a response to a challenge, and a fighting against, a refusal, an assertion of the unique independence and indestructability [sic] of the soul, the self, the idea.

So there is something heroic about the romantic and it is linked to what is most real, what is deeper and more meaningful than 'dust, wounds'. And poetry, it seems, belongs too to that area.

Lewis' ideas about the role of poetry in relation to the world were part of a wider and very lively debate in the Thirties about how political or how private poetry should be. Yeats, who died in January 1939, was one of his favourite poets and almost certainly the major influence on his own writing, and Yeats had attacked the Auden generation and their choosing "the man in the tube" as the arbiter of poetry. Yeats thought Auden and his followers were wrong to put politics at the centre of their poetry, wrong to reject "dream and personal emotion". Yeats also believed that poetry should be written out of the poet's sense of history, out of folk memories. MacNeice entered this debate in his 'A Statement'.[14] Although not so committed to such a transcendental poetry as Yeats was, MacNeice was critical of those who "decreed that from now on this [poetry] must come only from 'the people' and be written for 'the people'".[15] But he also did not think that poets should retreat to their Ivory Towers. MacNeice argued for a position in between the 'political pigeonhole' and the political 'vacuum'. Poetry cannot be severed from beliefs "but to let beliefs monopolise poetry is to be false not only to poetry but to life, which is itself not controlled by beliefs".[16] Lewis spent much of his first year in the army exploring these different positions, struggling to understand his role as a poet.

In December 1940, he went through a period of "passionate anger" directed at the boredom and futility of Longmoor. "If the soul is lost, the vigour of vision, what should one write about?" The camp's "engine sheds" and "the sidings filled with empties" appear in the short stories. His anger at the impotence of the common soldier drives a number of the stories. But such "facts" and attitudes barely surface in the poetry. What calms him most is once again being among the "wooded hills":

> And yesterday I stood high among the wooded hills on a steep bank with sixty-foot firs and beeches and elms below me ... And through the brown and many branched stillness of the glade the pigeons arrowed to their homing trees. And rested there. And I in all that peace stood watching, watching, almost forgetting the wretched failure of my spirit, the heaviness of my heart ... and then I moved along the lane and one by one the broken bits of misery reformed their old design in the broken window of my mind.

He is clear that the "walk is the reality", as much so as "The bomb screaming down".

During a very happy Christmas with Howell and Becky Davies and their children, Peter and Joan, and Bill and Lesley Sykes, walking alone in the dark, he sees that the war has nothing to do with truth: "The war isn't a war for truth, Jerry doesn't represent truth; Britain, U.S., Russia don't. The war is for independence, dominion, patriotism, communism, property. Not truth." Truth is linked to the natural world, and in particular to the body, both of which are beautiful. He is convinced once again of the centrality to the poet of beauty: "Beauty I am always aware of, I have an understanding, I am made to understand, I am, like a violin or a brush, an instrument for beauty."

Early in 1941, Lewis records an important conversation with a friend about poetry "and thence to Reality". He is still thinking about the role of the poet. Interestingly, he rejects Eliot and Auden: "Eliot is spiritual exhaustion. Auden is spiritual anguish. Eliot explores a cul-de-sac. Auden explores an arterial road." He recognises that, despite the tedium of Longmoor, "Subjective reality – romanticism and art – still dominate me". He particularly rejects the idea that reality is the same as what is most commonly accepted, "the L.C.M.

of life". Poetry should come out of a particular vision. How much notice should the poet take of the public? How far should the poet be a spokesman for the people? Lewis is still working out his position in this debate: "The balanced individual combines observation and imagination, others and self – his social conscience is the liaison officer. A person bitterly depressed by international affairs and poverty is in danger of losing his individual existence, his identity and his Proteus ..." The danger is that the imagination which helps make the person an individual will be suppressed by the world of 'observation' and 'others'. Reality may be reduced to the world of common objects. What happens then to the poem? "Is a railway engine more real than a poem?" Lewis asks whether both aren't "a projection in visible form of an idea? Is the railway driver more in touch with reality than a student of international affairs or literatures?" In his concern to keep the link between poetry and truth and beauty, Lewis wants to refute the claim that such a notion of poetry is unreal: "But am I unreal in my romanticism, my reading and writing and intro-spection and delight in word ideas? Or in my preoccupation with world affairs? Isn't the actual army life much more unreal – here in Longmoor at least than anything I have yet encountered?"

When Lewis thought about the poets of the First World War, he made the familiar distinction between the early poems of Brooke and Newbolt which were "patriotic, superficial" and which came before any real contact with war and the "poems of bodily agony, soul destruction, attrition, horror and revulsion". Then he makes the surprising claim that "very few poems have been written at all about war". He meant by this that most poems ostensibly about war still understated the reality, "concealing error, admitting only fortitude, seeking to perpetuate normality". Normality because for most people the façade / routine of normal life still carried on. But what had happened to heroism, that aspect of romanticism? He wondered whether it had declined because of the way events were now viewed. They were seen as part of a process almost beyond human control: "war is a social-economic crisis working itself out in terms of violence ... something scientific almost, to be endured scientifically, coolly, without jingoism, yet without bitter regret at irreparable loss, without a growing sense of waste, the economic truth being as real as spiritual truth, its contradiction as disastrous." Things were differ-ent in the war in the Middle East, where an element of heroism still lingered, not in the fighting itself but in the way war was viewed: "In the East the Seven Pillars, the spiritual, the long struggle with aridity and space and physical and mental deserts that must be crossed silently and unseen." But "the heroic war of desert stormtroops is a throwback"; the real war is where he finds himself, characterised by "tedium and its unemployment, its rigours and confinements, the normality that reveals the cruel ignoble motives and methods, no screens of blood and motion hiding them".

Despite the buffeting his romantic view of the poet was taking, he was still capable of an ironic aside at its expense. One blustery spring day, home on leave, while his mother is washing and hanging out the clothes, and his aunt is gardening, using her "little pruning fork to remove the dead aconites", he walks as usual noticing the "great firs" and the "ugly nissen huts", then stops in the warmth of the sun near daffodils "which Wordsworth converted into gilt-edged securities, paying a regular dividend". This is followed in his journal by a remarkable account of what it means to be a poet, in which he likens the writing of poetry to being taken over by madness or extreme passion: "the writer, attracted by wild (impassioned, coloured) words begins to write and quickens and goes mad with powerful driving words that circulate." What follows is a frenzied description in which the actual process of typing is seen as a painful exercise involving self-mutilation: "His fingers whip the keys; the swift machine throbs and leaps and cuts his fingers off. The fingers bleed; his bloodshot eyes droop, the murderer softly strokes his fallen head." Extraordinary, the degree of self-harm in this account, as though exploring depths of the self is not sufficient. Here, the writing of poetry suggests a process that goes beyond imagination into other aspects of the self that might seem to be almost outside the realms of poetry. It also suggests how damaging the effects of being in the army have become.

The peace and space that Lewis needed were constantly under threat. Lewis' journal entries have already indicated how the process of writing was for him very closely linked to his physical environment. The link between the actual process of writing and the environment in which it is carried out can be crucial for some authors. Hemingway wrote standing up, in long hand. Wordsworth composed while walking around his Lakeland home. In Wales, local tradition has it that whoever spends a night alone on the summit of the mountain Cadair Idris will come down mad or a poet. Lewis depended on a process that included walking, natural scenery and hills with views. Linking the poet to madman or to visionary has a long tradition. His description of typing above reminds the reader of the religious fanatic, but then it concludes: "He is gone among the words that would not speak. To the inarticulate depths of silence."

The process that lies behind Lewis' writing echoes in these sentences in 'words' (the woods and their darkness) and in "depths of silence" (the hills and their long views).

There are passages in his journal that strikingly reveal how separate Lewis kept the poet from the writer of prose. Passages such as this: "The guard tent. Rain, brownish luminous light. Two hours on, four off. Two trestle tables, old *Lilliputs* and *John Bulls*, a filthy novel, a week old popular *Weekly Post.*" This is a very different language from that of the poems and shows no attempt to approach the transcendental. Elsewhere in his journal, Lewis remarks "prose is factual". It seems that, as his year in the army continued, Lewis the soldier needed to maintain his romantic view of the poet, both to continue writing poetry and to maintain his sense of identity. At times, Lewis the poet and Lewis the prose writer seem to be different people.

Looking back after nearly a year in the army, Lewis decides that the "most basic enterprise of my being in uniform has been to preserve my identity, my individuality, my values against the artificially imposed caste laws of authority". And this has been done in three ways; one way has been to develop "my private life", another has been to concentrate on "the causes of the war, a more and more responsible attitude towards the world" and the third has been "the writing of poetry". When thinking about the latter and about the most "purely poetic experience" he has had, he talks, as he often does, of a familiar triumvirate, namely suffering, loneliness and vision. He writes in illuminating detail about a poem he has been trying to write which came to him first in "terms of music. I was walking across the barracks to dinner when I found myself singing the words. The words were at first expressions of tones and volumes and cadences, with an unexpressed harmony underlying it". He seems almost surprised at the effort the writing has cost him – "stress in the soul exhausts you like old age". This is the passage in his journals in which he comes closest to explaining the visionary experience which he often refers to as the most important part of the process of writing poetry.

> These words came out of me and they came up into me (perhaps that's the truth of it, though they came also from elsewhere, from heaven, earth, forms and fire and animals and state of being) and they were always active in my mind. I am in danger of exaggerating their effect – they were very gentle, very lovely – they didn't beat me with word truncheons; they insisted on nothing, but like beauty they were there for me to love and explore.

He goes on to describe a vision which slowly formed in his mind, which looked, unsurprisingly, like a Snowdonian landscape: "rather like a climbing valley in north Wales on the south-east approach to Snowdon – rising levels of meadow with a stream splayed and splashed over the rocks at the top of each meadow, falling down into the next." The words in his head tell him that this landscape is the home of the soul. Once again, he sees Yeats as the model of the poet: he "must rise above them [the people], climb into the literary hierarchy and be wonderful and lost like Yeats" (echoes of Cadair Idris perhaps); but he is in the middle of the people, in the army, so he must also "stay in the barrack room, in the ranks, in Cwmaman, in NAAFI and pub, in the 3rd class compartments" – and his short stories, collected in *The Last Inspection*, are a recognition of this other necessity.

It could be argued that this identification with Yeats at his most mystical, and taking Yeats as his role model for a poet, was very bad for Lewis. It could lead to an inability to develop new ways of writing, to an overindulgent romanticism and fondness for abstractions in his poetry. Yet it is clear from examining Lewis' journals and his comments on poetry that he needed the romantic model. It was embedded in the processes of his writing and it was linked to the values he believed in most. Perhaps, even more importantly, it seems clear from his own comments on writing that poetry was vital to the protection of his identity which he felt was threatened by army life.

★ ★ ★ ★ ★

In July 1941, fourteen months after enlisting, and despite all the difficulties he had experienced, Lewis' first collection of poems *Raiders' Dawn* was accepted for publication (though it didn't appear until March 1942). The collection is prefaced by 'Prologue: The Grinder', an opening poem which doesn't offer its war-time readers very much optimism. The lines in the opening verse, "Who carved the round red sun? / Who purified the snow?", with their echoes of Blake, suggest that Lewis thought the poet should be able to answer the deepest and most difficult questions. In the poem, the grinder (perhaps referring to the peripatetic workers Lewis might have seen going around the towns of his south Wales valley sharpening blades) stands for the poet (the 'grinder of words' and also now a soldier away from home, sharpening himself for war) who has used his strength "in striving for the vision", searching for a mythic language in which to express the situation of the poet in the changed world of war. In a number of the poems, Lewis certainly strives for 'the vision', particularly in the two longest and most ambitious poems in the book which are rarely included in anthologies and which do not appear in the popular *Selected Poems* (paperback 1981). Mythic language runs throughout the lament 'Threnody for a Starry Night', for instance, as Lewis strives to locate his individual pain and experience of the war within a structure made up of the universe ("the imperishable stars") and the myths and religions of the past ("The Babylonian planets", "the woman from the Egyptian rock-tomb", "Christ crucified", and "Socrates on the frozen lake") in a poem which reminds readers of the kind of anguish that Lewis disliked in Eliot. The poet / grinder, the 'Prologue' continues, cannot make "the perfect statements of the truths" out of "patched umbrellas and his notched old knives" (an echo of Yeats' "Old kettles, old bottles, and a broken can"[17]) and by the poem's end failure is seemingly acknowledged with the hope for poetry reduced to "sparks [that] can warm the night". (There are echoes here of a familiar note at the time: Auden, who left England for the USA in 1939, ends his poem 'September 1, 1939' with the line, "Show an affirming flame".) Yet the poem also tells us that, however painful the process, the poet must not give up. The poem begins with a question from the poet: "Nothing to grind? Then answer, and I'll go". A different voice, perhaps intended to be the reader's, answers in the last verse: "Keep grinding then, though nothing's left to whet – / bad luck unless your sparks can warm the night". "Keep grinding then" – for Lewis the process of writing poetry was a commitment he could not afford to give up.

Lewis tells us in his 'Author's Note' to *Raiders' Dawn* that "Practically all these poems have been written since September, 1939; two-thirds of them have been written on active service". Most of the latter are grouped in the opening section of the book, 'Poems in Khaki', and the reader working through them is soon struck by the centrality of the themes of beauty and love. But another quality also stands out alongside the pervading romantic and Yeatsian influences. An element of the documentary realism of the stories appears in some of the poems. This element is not so much made up of the details of the soldier's life, such as uniform, food, weapons and training, but more of the visual details of places Lewis visits and walks through, mostly near Longmoor. And these details are invariably linked to the natural world; they are precise observations, in particular, of trees and landscape. So Lewis' most anthologised and recognisable poem, 'All day it has rained', locates soldiering within a framework of place and typically includes walking through woods to a high spot, the Shoulder o' Mutton, above Steep in Hampshire.

Lewis' walks were central to his process of poetic composition. His finest poems, those where a voice develops that has moved on from the huge influences of his omnivorous reading (in particular Yeats, and the romantics Blake and Keats), are based on walks and his experience, especially visual, of the natural world. In 'All day it has rained', the oaks' 'acorns' among the "gorse and heather" play a refreshing role: "the acorns that suddenly / Snatched from their cups by the wild south-westerly / Pattered against the tent and our upturned dreaming faces." The happiest moment in the poem is linked to trees as he watched the children "in the woods on Saturday / Shaking down burning chestnuts". 'Wild south-westerly', 'on Saturday', these factuals are essential to this distinctive new voice.

It also seems clear that those poems that are most distinctively Lewis' own come from looking outwards, come as a result of getting away from the camp and its training and tedium and all the self-alienation linked to that. 'The Public Gardens', the fourth poem in *Raiders' Dawn*, vividly recreates another "Saturday evening" out of camp through an accumulation of fluently controlled, precisely observed details: "a few top-heavy hollyhocks", "twin sycamores", "thin little woman in black stockings and a straw hat with wax flowers", creating a tangible atmosphere and pathos. The poet directly admits in the poem that looking outwards has helped him forget "my khaki, my crude trade". Despite the isolation of the characters in the poem, despite the undermining of the "public" caused by the war, and despite the fragility of the human connections, there are still lines linking people; a "pattern emerges" and "the park is a maze of diagonal lines".

In Lewis' poetic subconscious, familiar trees are very important. They can act to protect him from the soldiering, the war and the threats war brings: in 'The Public Gardens', the "twin sycamores storing the darkness massively under balconies of leaf" keep the threats under control – though they are still present. 'Lanes', the walked paths, are also a form of salvation. In 'The Sentry', referring to one of the soldier's regular duties, the soldier begins to die when he has "left / The beautiful lanes of sleep".

The clearest example of realism linked to walks comes in 'To Edward Thomas' where it is not so much the influence of Thomas' writing – much remarked upon by critics – but the influence of Lewis' own practice of walking which is significant. The opening of the poem is like a set of instructions on how to find Thomas' memorial stone. Once again the happiest moment is reached when the mind engages

with the natural world, goes out into it, letting the sunlight direct eyes
onto the named trees, "yew-trees ... beech and ash to birch and chest-
nut", over the Downs and "soft green pastures" to the sea. The
poet/observer reaches a point where the eyes search for the external
world but only the mind can find it and the mind becomes, as it were,
the external world, emptied of the person.

* * * * *

Just after a year of soldiering, Lewis attended Officer Cadet Training
at Heysham Towers in Lancashire, then joined the Sixth Battalion of
the South Wales Borderers at Woodbridge in Suffolk as a Second
Lieutenant. In May 1942, the Borderers went for tank training at
Bovington in Dorset before finally being posted to India in October.
On 17th December, Lewis arrived in Bombay. The poems Lewis
wrote after autumn 1941 are collected in *Ha! Ha! Among The
Trumpets* published in 1945, the year after his death in Burma. The
book is arranged in three sections according to the path his soldiering had taken: 'England', 'The Voyage' and 'India'. 'On
Embarkation', the longest poem in the book, is similar in form and
structure to 'To Edward Thomas'. It is a poem which contains
elements of the documentary realism style so characteristic of his
stories in details such as "the cargo / The cranking derricks drop into
the hold", "one man wrapped in blankets", "sick with injections". It
is also another looking outward, walk poem. Speaking of "Some
things you see in detail, those you need", Lewis visits Penbryn, the
source of some of his most important memories, before embarkation. After getting off the train, he directs us precisely the way to go,
and eagerly encourages us with the repeated 'here's: "Just here you
leave this Cardiganshire lane, / Here by these milk churns and this
telegraph pole." Then, after a walk crossing the fields, described in
extraordinary detail ("The wheat as thin as hair on flinty slopes"),
he (we) approach "The green Atlantic, far as the eye can reach" as
the restful point of the poem, which is all about journeys, is reached.

In a letter to Robert Graves[18] which Graves quotes in the
Foreword he wrote for the book, Lewis stresses once more how, even
in the very different landscape of India, looking outwards, travelling
through the landscape (though here walking had often to be
replaced by motorised transport) remained crucial to his poetic
methods, to enable him to continue as a poet: "I think I'm most
completely normal when I'm roaring across the country on a motor-
bike, aware of the flow and the tradition of peasant life, passing gay
funerals with beautifully attired corpses propped up on canopied

platforms, or when I'm peeping at Victorian-Gothic princely palaces in corrupt Native State towns, or eating a coconut in a jungle village in communion with the dancing and chanting youths before the pot-bellied elephant-god of luck." The second longest poem in the book, placed prominently near the end, and probably the last poem Lewis wrote, is 'The Jungle' which focuses more on the pool in the jungle than the jungle itself. No familiar path to the pool is traced in this poem. There is a clear sense of having been brought here by undesired means: "Wandering and fortuitous the paths / We followed to this rendezvous today." This is a different pool from the restful pools ("dragonflies' blue flicker on quiet pools"[19]) that Lewis met on his walks at home, such as the pool he walked around near Longmoor camp. In India, the dragonfly has given place to "the crocodile", "grey monkeys" and "Annihilating paws". The familiar trees are replaced by the "banyan". Instead of a widening horizon, there is a narrowing of the view as "the black spot in the focus grows and grows". And instead of looking out, he stares at "The face distorted in a jungle pool / That drowns its image in a mort of leaves". It seems from reading this cold disturbing poem that looking outwards, resting his eyes on trees and views, getting beyond the soldiering and the war, has become very difficult for Lewis. He now feels himself to be in a 'wilderness', speaks of being 'imprisoned' and, most disturbing of all, sees himself as one of 'the ghosts'. Ominously the poem keeps on coming back to the poet himself, to his self. Up to now, it has been the ability to see what is outside himself, by walking the paths through the trees, often to get above the world of soldiering that has given Lewis the process that enabled him to continue as a poet. A couple of months after writing 'The Jungle', on 5th March 1944, Lewis was found dead.[20]

Notes

1. Alun Lewis, *Collected Stories* (ed. Cary Archard). Bridgend: Seren, 1991, p.169. From the story 'They Came', the last story in *The Last Inspection* (1942, though the book did not appear until 1943).
2. On 15th May 1940 Lewis enlisted with The Royal Engineers and was sent to No.1 Railway Training Centre at Longmoor, Hants.
3. Lewis' thesis was on the work of the thirteenth century Papal Legate Ottobono.
4. Alun Lewis, *Collected Journals*. Bridgend: Seren, 2008. (And all subsequent journal extracts.) The journals begin in autumn 1937, and contain brief entries for spring and autumn 1938. There are some fuller entries for 1939. The much fuller Longmoor journal begins in May 1940. Entries continue, most undated, up to autumn 1943.

5.   Lewis worked at the school from November 1938 until a classroom accident to his hand in March 1940.

6.   *Collected Stories*, p.166.

7.   Dylan Thomas, *The Collected Letters* (ed. Paul Ferris). London: J.M. Dent & Sons, 1985, p.279. To Vernon Watkins, 21st March 1938.

8.   In *Horizon*: 'All day it has rained' (January 1941); 'The Soldier' (May 1941). In *Life and Letters Today*: 'Fever' (March 1940); 'River Rhondda' July 1941. In *Poetry London*: 'Christmas Holiday' (March 1941); 'Easter at Christmas' April 1941.

9.   *Collected Stories*, pp.68-9.

10. Unpublished novel about student life in Aberystwyth. Lewis was working on it in early 1940.

11. In: Robert Hewison, *Under Siege: Literary Life in London, 1939-45*. London: Weidenfeld & Nicolson, 1977, p.74.

12. Lewis first visited the Red House in Steep where Thomas had lived in October 1940.

13. Howell Davies had edited *The Dragon* when he was at the university at Aberystwyth. He had become a journalist in London.

14. Louis MacNeice, *Selected Literary Criticism* (ed. Alan Heuser). Oxford: Clarendon, 1987, p.98.

15. *Ibid.*, p.111.

16. *Ibid.*, p.114.

17. 'The Circus Animals' Desertion' from *Last Poems* (1939).

18. Lewis first corresponded with Graves in 1941. In his Foreword, Graves tells us: "he asked me to read the manuscript and decide for him how much should be included and whether any rewriting was needed. In doubtful cases his wife Gweno was to have the casting vote". The letter quoted was written on 23rd January 1944.

19. 'Lines on a Tudor Mansion' from *Raiders' Dawn* (1942).

20. For the details of Lewis' death and a discussion of whether it was by his own hand, see: John Pikoulis, *Alun Lewis: A Life*. Bridgend: Seren, 1991, pp.234-243.

Dylan Thomas and War

James A. Davies

Dylan Thomas lived his comparatively short life through a period dominated by war and preparations for war. He was born on 29th October 1914, during, as he later wrote, the first Battle of Ypres. He was four on Armistice Day. Though he wrote in *Reminiscences of Childhood* of 'the Front' from which so many never returned and which he had confused with the small lobby behind his home's front door, effectively he had few if any direct memories of the Great War.[1] But his formative years, from the mid 1920s onwards, were dominated by that war's literary consequences: the outpouring of memoirs, novels and volumes of letters, plus the abiding and increasing influence of the war poets, particularly that of Wilfred Owen. In his late teens and early twenties Thomas filled his notebooks and began publishing poems and stories against the darkening and violent background of the rise of fascism in Germany and elsewhere. On 18th July 1936 the Spanish Civil War began that ended with a victory for General Franco's fascist nationalists on 1st April 1939. Five months later, on 3rd September, Britain declared war on Germany. This, World War Two, ended in Europe on 8th May 1945. Japan surrendered on 14th August 1945, following the dropping of atomic bombs on Hiroshima and Nagasaki. The Cold War and the age of nuclear deterrence followed with its several alarms. The Korean War began in 1950 and ended with the signing of an Armistice on 27th July 1953. The Cold War was to continue long after Thomas' death on 9th November 1953.

Though Dylan Thomas never fought in a war, the wars of his lifetime – in particular the two World Wars – influenced him greatly. His attitude to war in general and to military service is a complex mixture of pacifism, fascination, compassion, violent propensities, solipsism, some guilt and some arrogance. In particular, there is a strange dichotomy between the attitudes and opinions of his personal life and how he writes about war.

Thomas' reactions to the Great War have been well documented.[2]
They begin with three poems in his school magazine, poems mainly
influenced by his youthful reading of aesthetes, Georgians and war-
poets of the Laurence Binyon school. 'The Watchers' is about the
"mighty dead ... who rest by Ypres and Posières by Vimy and
Cambrai" listening to the armies advance and the attacks succeed.
'Missing' was written for the tenth anniversary of the Armistice; a
soldier dead and lost on the battlefield is caressed by the sun whilst
the wind "whisper[s] a benediction for the dead". A third poem,
'Armistice', is also a venture into technically assured sentimentality:

> But a wise, new love shall ascend,
>   From the dust to the clouds of the sky;
> It shall never grow weary, nor end,
>   Nor, like us who are left, shall it die.[3]

These are poems for readers – mainly grammar school pupils and
parents – so often bereaved and remembering. So, too, in one sense,
is Thomas' assured essay of 1929 on 'Modern Poetry'; though the
Great War had changed English poetry, he wrote, its brutality had
"failed to warp man's outlook and ideals ... Out of the darkness came
the clear light of genius ... Wilfred Owen, Robert Graves, Julian
Grenfell, and the other heroes who built towers of beauty upon the
ashes of their lives."[4] The essay here confirms what the poems assert.
Both former and latter, juvenilia though both are, offer a basic
optimism: war did not, will not, crush man's essential creative spirit.

The school magazine poems and essay show Thomas fascinated
by the Great War. That fascination – within which was one for violence
itself – is an important element in his first two published volumes of
poetry, *18 Poems* (1934) and *Twenty-Five Poems* (1936). These
appeared during the ominous rise of fascism in Europe and in Britain.
The British Mosleyite variety was experienced directly by Thomas
and his friend Bert Trick, the British Union of Fascists having opened
an office in Swansea in 1931. In 1934 the Union brought Sir Oswald
Mosley to the town to speak at a mass rally. Thomas attended in
support of anti-fascist groups; he and Bert Trick witnessed the
violence generated by the meeting.[5] But though they both favoured
direct action again fascism, during the same year they offered their
services as 'active propagandists' to the Swansea branch of the pacifist
No More War Movement.[6] This appears to have come to nothing.

The Great War is a recurring motif in *18 Poems*. 'I see the boys of
summer', the first poem in a carefully arranged volume, though
mainly focussing on 1930s economic casualties, in its use of explo-

sion imagery – "love and light bursts in their throats" – suggests the boys may also be among the psychological casualties of war. In 'Before I knocked', a poem at once about the Incarnation as well as secular suffering, to convey the suffering of Christ during flagellation and thorn-crowning Thomas reaches for Great War imagery of cutting wire to penetrate enemy defences:

> And flesh was snipped to cross the lines
> Of gallow crosses on the liver
> And brambles in the wringing brains.[7]

In the same poem the line "And I was struck down by death's feather", together with further 'death's feather' references throughout the volume, may well reflect the wartime practice of handing white feathers to those men not in uniform. This may have happened to Thomas' father in his reserved occupation: his wife, Florence, considered that during the war he had a hard time.

In *18 Poems* three poems in particular have substantial links with the Great War. One is 'When once the twilight locks no longer', written on Armistice Day 1933. The first draft was sent to Pamela Hansford Johnson with a letter that in its imagery of branding, bayoneting and mutilation conveys the extent of Thomas' hatred of what the Great War did and continued to do, and the extent to which it seized his sympathetic and fascinated imagination.[8] The poem itself offers a lurid dream sequence and much war imagery. But its emotional effect is controlled by a strict rhyme scheme as the poem moves to a final line – "And worlds hang on the trees" – optimistic in its sense of prizes still to be won.

The second poem is 'I dreamed my genesis'. It reflects Thomas' awareness of his wartime birth:

> I dreamed my genesis and died again, shrapnel
> Rammed in the marching heart, hole
> In the stitched wound and clotted wind, muzzled
> Death on the mouth that ate the gas.

This last line, its use of "ate", suggests the extent to which he was drawn to the violence he described.

The third poem is 'My world is pyramid', part of which describes the fate of the Austrian Social Democrats, massacred during 1934 by forces loyal to Dolfuss, Austria's fascist Chancellor. Thomas' language:

> the riddled lads
> Strewing their bowels from a hill of bones,
> Cry Eloi to the guns.

– could have been used to describe events in the Great War. The final stanza, like that of 'I dreamed my genesis', offers optimistic possibilities: death's feather blown away and the power of physical and sexual life asserted forcefully.

The first poem of *Twenty-Five Poems* (1936), 'I, in my intricate image', continues Thomas' obsession with the "war to end all wars". Death is dramatised as a "black patrol" with "monstrous officers and the decaying army" and

> The sexton sentinel, garrisoned under thistles,
> A cock-on-a-dunghill
> Crowing to Lazarus the morning is vanity.

Here the sentiment is bleak: death as finality in a world losing faith in any kind of resurrection.

'The seed at zero' is about bombarding a town; 'Out of the sighs' offers a moving image of the protagonist "leaving woman waiting / For her soldier". But the key poem in any consideration of war themes in *Twenty-Five Poems* is 'And death shall have no dominion'. I have described elsewhere the evolution of this poem from Thomas' notebook to its first publication in *New English Weekly* in May 1933 to the revised and final version that appears in *Twenty-Five Poems* and subsequent collections.[9] This final version jettisons suggestions that "Beauty may blossom in pain" and that religious consolation may be effected through death and Judgement Day resurrection. The final version ends with a consoling pantheism: life after death here means that life continues as part of nature:

> Though they be mad and dead as nails,
> Heads of the characters hammer through daisies.

The continuing and strangely violent power of the dead enables them to "Break in the sun" and so control the main source of natural energy. It is a power directly contrasting with the helplessness of the living and dying.

The absence of the earlier Christian ending and the increased stress on the dead – conveyed by Thomas' use of the body-in-the-open-air motif – could seem to darken this final version. That they do not is due to two factors: the poem's tight form, which, as so often in Thomas' poetry, prevents over-emotionalising, and the optimistic repetition. We are reminded of the school magazine poems; to some extent here is another poem for bereaved survivors still desperately clinging to consoling ideas of worthwhile heroism.

Twenty-Five Poems was published in September 1936, by which time the Spanish Civil War was in its second month. Writer friends went to Spain; some fought and died with the International Brigade. At times Thomas felt he should do something to help the anti-fascist cause but his guilt was never sufficient to make him volunteer to fight. Nevertheless, he had strong feelings about Spain, intensified by Swansea's strong links with the Basque country. In 1937, shortly after the Guernica bombing, eighty Basque children were brought to Swansea for a holiday. They were billeted at Sketty Hall. Bert Trick was part of the reception committee and arranged a visit by Thomas and Caitlin. Thomas lent a hand and amused the children by getting stuck in an air-raid shelter tunnel and having to be rescued.[10]

His emotional involvement in the Spanish War was well seen in March 1939, when he was outraged at the fall of Madrid. All such feelings were channelled into poems and stories in *The Map of Love* (1939), the background to the writing of which included Italy's invasion of Abyssinia and German annexations in Europe, as well as Spain.

In *The Map of Love* there is still occasional harking-back to the Great War, for instance in 'When all my five and country senses', where "love drummed away" is "lashed to syllables", a reminder of Army punishment in 'And death shall have no dominion'. But this volume is now dominated by apocalyptic moments. One example is in 'Because the pleasure-bird whistles', the opening poem written for the new year of 1939, and which describes, in part,

> an old year
> Toppling and burning in the muddle of towers and galleries.

This burning world is found again at the end of the volume in the conclusion to 'The Orchards': "The trees were fireworks and torches, smouldered out of the furnace of the fields into a burning arc, cast down their branded fruit like cinders on the charred roads and fields."[11]

Poems written during the Spanish Civil War demonstrate the extent to which Thomas was psychologically and emotionally involved in the conflict. His viewpoint is secular-socialist, at times extremely so: a hatred of fascism and of the Spanish Catholic Church that supported Franco against the godless left. Hence the fire-gutted cathedral and the priest as a devil ("a sulphur priest, / His beat heel cleft in a sandal") in 'It is the sinners' dust-tongued bell', and the priest as beast in 'I make this in a warring absence'.

'A saint about to fall' is Thomas' most important poetical response to the war in Spain. Though inspired by the imminent birth of Llewelyn, the Thomas' first child, the poem was first entitled 'In September'. This referred to September 1938, described by Thomas as "a terrible war month". It was the depth of appeasement; during the month Chamberlain had visited Hitler, made disgraceful concessions regarding Czechoslovakia, and returned to Britain crying "Peace in our time".[12] But Thomas' description of the month suggests that events in Spain may well have been foremost in his mind; the Republican Army was suffering heavy losses, it was decided to withdraw the International Brigades from front-line duties, Franco was moving inexorably towards victory.

As the title suggests, 'A saint about to fall' is a version of the Fall. The child's birth necessitates leaving a bombed heaven ("The stained flats ... hit and razed") for a world of violent atrocities: "The skull of the earth is barbed with a war of burning brains and hair." The final stanza draws upon imagery that ranges from the womb as refuge or asylum to linking Herod's massacre of the innocents to modern atrocities against children:

> Lapped among herods wail
> As their blade marches in

Yet, even here, faced with such a world, Thomas finds joy in imminent creation, a cause to 'Cry joy' even in the 'thundering bullring' of Spain in 1938.

The Spanish Civil War ended in 1939, only months before World War Two began. Conscription was in the air and Thomas' response was not his finest hour. "I don't know what to do," he wrote to Desmond Hawkins, jocularity masking his concern, "declare myself a neutral state, or join as a small tank."[13] To Vernon Watkins he was franker: the prospect of war, he told his friend, filled him with "horror & terror & lassitude".[14] To his father he wrote: "If I could pray, I'd pray for peace. I'm not a man of action; & the brutal activities of war appal me – as they do every thinking person."[15] Thomas resented the war – he seemed, at times, to take matters personally – because it interfered with his literary life. Certainly, initially, it left him penniless: magazines were closing, sales of *The Map of Love*, published only nine days before war was declared, were decimated by events, as were those of *Portrait of the Artist as a Young Dog*, which appeared in 1940 during the Battle of Britain. Meanwhile, Laugharne became a military transit centre, his friends (Daniel Jones and Vernon Watkins amongst them) were preparing for military call-up. Thomas tried frantically to avoid military service, scheduled for April 1940.

At first he considered reviving his pacifist connections and wrote to Gwynfor Evans, Secretary of the Welsh Pacifist Movement. Evans saw only evasion and opportunism and responded accordingly.[16] Thomas tried, unsuccessfully, to involve writer friends in an orchestrated 'Objections to War' campaign. This came to nothing. He tried to pull strings – letters to Edward Marsh, Humbert Wolfe, Sir Kenneth Clark, all influential civil servants with literary inclinations – to obtain a reserved occupation. Nothing came of such efforts. Even Victor Cazelet's anti-aircraft battery of writers and artists turned him down.[17]

He was temporarily reprieved by the army medical, which took place at Llandeilo near Carmarthen. In circumstances that have never been satisfactorily explained – Caitlin always insisted that he smoked and drank so much during the previous twenty-four hours that doctors were fooled into thinking him permanently unfit – he was graded C3. This meant that, though capable of military service, he would be one of the last to be called up. In the meantime he could be allocated to non-combatant war-work.[18]

Whilst waiting for the latter and ever hopeful that a congenial something would turn up, Thomas lived in Laugharne and completed *Portrait of an Artist as a Young Dog*. Oddly and unwisely he boasted about his avoidance of the draft, picked fights, sometimes with soldiers, and was at times beaten up by those infuriated by his attitude. All this notwithstanding, the first years of the war, 1939 to 1941 were, by Thomas' standards, prolific: he completed eleven poems and what we now have as *Adventures in the Skin Trade*. In 1941 Donald Taylor hired him as a scriptwriter for Strand Films, (later Gryphon Films) in Golden Square, Soho, which not only made general documentaries for industry and the Government but also, increasingly, propaganda films.

The would-be pacifist, war hater and evader seemed to find nothing amiss in serving the war effort through his scriptwriting. As well as writing the scripts he supplied voice-overs for two films of Welsh interest: *Wales: Green Mountain, Black Mountain* (1942) and *Our Country* (1944). The former was designed to further the war effort in Wales by suggesting the value of work and community and the way in which Welsh traditions could combine with industrial vigour. *Our Country* follows a sailor on shore-leave travelling through Britain and observing the country at war. The script, at times too literary, has some successful moments. One is a scene on Dover cliffs, in which Thomas offers an (in context) appropriate neo-Shakespearian patriotism:

> and from this island end white faced over the
>   shifting sea-dyes
> a man may hear his country's body talking
> and be caught in the weathers of her eyes.[19]

Secondly, in a scene in Sheffield, a factory girl speaks of the nightly blackout, fear of air raids and a new world beginning again the following morning. Here, possibly, is a precursor of stanzas three and four of 'Fern Hill'. Less successful is *These Are the Men* (1943) which, too glibly, superimposes self-denouncing speeches on Nazi leaders speaking at Nuremberg. These propaganda films, of course, simplify issues in the interests of popular persuasion, suppress complications, stereotype, cheer, and encourage. As such, to an extent, they effect a link with Thomas' poems of the Blitz.

His film work meant that Thomas – sometimes with his family – was in London for much of the war, enduring the bombing at first hand, often frightened, always nervous. He became famous among the bars and bedrooms of the chaotic city. From 1941 until 1944 such, with scriptwriting, was his London life. He wrote little or no poetry until, during 1944 and 1945, he had what turned out to be his last prolific period.

Deaths and Entrances (1946) collects his poems of the 1940s. The most important group is that on the London Blitz, necessarily from a civilian's perspective. The earliest is the eponymous 'Deaths and Entrances', written during 1940-1941 when staying in John Davenport's house in Wiltshire. The poem makes a disturbing connection between the bomber pilot striking fear into the waiting populace and the poet penetrating to his reader's heart. The poet, as much as the pilot, is

> One enemy, of many, who knows well
>   Your heart is luminous
> In the watched dark, quivering through locks and caves,
>   Will pull the thunderbolts
> To shut the sun.

The poem is equally striking in its essentially heroic assertion of the value of poetry in defying war; the poet will "load the throats of shells / With every cry". The poet's 'wound' – invariably, for Thomas, a reference to the source of his poetic inspiration – requires him to "bathe his raining blood in the male sea". Ultimately, the poem links the poet with Samson in a final line that suggests disturbance and destruction but does not exclude strength and support. Ambiguity generates optimistic possibility.

'Among Those Killed in the Dawn Raid was a Man Aged a Hundred' was written in July 1941 and is perhaps the strangest of the war poems. To an extent the poem looks back to those of the Great War: the body lying in the open air, the spade and the common cart. Yet the old man 'died', rather than being killed; death itself is seen as liberation; resurrection is suggested, slightly humorously, by the perching of 'a hundred storks'. In one reading, the old man's death becomes part of the natural cycle, the power of which counters that of war.

'Ceremony After a Fire Raid' and 'A Refusal to Mourn the Death, by Fire, of a Child in London', have at their centres a burning child. This last, symbolising outrages against vulnerable civilians in World War Two, displaces the soldier's dead body lying on open ground that features so strongly in Thomas' poetic responses to World War One. Both end with Thomas' now-familiar consoling ambiguity: life reasserting itself in 'Ceremony After a Fire Raid' as "The masses of the sea ... / Erupt, fountain and enter to utter for ever / Glory glory glory" and the eternalising suggestiveness of "After the first death, there is no other", the final line of 'A Refusal to Mourn'.

Two other poems complete the war poems group. One is 'Holy Spring', which discards its Great War origins – it began life as a notebook poem[20] – to dramatise Thomas' existential despair as he "climb[s] to greet the war in which I have no heart". In this poem of late 1944 Thomas derives no consolation from spring or from the morning that emerges "out of the woebegone pyre" that is Blitzed London. Such natural forces are vulnerable in the world of war. His only comfort, it seems, is that the "hail and upheaval" of war leads to poems.

'Lie still, sleep becalmed', written during the last months of the war, describes a wounded man in a boat floating on the sea. To a degree this is a war poem. But the wound is in the throat and so a likely reference to Thomas' father, who suffered and recovered from cancer of the throat during the mid 1930s. Further, as has been noted, in making use of Thomas' view of poetic inspiration as a 'wound', here "wrapped in the salt sheet" that is the poet's page of bitter difficulty, the poem is also about Thomas' struggles to write. The poem ends with the possibility of survival.

In March 1945 Thomas had his only experience of being under fire. The family, then living in Majoda, a bungalow near New Quay, were submachine gunned by William Killick, an angry and drunken commando captain with whom Thomas had argued earlier that evening in New Quay's Black Lion pub. Thomas behaved so coolly as to suggest he had lost any concern for himself.[21] Certainly he was beset with worries about money, his marriage and his future. The end of the war meant the end of his lucrative scriptwriting. Further, as Gwen Watkins reported, the war's end contributed to an existential crisis:

> Vernon always felt that the War made a terrific chasm in Dylan's life. That before that Dylan found life good and interesting, and after that life had a kind of horror about it that he could never get across. He looked back across the chasm; he could write great poems about childhood, but he couldn't go forward to an adult world in which such horrors could exist.[22]

This is not wholly persuasive, given that such great poems as 'Over Sir John's Hill' and 'Do not go gentle', both products of the post-war period, are not about childhood. But there is no doubt that, after World War Two, during the last eight years of his life, he was troubled by consequences and fearsome possibilities.

One of the former was the discovery and liberation of the death camps, passing references to which can be found in Thomas' letters. Thus, in May 1945 he described life in Majoda, New Quay, and concluded, enigmatically, that he was experiencing "nature serene as Fats Waller in Belsen"; a month later he was in "worse-than-Belsen London".[23] Belsen, and all it represented, was so often on his mind. Even the early versions of *Under Milk Wood* reflect this: 'The Town that was Mad' is cordoned off with barbed wire and sentries, the rest of the world – and not the town – becoming the concentration camp.

Secondly, during August 1945 he was devastated by Hiroshima and Nagasaki, the beginning of the nuclear age. Occasional jocularity does not hide underlying horror. "There was nothing in my head but a little Nagasaki", he told Oscar Williams during late 1945.[24] "Atom willing", he said to Vernon Watkins during 1946, promising to write more regularly.[25] The late poems demonstrate Thomas' fears that, as he put it in 'In Country Sleep', "the world falls, silent as the cyclone of silence". The sad fatalism of 'Over Sir John's Hill' further dramatises Thomas' existential despair. 'Poem on his Birthday' describes a world that is now "the earth of the night" and in which

> The rocketing wind will blow
> The bones out of the hills,
> And the scythed boulders bleed, and the last
> Rage shattered waters kick
> Masts and fishes to the still quick stars.

'In the White Giant's Thigh', ending as it does with the destruction of whole communities (even though, here, through the passage of time), is a third poem responding, partly, implicitly and obliquely to Hiroshima and Nagasaki. Thomas first read the poem on air, together with 'In Country Sleep' and 'Over Sir John's Hill', other parts of an unfinished sequence to be entitled 'In Country Heaven'. The readings were preceded by a commentary, part of which became a note to the publication of 'In the White Giant's Thigh' in *Botteghe Oscure*. The note explained that the whole sequence would be about the death of the world:

> The earth has killed itself. It is black, petrified, wizened, poisoned, burst; insanity has blown it rotten; and no creatures at all ... shortly and brutishly hunt their days down like enemies on that corrupted face. [Earth is] ... that self-killed place ...[26]

Yet, having said this, Thomas ends with affirmation and hope; a destroyed community can still "teach [him] the love that is evergreen after the fall-leaved grave", a small counter – a moment, perhaps, of propaganda – to the idea of nuclear catastrophe flowing determinedly through these last poems. 'Prologue', the last completed poem, ends with final gestures towards Armageddon: the world flooded by a new Deluge, the poems as arks which may (or may not) survive the flood's flowering.

Thirdly, in these post-war years Thomas returns to his early obsession with the Great War. *Reminiscences of Childhood* is one instance, as has been noted. Two others also occur in broadcasts. In 1946, in a programme on Welsh poetry, Thomas wrote of Wilfred Owen:

> It is a miracle how, in his short and warring life, in the dirt, the blood, the despair, the scarcely tolerable cold, the fire and gas and death of France, he contrived to achieve all his ambitions and to perfect his original technique.

In the same broadcast he wrote of Edward Thomas that when he was killed in Flanders, "a mirror of England was shattered of so pure and true a crystal that a clearer and tender reflection can be found no other where than in [his] poems". The broadcast ended with Alun Lewis' war poems. Here was another poet, Thomas considered, who knew that the poetry was in the pity.[27]

Later in 1946 Thomas wrote a BBC programme wholly devoted to Wilfred Owen.[28] The text reflects Thomas' preoccupations. One such is nuclear annihilation; Owen's work will survive, writes Thomas, "if there are men, then, still to read – by which I mean, if there are men at all". Owen speaks to the present, a time which "insist[s] upon chief actors who are senseless enough to perform a cataclysm". In what "may never be known to historians as the 'atomic age'" Owen becomes a poet for "all times, all places, and all wars". Most striking of all about this broadcast, and the earlier references to Owen, is the strength of Thomas' feelings for the suffering of those who served in 1914-18. He writes of "the foolishness, unnaturalness, horror, inhumanity, and insupportability of War ... so that all could suffer and see, the heroic lies, the willingness of the old to sacrifice the young, indifference, grief, the Soul of Soldiers." Thomas continues:

> To see [Owen] in his flame-lit perspective, against the background, now, of poxed and cratered war-scape, shivering in the snow under the slitting wind, marooned on a frozen desert, or crying, in a little oven of mud, that his 'senses are charred', is to see a man consigned to articulate immolation. He buries his smashed head with his own singed hands ...

To the end Thomas raged against war. The Korean War led him to write to Oscar Williams in October 1952:

> Our love from us, looking over wet sand at nothing with some birds on it, to you eagled there looking out at the Statue of – what's its name? I think it has something to do with what Our Side gives to people after it has napalmed them.[29]

Even the proposed collaboration with Stravinsky – cut short by Thomas' death – was on an opera that, as Thomas put it to the composer, "was to be about the rediscovery of our planet following an atomic misadventure".[30]

Dylan Thomas' concern with the violence of war and the possibility of annihilation, as he once said in another context, runs like a 'moving column' through his life and writing.[31] It affects so much of his work, one example being his 'fatherly' poems fixated on the violence of his father's part in the sexual act, war and conception linked, for example, in 'I dreamed my genesis'. His concern with writing and the nature of his own draws on the imagery of war: poetic inspiration as a 'wound' from which poetry flows like blood.

Thomas wrote further of his poetry that it emerged

> Out of the inevitable conflict of images – inevitable, because of the creative, recreative, destructive, and contradictory nature of the motivating centre, the womb of war – I try to make that momentary peace which is a poem.[32]

The tempestuous nature of many of Thomas' poems, the fierce dialectic of, say, 'I make this in a warring absence', can make us hesitate over 'momentary peace'; even 'Fern Hill' is shot through with unease and vulnerability. But the meaning of this phrase can emerge out of the difference between reactions to war in Thomas' private life – chaotic, fearing, harassed, hating, at times close to cowardly – and what the writings, particularly the poems, actually say. Again and again, Thomas' war poems either insist on positives emerging out of war's brutality, or refuse to exclude that sustaining possibility. In this sense they are poems that search for reconciliation, poems that seek to put war in its place. In 1941 he told Vernon Watkins that both were "prisoners now in a live melodrama". Given the complexity of Thomas' reactions to war, 'melodrama' seems inadequate. The prison metaphor is more apposite, for Thomas never escaped an obsession with war and the violence of war. It is at the heart of his literary achievement.

Notes

1. Dylan Thomas, *The Broadcasts* (ed. Ralph Maud). London: J.M. Dent & Sons Ltd, 1991, p.3.
2. See James A. Davies, "'A Mental Militarist": Dylan Thomas and the Great War' in Tony Brown, Jane Aaron and M. Wynn Thomas (eds.), *Welsh Writing in English: A Yearbook of Critical Essays* (Vol.2, 1996), pp.62-81, and his *A Reference Companion to Dylan Thomas*. Westport, Conn.: Greenwood Press, 1998, passim. See also Jacob Korg, *Dylan Thomas*. New York: Twayne, 1965. Most critical studies of Dylan Thomas have something to say on this subject.
3. 'The Watchers', *Swansea Grammar School Magazine*, (24 No.1, March 1927), pp.16-17. 'Missing', *SGSM*, (25 No.2, July 1928), p.43. The poem is reprinted in Dylan Thomas, *The Poems* (ed. Daniel Jones).

London: Dent, 1971, p.222. 'Armistice', *SGSM* (Vol 27 No.3, December 1930), p.75.

4. 'Modern Poetry', *SGSM*, (26 No.3, December 1929), p.84. The essay is reprinted in Dylan Thomas, *Early Prose Writings* (ed. Walford Davies). London: J.M. Dent & Sons, 1971, pp.83-86.

5. Andrew Lycett, *Dylan Thomas: A New Life*. London: Weidenfeld & Nicolson, 2003, p.67, pp.96-97.

6. Dylan Thomas, *The Collected Letters, New Edition* (ed. Paul Ferris). London: J.M. Dent & Sons, 2000, p.192.

7. All quotations from Thomas' poetry are taken from *Collected Poems 1934-1953* (eds. Walford Davies and Ralph Maud). London: J.M. Dent & Sons, 1988.

8. *Collected Letters*, pp.71-73.

9. *A Reference Companion to Dylan Thomas*, pp.128-133.

10. *Dylan Thomas: A New Life*, p.150, p.154.

11. Dylan Thomas, *The Collected Stories, Everyman Edition* (ed. Walford Davies) London: J.M. Dent & Sons, 1993; reprinted 1995, p.49.

12. See the note to the poem in *Collected Poems 1934-1953*, pp.229-230.

13. *Collected Letters*, p.461.

14. *Ibid.*, p.453.

15. *Ibid.*, p.455.

16. See ed. David N. Thomas, *Dylan Remembered, 2 (1935-1953)*. Bridgend: Seren / National Library of Wales, 2004, pp.93-94.

17. A recent detailed account of this period of Thomas' life is *Dylan Thomas: A New Life*, Chapter 12 passim.

18. See Paul Ferris, *Dylan Thomas: The Biography, New Edition*. London: J.M. Dent & Sons, 1999, pp.171-172.

19. Dylan Thomas, 'Our Country' in *The Filmscripts* (ed. John Ackerman). London: J.M. Dent & Sons, 1995, p.69.

20. 'Out of a war of wits, when folly of words' in *Poet in the Making: The Notebooks of Dylan Thomas* (ed. Ralph Maud). London: J.M. Dent & Sons, 1968, pp.171-172.

21. For the fullest account of this incident, see David N. Thomas, *Dylan Thomas: A Farm, Two Mansions and a Bungalow*. Bridgend: Seren, 2000, Chapter Four passim.

22. *Dylan Thomas Remembered 1935-1953*, p.94.

23. *Collected Letters*, p.617, p.619.

24. *Ibid.*, p.639.

25. *Ibid.*, p.658.

26. *The Broadcasts*, pp.223-226.

27. Quotations are from 'Welsh Poetry' in *The Broadcasts*, pp.29-50.

28. 'Wilfred Owen' in *The Broadcasts*, pp.93-101.

29. *Collected Letters*, p.938.

30. Igor Stravinsky and Robert Craft, *Conversations with Igor Stravinsky*. London: Faber and Faber, 1959, p.78.

31. *Early Prose Writings*, p.150.

32. *Collected Letters*, p.329.

33. *Ibid.*, p.555.

"All Change!": Dannie Abse and the Twentieth Century Wars

Tony Curtis

Herr Doktor, an S is but a straight line bent." This final line from the poem 'One of the Chosen', published in 2003, shows that Dannie Abse in his ninth decade and at the beginning of the new century was still reflecting on the Second World War.[1] There is a sense in which the events of the 1930s and 1940s not only determined the course of his life, professionally and creatively, but were of profound, existential importance to this significant writer from Wales.

In his autobiographical novel *Ash on a Young Man's Sleeve*, written over fifty years before, Dannie Abse had fictionalised his boyhood and early manhood years in Cardiff.[2] He grew up in a warm, supportive and highly stimulating family: brothers Wilfred and Leo were exemplars of energy and intellect in medicine and the law and politics. The clash of ideologies and the rise of Fascism in the 1930s were articulated and manifested in that household. The two decades of *entre deux guerres* are haunted by horrors past and materialising threats. The young boy's Auntie Cecile and Uncle Bertie never lock their front door in case their son Clive should eventually return from the Great War; this is a figure who reappears as 'Cousin Sidney', actually missing in combat at Dunkirk, in a later poem. The impressionable boy is taken by Leo to the Memorial Meeting for Jimmy Ford, a Cardiff man who has died fighting Franco in Spain: "The Fifteenth Brigade, ragtime idealists, advanced; but Jimmy Ford lay horizontal, akimbo, on the dusty road near the tobacco fields, the vision of a white deserted farmhouse leaking out of his surprised eyes."

Despite his youth Dannie understands the significance of this loss and the political context of armed struggle: "If I was bigger perhaps I could go to Spain. It was worth fighting for. Maybe if I got killed they'd have a memorial meeting for me. It was very sad all these young men dying. One week Leo would show me a short story by Ralph Fox in *Left Review*. The next week there would be his obituary. There'd been an article by Christopher Caudwell, then a week later his obituary also. One week a poem by John Cornford, the next another obituary, and so on and so on. Nobody seemed to care except Leo and some of his friends."

He writes later of the effect of reading the poet Miguel Hernandez "with rapt and growing anger".[3] Though he also recognised that, "Righteous the rhetoric of indignation, / but protesting poems, like the plaster angels, / are impotent". He remembers, too, his disaffection with "the fashionable 'pink' poets of the day: W.H. Auden, Stephen Spender, Louis MacNeice, and Cecil Day Lewis" who "were content to compose poems that were ordered carnivals of the interior life ... to give readers pleasure". The young Abse "owned no religious commitment", but, like the seventeen century divine George Herbert, "wanted my poems to change the world".[4]

Of course, Dannie Abse was too young to be engaged in active service. He followed his brother Wilfred into medicine and was training in Westminster Hospital as the war was drawing to a close. He speaks of being left out of the assignment of trainees who went to Germany to treat the victims of the death and concentration camps, possibly because he was a Jew. Ironically, after qualifying he was sent on military service as a National Serviceman. His experiences as a commissioned officer in the RAF were later fictionalised in *Some Corner of an English Field*.[5] The central character, Henderson, gives a confessional speech at his 'dining out' dinner:

> A doctor – but a National Serviceman nevertheless, who has not been quite at ease, quite at home ... one had to face up to realities. I mean the external reality that is visible around us: the uniforms, the barrage balloons, the homesick faces – the internal reality: the longing to love someone and to be loved, the need for faith in each other and in God, and the terror of longing for something that one can't quite understand ...

Dannie Abse rose, briefly, to be a Squadron Leader when his commanding officer fell sick. His experiences of service were, as might be expected, underpinned by boredom and frustration. That slightly inebriated speech by Henderson carries the weight of a post-war, post-Holocaust existentialist crisis; it is surely not too far removed from the writer's own feelings. It is difficult not to read into Henderson's experiences and attitudes those of the writer:

> Somebody had written: a man's destiny is what he is. That was a lie. Fate was the accident that happened to one, a bomb

falling, being called up, conscripted into boredom. It's not
what you are that matters so much, thought Henderson, but
where you are at a given time. One walked down a dark corri-
dor, with all the vision and wisdom that one had, but if there
was an open trapdoor there you fell right through, whoever
you were. That was the morality of things, the biological
morality of things.[6]

Actual conflict, experienced and imagined, was more acutely
realised in the earlier novel: bombs fall in the young Abse's neighbourhood of Roath and his friend Keith is carried dead from the
debris. The young Abse walks away from that boyhood sobered by
the loss: "Near the air-raid shelters I heard, also, the waterfall crash-
ing down into its disaster and saw, in the harp of wind, pools of
rain-water trembling on the gravel pathway, reflecting shuddering
fragments of sky. Pieces of sky, water leaves, hands all fallen, falling
in the convalescent sunlight." He strolls "home that was never to be
home again".[7]

Much later he would claim: "Hitler made me more of a Jew than
Moses."[8] Clearly, a childhood spent in the shadow of Fascism and a
young adulthood in blitzed Cardiff and London as a medical
student would characterise and focus the professional man and the
professional writer. The two ladies who occupied the room next to
his in his student digs in Aberdare Gardens, NW6, Mrs Schiff and
Mrs Blumenfeld, were refugees from Nazi Germany; only later
would he fully realise the roots of their sadness:

> After the war years, I, like so many others, in Britain and
> elsewhere, learnt more and more about the death camps of
> Europe. I came to realise that what had happened to the
> relatives of Blumenfeld and Schiff was something that could
> not be irrevocably suppressed from consciousness, that in
> one sense I, too, was a survivor, that I could never encounter
> a German of a certain age-group without seeing him as a
> one-time inquisitor, that ordinary smoke towering over
> autumn gardens could trigger off a vision of concentration
> camps, false teeth, soap.[9]

One of the most memorable sections in *Ash on a Young Man's Sleeve*
is the "All change at Auschwitz-Dachau" passage:

> Near the Refreshment Room stood a hygienic-looking shed
> containing a few gas chambers, inside one of which a stray
> passenger now found himself. The rest of the passengers sat

in the train, their luggage on the rack of pain. These suitcases were labelled Munch, Berlin, Vienna, Madrid, Prague. When the engine gave its plaintive shriek in the still air, no passenger moved, no passenger spoke. They merely sat, the hook-nosed ones, gazing straight ahead, waiting for the train to move out. Not looking at the pictures lining the carriages. Neither that of Hitler addressing a huge crowd, nor aeroplanes over Barcelona, nor troops goose-marching through Austria. Nobody looked, nobody spoke, nobody waved a last farewell.

A guard came and opened the door, 'All change!' he screamed. They changed into skeletons. Skeletons row after row sitting bolt upright in the carriages of Time.

The loudspeaker crackled again. The next train to arrive at platform two will be the London train.

The engine pulled in.

'There they are,' said Uncle Bertie.

Leo bundled out of the train, mother and father after him, smiling.

'All change!' a porter shouted.[10]

There is a mixture of nightmare and guilt in that passage. There, but for chance, go the Abses.[11] The writing strains a little – "the rack of pain", "the carriages of Time" - but the imaginative force, be it the young boy's or the reflective adult's, is compelling. Dannie Abse is in Wales, not Poland, Roath, not the Warsaw ghetto, but the trauma of the Holocaust is felt and shared. Over the next fifty years the poet, dramatist, essayist and novelist will return to that dilemma and that consideration: "the biological morality of things".

Of Abse's work in the theatre it is *The Dogs of Pavlov* which poses profound questions regarding the Holocaust and the culpability of the German nation.[12] Twenty years after the war it is the report of an experiment in psychology at Yale which offers the writer a narrative through which he can explore the dilemmas of guilt and blame rooted in the Second World War. Professor Stanley Milgram working at Yale wanted to explore the relationship between command structures and the individual conscience. Volunteers were asked to administer electric shocks of increasing severity to others strapped in a glass booth. As a question posed to the victim was wrongly answered the electric charge was increased, to the point of seriously threatening that person's health. No matter how reluctant the administrator of the shocks felt themselves, the orders to proceed with the shocking became more insistent and bullying. No-one refused the commands to punish the victims. Of course, Milgram was, unknown to the controllers of the electric shocks, using actors who faked their pain, their torture. *The Dogs of Pavlov* dramatises these events.

Dannie Abse had worked on a version of the Balzac story 'El Verdugo' as early as 1948 and this, and other work in the theatre, developed into *House of Cowards* and *Pythagoras (Smith)*, as well as *The Dogs of Pavlov*, all of which deal with the moral crises of characters in authoritarian states. The play was regarded as a serious response to his experiments by Professor Milgram who wrote a preface to the published work.

In 1949 Dannie Abse started the magazine *Poetry and Poverty*; it ran for six years and pre-figured the *New Lines / Mavericks* rivalry and debate of the later 1950s concerning the form and subject-matter of contemporary poetry. He wanted to argue against "The new choir ... Proudly English they sing with sharp, flat voices / but no-one dances, nobody rejoices"2, preferring the "Dionysian sin" of Dylan Thomas, the risk-taking of vision and language:[13]

> ... I did not want to publish civilised, neat poems that ignored the psychotic savagery of twentieth century life. Why, only the previous decade there had been Auschwitz and Belsen, Hiroshima and Nagasaki – so shouldn't poetry be more vital, angry, rough, urgent – in short, Dionysian? Should not poets write out of an urgent, personal predicament rather than compose neat little, clever exercises?[14]

Clearly, as with Ceri Richards in his art, Dannie Abse's work in the decades following the war had, close to its centre, a need to form an objective correlative, narratives and imagery for the mid-century's world war and its subsequent, consequent lurch into the Cold War. Over twenty years later he would characterise the poet's role in the world:

> They were the poems of a much-married man who was almost as happy as possible – yet felt threatened sometimes, and uneasy. For, as a doctor, he was clearly aware of other people's dissatisfactions and suffering. He was increasingly aware, too, of his own mortality – how the apple flesh was always turning brown after the bite. In addition, there were those man-made threats: he took his wife to the Academy Cinema in Oxford Street only to be assaulted by a film about Auschwitz; or he would be exposed to the obscene, derelict war images of Vietnam. There was no running away. Writing poetry, too, was an immersion into common reality not an escape from it.[15]

That visit to the Oxford Street cinema is narrated in the poem 'A Night Out'.[16] Written in the 1960s, it is the narrative of a visit to see "a new Polish film" about the Holocaust. After the depiction of "the spotlit drama of our nightmares: / images of Auschwitz almost authentic" and the "trustful children, no older than our own, / strolling into the chambers without fuss, / while smoke, black and curly, oozed from chimneys", Dannie and Joan Abse and their friends sip coffee "in a bored espresso bar nearby" and return home to the comfortable surburbs, where the Abses make love "in the marital bed". That act may be directly referencing a Kabbalistic belief in the need to re-balance the universe when moral chaos threatens; it is a clear, positive response to the negative images the film has planted in their minds.[17]

The world is healed, to an extent, to its only possible extent, by the union in marriage. The suburban safety, the reassuring banality of garaging the car and checking on their sleeping children is undercut by the mention of their "au pair girl from Germany". This is unlikely and unnecessary; an emblem of the new Europe and post-war unity and forgiveness. The irony is too heavy and the burden of their guilt in subscribing to a fictional, filmic depiction of the Holocaust has already been more than adequately signalled in the poem's middle section. Nevertheless 'A Night Out' is significant in the context of Dannie Abse's writing; having spent the war as a medical student, and his National Service in the comparative comfort of a medic's commission, the writer is interrogating his right, any survivor's right, to re-enact the horrors of the Final Solution. He asserts that right, that responsibility, more positively in other, later poems, including, 'Not Beautiful', 'Uncle Isidore', 'Case History', 'One of the Chosen' and 'More Mozart – Germany 1970' in which "The German streets tonight / are soaped in moonlight ... And twelve million eyes / in six million heads / stare in the same direction".[18]

In the 1950s the demobbed Dr Abse re-entered civilian life and began to build his professional career and family life; this was done against the backdrop of the developing Cold War and the increasingly urgent threat of nuclear war. His experiences in the RAF, as well as the growing public discussion of the issues of atomic weapons as the wreckage of European cities and societies being re-ordered, must have meant that he was particularly aware of the fragile hope of the post-war period. As early as the third collection, *Tenants of the House*[19], there is a poem which expresses that very real fear of imminent catastrophe, a second holocaust, a nuclear holocaust:

> Oh how much like Europe's Gothic Past!
> This scene of my nightmare's protoplast:
> glow of the radioactive worm.
> Future story of the Blast?

The threat of impending "leukaemia in the soul of all" is at the core of a nightmare that, on this occasion, the presence of his wife by his side cannot allay:

> the grey skin shrivelling from the head
> our two skulls in the double bed

'Verses at Night' records the deep insecurity of the post-war decade; that was to run in parallel in Dannie Abse's work across the genre with a need to revisit the Nazis' Holocaust, to try again and again to make sense of what had happened in the concentration and death camps.

In the same collection 'The Emperors of the Island – *a political parable to be read aloud*' more successfully, because less specifically, creates a trope for the relentlessly destructive nature of humankind:

> There is the story of a deserted island
> where five men walked down to the bay.

One by one they dig a grave and each time one fewer returns until

> Four ghosts dug one grave in the sand,
> four ghosts stood on the sea wet rock;
> five ghosts moved away.

It is polemical, but works both on the page and in performance because it has a lyrical pattern, and it remains as relevant and effective today as fifty years ago. This poem is pertinent to a wide range of political and war situations, whereas 'Verses at Night' seems locked into a mid-century crisis: long may it remain there.

In Dannie Abse's next collection, *Poems Golders Green*[20], he included a response to the release from prison of the collaborator and broadcaster for Mussolini, Ezra Pound, entitled 'After the Release of Ezra Pound'. Pound the poet was, of course, also the collaborator, editor, mentor of T.S. Eliot, an especially important figure at the time of *The Waste Land*; one of the more significant poets in English before the Second World War, in fact. Abse's poem takes the form of a reply to Paul Potts' poem and forgiveness of Pound; he says that "Pound did not hear the raw Jewish cry, / the

populations committed to the dark ..." and that if his journey of
release between prison cell and his coffin was surely short

> ... that ticking distance between
> was merely a journey long enough
> to walk the circumference of a Belsen,
> Walt Whitman would have been eloquent,
> and Thomas Jefferson would have cursed.

He finds it impossible to forgive absolutely. In 'Ezra Pound and My
Father', a chapter in *A Poet in the Family*, the poet describes how his
father would "persevere with the crackling signals" from Italy and
Pound's "gibberish and rhetoric and near obscenity" because they
might glean some alternative news on the progress of the war in
which brothers Leo and Wilfred were actively fighting in Europe.
That "lousy anti-Semite" uttering the "ravings of an eccentric poet,
the paradox of a sensitive Fascist" and his irritating "nasal
harangue" made an impression in that summer of 1943 quite
contrary to the enthusiasm which the young poet had for the work
in *Selected Poems* borrowed earlier from Cardiff Central Library.[21]

The 'Red Balloon' in the same collection presents an image of
anti-Semitism from Abse's boyhood and that sense of anger at such
racism is continually expressed in Abse's poetry; the most effective,
shocking work is 'Case History':

> 'Most Welshmen are worthless
> an inferior breed, doctor.'
> He did not know I was Welsh.
> Then he praised the architects
> of the German death-camps –
> did not know I was a Jew.
> He called liberals, 'White blacks',
> and continued to invent curses.
>
> When I palpated his liver
> I felt the soft liver of Goering;
> when I lifted my stethoscope
> I heard the heartbeats of Himmler;
> when I read his encephalograph
> I thought, '*Sieg heil, mein Fuhrer.*'
>
> In the clinic's dispensary
> red berry of black bryony,
> cowbane, deadly nightshade, deathcap.
> Yet I prescribed for him
> as if he were my brother.

Later that night I must have slept
on my arm: momentarily
my right hand lost its cunning.[22]

The two aspects of Abse the man – doctor and writer, the wearer of
the "white coat and the purple coat" – inform many poems and
much of the fiction, autobiography and journal writing; however,
there is too the dilemma of the professional doctor who trained
through the 1940s and the Jew whose accident of birth meant that
he was relatively safe in Britain while the Nazis embarked on their
Final Solution to "the Jewish problem". At the point of initial quali-
fication the young doctor was not included in the contingent from
Westminster Hospital who travelled over to Germany to help with
the victims of Belsen and other camps:

> In April 1945, when the war seemed almost as good as over,
> our firm was called together. Would any of us volunteer to
> nurse and treat critically sick prisoners in a camp that the
> Germans has abandoned? We were not told the name of that
> camp. Of course I volunteered. But unlike Russell Barton,
> Titch, Eric Trimmer, Hargreaves and others, inexplicably I
> was not accepted. 'They must think I'm a duffer,' I told Titch
> gloomily.
> Soon after, Titch and the rest were flown from an RAF camp
> near Swindon. Their destination hell. Some called it Belsen.
> They flew from RAF Lyneham on April 28th, the day the
> Italian partisans hung Mussolini and his mistress head
> downwards from meat hooks in a Milan garage. Two days later
> Hitler committed suicide and my friends in Belsen heard his
> emaciated victims cry pleadingly, 'Herr Doktor, Herr Doktor'.
> They were covered, these barely living skeletons, with sores
> and ulcers and infested with every kind of body parasite.
> Hargreaves contracted typhus and became seriously ill.
> None of this I knew until much later when I guessed that I
> was not allowed to join the Belsen team because I was a Jew.
> Meanwhile, on May 8th, it was Victory Day. With Nan I joined
> the effervescent singing crowds in Trafalgar Square who were
> wearing paper hats as at a party.
> I often think about not going to Belsen.[23]

There is regret and an irrational guilt: Abse was not a witness, did
not almost share the fate of the camp inmates, as Hargreaves did;
this month of May 1945 was, in retrospect, a dance macabre, a
James Ensor painting. Abse the writer becomes a passionate and
angry survivor; of course, the patient in 'Case History' is a collec-

tive personification of all those bigots, racists and revisionists who deny the Holocaust and would not stand in the way of another genocide. A doctor's role is to treat patients without prejudice; to treat the symptoms and the sick person in a concerned but largely objective way. The moral dilemma holds too: at what point may the right hand "lose its cunning"? And what exactly does that mean? It is ambiguous and deeply unsettling. At what point and in the light of what knowledge may one's professional duty be swayed and overridden?

The wars of his century, our century, form the man and inform the writer. The First World War casts a shadow over the decade of Dannie Abse's boyhood, as does the rise of Fascism and the Spanish Civil War; he is more directly involved with the Second World War – his brothers are on active service, he is bombed in Cardiff and witnesses the Blitz as a student in London – but he is not in the front line, as a Jew, as a doctor, even as an RAF officer on National Service in the 1950s. 'Three Street Musicians'[24] play 'Roses of Picardy' and "now, suddenly, there are too many ghosts about". In 'Not Beautiful' Dr Abse gives the lie to a man who would show optimism in the face of the twentieth century horrors: "... all hiroshimas, in raw and raving voices, / live skeletons of the Camp, flies hugging faeces, / in war, in famine, he'd find the beautiful."[25] It is better to feel anger, the poet says: "... to curse is more sacred / than to pretend by affirming. And offend."

In 'Llandough Hospital' Dannie Abse's dying father is "thin as Auschwitz in that bed".[26] In 'Exit' his mother is in "this concentration camp for one".[27] It as if our own natural mortality can deal us a blow as terrible as that of the Nazis' victims: the practice of medicine brings one up against that realisation more acutely than reading. 'Uncle Isidore', "smelly / schnorrer and lemon-tea Bolshevik" has the answer though: he plays on, after the pogroms and the camps, after the doctor's visit, through the thunder and rain on his violin, "some notes wrong, all notes wild".[28] That seems like a manifesto for the writer, too.

In that poem from the time of his mother's death, 'Exit', Dannie Abse takes solace in the story of David and Bathsheba, for "out of so much suffering / came forth the other child / the wise child, the Solomon". That Old Testament story would inform a later poem, one of his mature, significant achievements; 'Events Leading to the Conception of Solomon, the Wise Child' is Abse's most direct response to the continuing crisis in the Middle East.[29]

Here Dannie Abse reworks the Bible story of David and Bathsheba: a king's infatuation, pursuit and seduction of one of his military commander's wives, Bathsheba the wife of Uriah. The implications of this act for the central characters are echoed in a demotic chorus in the manner of T.S. Eliot's Chorus in *Murder in the Cathedral*:

> Since scandal's bad for royal business
> the King must not father the child;
> so he called Uriah from the front,
> shook his hand like a voter. Smiled.

The language of this long poem swings from the Biblical to the ballad, from lyrical poetry to wise-crack innuendo. The narrative progresses from Ancient Israel to the present day. Tribes still fight over the same land; lives, personal and public, are enacted against a constant backdrop of violence. Prayers and pleas rise from all sides, all cultures and beliefs:

> Allah Akbar!
> Sovereign of the Universe!
> Our father in Heaven!
> Father of Mercies!
> Shema Yisroael!

And then the hush of the land, the desert land:

> after the shadow of an aeroplane
>   has hurtled and leapt
> below the hills and on to the hills
>   that surround Jerusalem.

The position which a British Jew takes on the Middle East is a difficult one; this is the only piece by Dannie Abse to deal with the issue. Through the previous decades and other collections, however, there have been a number of writings which engage with the Cold War and the Vietnam War. Joan Abse and their daughter Keren were personally engaged in protests at Britain's nuclear arsenal. CND and specifically the Greenham Common Women's demonstration are mentioned.[30] His *Ham & High* journals record a "die-in" organised by Hampstead CND in which "everybody would lie down signifying that the Heath was planned as Hampstead's Mass Grave" in the event of a nuclear holocaust; at which he, reluctantly, agreed to read a poem from the 1950s: "I dislike participating in public protests, especially if one is asked to be ostentatious in them. I wish I did not feel that way, but I do." More explicit and showing more direct anger is his piece about the Chemical Warfare Centre at

Porton Down in Wiltshire: "I confess that such facts [the shooting of animals in wounding tests] remind me of the medical atrocity experiments of the Nazis in 1942 in Ravensbruck Concentration Camp for women." Both experimenters used the justification of research into saving the lives of their own army's casualties.

The Vietnam War was also a continuing concern for Dannie Abse: 'On the Beach', 'Give Me Your Hands', 'Forgotten' and others. That war was, obviously, a televisual war, recorded, observed, mediated, at a distance from us. It was a decade-long, increasingly absurd conundrum into which our natural ally, the USA, had been drawn and then plunged fully.

> I know the geography of the great world
> has changed; the war, the peace, the deletions
> of places – red pieces gone forever,
> and names of countries altered forever:
> Gold Coast Ghana, Persia become Iran,
> Siam Thailand, and Hell now Vietnam.[31]

The world has changed, as its map has changed from the simplicity of his boyhood atlas.

> In Vietnam, beneath scarred trees,
> unreal the staring casualties.
> Of course I care. What good is that?[32]

But it is a distant war, someone else's war, about which we are powerless:

> Yawning, I fold yesterday's newspaper
> from England, and its news of Vietnam
> which has had, and will have, a thousand names.
> Then I lie back on the tourist sand.[23]

In his recent collection Dannie Abse groups twelve poems which deal with war and its consequences: from 'The Other Story about the Angel of Mons', where the apparition causes the horses to bolt and the carrion crows to take flight[34]; through the dubious political conversion by a soap-box orator[35]; to "the statues of forgotten heroes, / nameless soldiers and generals on horseback"[36] and an 'Advert' for the 'Devil / Violent Death':

> Impeccable references will be provided.
> Men such as Haman and Hitler,
> Saladin and Saddam,
> Domitian and Shaka,
> have not found me wanting.
>
> ...
>
> As for you premature punters,
> you kinky Suicide Bombers,
> don't worry, I like you all.

While the poet is still uncertain about his role, "the ineffectual poet strums his lyre"[37]; whether, surely, he might have done more to protest, as his "gentle wife, convinced pacifist"[38] had consistently done, instead of simply staring "at the highest, jubilant, silver / sunlit point of a fountain" in the park.[39]

That group collects 'One of the Chosen' which through the persona of a Nazi explores the context of the rise of Hitler who "candled away my fears one by one":

> You sneer. I did my duty. What I was I am,
> one who knew the sequel to *Non Serviam*.
> Elect I was chosen as his instrument.
> Herr Doktor, an S is but a straight line bent.

The Holocaust remains the pinnacle of evil manifest in the twentieth century; coming to terms with a life lived through and beyond that period is one of the challenges which Dannie Abse has tried to answer in his poetry.

In his substantial body of writing – poetry, fiction, drama and journals – Dannie Abse has witnessed, recorded, recreated and debated the wars which have formed his century. In 'A Letter from Ogmore-by-Sea' he says:

> Goodbye, 20th Century.
> What should I mourn?
> Hiroshima, Auschwitz?
>
> ...
>
> Goodbye, 20th Century,
> your trumpets and your drums,
> your war-wounds still unhealed.
> Goodbye, I-must-leave-you-Dolly,
> goodbye Lily Marlene.

> Has the Past always a future?
> Will there always be
> a jackboot on the stair,
> a refugee to roam?[40]

The century of his life has been one formed and spoiled by war and the threat of war. War and the suffering of war has been one of his themes; Dannie Abse has interrogated the causes and effects of war as effectively as any writer of his generation, or ours.

Notes

1. Dannie Abse, 'One of the Chosen' in *Poetry Wales* (Vol. 36 No.1., July 2000); first collected in *The Yellow Bird*. New York: The Sheep Meadow Press, 2004.
2. Dannie Abse, *Ash on a Young Man's Sleeve*. London: Hutchinson, 1954; later Penguin.
3. Dannie Abse, *A Poet in the Family*. London: Hutchinson, 1974, pp.6-8.
4. *Ibid.*, pp.10-11.
5. Dannie Abse, *Some Corner of an English Field*. London: Hutchinson, 1956.
6. *Ibid.*, p 82.
7. The young Abse was himself injured when a bomb fell close to his house in Windermere Avenue, Cardiff. *A Poet in the Family*, pp.43-44.
8. Dannie Abse, 'Replies to an Enquiry' in *The Two Roads Taken*. London: Enitharmon, 2003.
9. *A Poet in the Family*, p.78.
10. *Ash on a Young Man's Sleeve*, pp.127-128 (in the Penguin edition).
11. He later wrote: "I often think of my not going to Belsen". *A Poet in the Family*.
12. Dannie Abse, 'The Dogs of Pavlov' in *The View from Row G: Three Plays* (ed. James A. Davies). Bridgend: Seren Books, 1990. The editor's notes and Introduction are a valuable source for criticism of Abse as a playwright.
13. Dannie Abse, 'Enter the Movement' in *Poetry and Poverty*.
14. *A Poet in the Family*, p.153.
15. *Ibid.*, p.198.
16. All poems are to be found in Dannie Abse, *New and Collected Poems*. London: Hutchinson, 2003.
17. This is discussed in more detail by Joseph Cohen in his Introduction to *The Poetry of Dannie Abse: Critical Essays and Reminiscences*. London: Robson Books, 1983.
18. Dannie Abse, *Funland and Other Poems*. London: Hutchinson, 1973.
19. Dannie Abse, *Tenants of the House*. London: Hutchinson, 1957; reprinted in 1958, published in the USA in 1959.
20. Dannie Abse, *Poems Golders Green*. London: Hutchinson, 1962.

21.   *A Poet in the Family*, pp.58-63.

22.   Dannie Abse, *Ask the Bloody Horse*. London: Hutchinson, 1986.

23.   Dannie Abse, *Goodbye Twentieth Century: An Autobiography*. London: Pimlico, 2001, pp.86-87.

24.   *Funland and Other Poems*.

25.   Dannie Abse, *A Small Desperation*. London: Hutchinson, 1968.

26.   *Ibid.*

27.   *Ask the Bloody Horse.*

28.   *New and Collected Poems.*

29.   Dannie Abse, *Arcadia One Mile*. London: Hutchinson, 1998.

30.   Dannie Abse, 'April 1984' in *Journals from the Ant-Heap*. London: Hutchinson, 1986. Republished in *Intermittent Journals*. Bridgend: Seren, 1994.

31.   'Forgotten' in *The Yellow Bird*.

32.   'Give me your Hands'.

33.   'On The Beach'.

34.   'Terrible Angels'.

35.   'Politics in the Park'.

36.   'Heroes'.

37.   'War Poet', a poem of saddened irony.

38.   'Ants'.

39.   'Politics in the Park'.

40.   *Arcadia One Mile.*

Welsh Women Writers and War

Katie Gramich

Stafell Gynddylan ys tywyll heno,
Heb dân, heb wely;
Wylaf wers, tawaf wedy.[1]

Dark is Cynddylan's hall tonight
With no fire, no bed.
I weep awhile, then am silent.[1]

The ninth-century middle-Welsh poems known as *Canu Heledd* consist of a series of laments and elegies spoken in the voice of a woman called Heledd who is mourning the death of her brother and the destruction of her home in a disastrous battle against the Mercian enemy. The verse is poignant and suffused with a tangible sense of personal loss and dispossession. War itself is represented as extreme savagery, though there is no humanitarian questioning of the heroic ideal of the great warrior. Cynddylan himself is lauded as one of the most efficient and successful butchers of them all before his own defeat. Yet such is the power of the verse and the intensity of the feeling expressed, we mourn with Heledd over the loss of her brother. Whether the poem was actually composed by a woman remains in doubt; nevertheless, *Canu Heledd* may be regarded as prophetic of one of the main literary responses of Welsh women writers to war: the impulse to mourn and to express irreplaceable loss. Nor is this, of course, a response confined to Welsh women; the notion of the suffering woman remaining behind to deal with the aftermath of war and to commemorate what has been lost is one which is repeated in diverse cultures and ages, from the voice of Antigone to that of Vera Brittain.

Wars and conflicts of previous ages, such as the rebellion of Owain Glyndŵr and the tithe wars, feature in early twentieth-century Welsh women's writing[2] but they do so largely as off-stage events or as an historical background against which the main plot unfolds. It is really only with the outbreak of the First World War that war becomes not just a backdrop but an all-involving, formative experience in some Welsh women's writing. Although World War One features only in the last five chapters of Kate Roberts' 1936 novel *Traed mewn cyffion* (*Feet in Chains*), it is nevertheless central to the book's conception and impact. Roberts herself stated that the catalyst for her becoming a writer in the first place was the loss of her brother, who was killed in that war. The experience of that loss is given fictional form in the novel. Her writing, then, springs from a sense of loss and disillusionment (*'siom'*); the novel may be regarded as an attempt at personal catharsis and as a commemoration of the dead and their lost world.

Feet in Chains is, therefore, a highly autobiographical novel, though it is more the autobiography of a family than a single individual. It is set in the slate quarrying / smallholding community of Caernarfonshire between the 1880s and the middle of the First World War. It focuses on the people of Moel Arian, who live a life of austerity, incessant labour and rigid self-discipline. The novel draws attention to their stoicism but at the same time shows how enchained they are both by their sense of duty and by their political naivety. The war functions in the novel, as it did in the author's life, as a catalyst for change.

At first, the people of Moel Arian regard the War as something distant and incomprehensible: "they did not understand its causes; they believed in what the papers said, that Great Britain was going to the help of smaller nations."[3] The family at Ffridd Felen connect it initially with the Boer War of which they remember "how the headmaster had made them march through the village in procession with their banners flying when Mafeking was relieved, but it had not meant anything to them."[4] The wars of the British Empire are clearly of no interest to these people, nor do they admire the warrior hero – the local militiaman is an object of scorn rather than awe. They are, at best, indifferent colonial subjects, unaware of their own abject status or their own stake in the colonial enterprise. However, the novel demonstrates how an awareness of subjection begins to grow in the general consciousness and it is the War which, unexpectedly, effects this political awakening.

When Twm, one of the sons of Ffridd Felen joins up, his family is at first shocked by his dereliction of familial duty: "here was Twm playing such a shabby trick! When he could be sending a little money home each month, he had gone and joined the army ..."[5] Such a reaction underlines the people's naivety, since at this point they still believe that the war will soon be over and that there is no danger of any of the local boys who join up actually being required to fight. Life goes on as usual on the smallholding only disrupted by Bet, one of the daughters, who "kept saying she would like to go away to work in an ammunition factory".[6] Soon, though, the shocking news comes that Twm is to be sent to France. His mother, Jane, consoles herself by sending him two packages of home-made food every week; Roberts is an astute observer of her people's reactions – generally taciturn and often unable to articulate their emotions verbally, the women at least have an outlet in the ability to express love by means of food. Gradually, the people of Moel Arian begin to awake from their stoical quietism; they

> began to ask what was the meaning of it all ... They did not
> believe at all now that the war was being fought to save the
> smaller nations, or that it was a war to end all wars ... They
> came to realize that, in every country, there were people who
> regarded war as a good thing, and were taking advantage of
> their sons to promote their own interests. These were 'The
> Ruling Class', the same who oppressed them in the quarry,
> who sucked their blood and turned it into gold for themselves
> ... their views began to change. Their faith in preachers and
> politicians was shaken ... But the war continued.[7]

The well-known climax of the novel occurs when the mother, Jane Gruffydd, receives an official letter informing her of the death of her son, a letter which she cannot understand because it is written in English. Kate Roberts' writing here is deceptively simple and emotionally explosive. The experience of Jane Gruffydd is intensely personal and yet the whole episode is emblematic of the experience of many Welsh people during World War One. Roberts' realist technique, focusing on the materiality of the object, "sheets of paper, written in English"[8] in which Jane recognises only Twm's name and his army number, forces the reader into sharing her bewildered, panicky incomprehension. At the same time, the political undercurrent of the scene is unmistakable: Welsh-speaking Wales is being sacrificed for an alien cause by an imperial power which is both ruthless and insensitive.

The family's period of shock and mourning after the bereavement is memorably evoked: "time stood still in Ffridd Felen ... There was no tomorrow. There remained only yesterday."[9] The loss caused by the war in a way consecrates the past; this is a feeling shared by Kate Roberts herself, who said in a 1961 letter to Saunders Lewis, referring to the 'rootless' young people of the day: "the past isn't important to them at all. It means everything to me."[10] This period of numb suffering after the death comes to an end in the novel with the visit of a military pensions officer, who smugly informs Jane and her son, Owen, that he reduced a neighbouring widow's pension when he discovered that she earned some money by selling eggs. The self-congratulation of this representative of the British State is soon dispelled, however:

> At that moment a strange feeling came over Jane Gruffydd. For fifteen long months, a deep resentment had been gathering in her very soul against everything that was responsible for the war, against man and against God. And when she saw this plump man in his immaculate clothes preening himself on the fact that he had reduced a widow's pension, she lost control of herself. It was like a dam bursting. At that moment, the man standing before her represented all that was behind the War. She grabbed the nearest thing to hand – a clothes-brush – and struck him on the head with it.
> "Get out of this house at once," she shouted.[11]

The final vision of the novel is that of Owen, who belongs to Kate Roberts' own generation: "his eyes were opened to the possibility of doing something instead of simply enduring like a dumb animal."[12] The novel shows a nationalist and a socialist consciousness being born in the people of one corner of Wales as a direct result of their bitter experience of war. Historians of Plaid Cymru, founded in the 1920s by Kate Roberts among many others, concur that war experiences greatly influenced the nationalist feeling which gave rise to the party. Particularly galling for many was the idea that the war was allegedly fought, as the novel puts it, to "help the small nations", a slogan which naturally encouraged many young Welsh people to join up. Gradually, like the characters in the novel, the people who would go on to found and support Plaid Cymru realised not just the falsity of the claim but the oppressive weight of the colonial edifice which that political banner concealed. Thus, Kate Roberts' novel is not only another in a long tradition of female-authored elegies for the death and destruction of war; it is also an eloquent expression of political protest. Emblematically, near the end of the novel, the archetypal Welsh Mam takes up her brush not to scrub and scour but to attack the representative of the oppressive British state, which extends its tentacles even as far as her own domestic hearth.

A Welsh novelist of a younger generation, Siân James, offers another view of rural west Wales during the First World War in her 1979 novel, *A Small Country*. Rather than focusing on the role of the mother of the family, who dies at an early stage of the war, James renders the work of the young women actively involved in the war effort. Catrin, coming to adulthood, longs vaguely to follow an artistic vocation but resigns herself to training as a nurse; the advent of war strengthens her resolve:

> Now that the war had come, it seemed the appropriate time for putting aside personal vanities like love affairs and painting and drawing, and for making a serious commitment. It wasn't so much patriotism that moved her as a foreboding ... that life was earnest and might be grim. The outbreak of war enabled her to forget herself and really think of herself as a nurse. [13]

Another female character, an ardent young English suffrage campaigner called Rose, also becomes a nurse, switching her energies to a patriotic and idealistic "struggle to defend the civilisation of the world".[14] However, her first contact with real wounded soldiers and their terrible personal testimonies rid her of her illusions: "Her ideas of warfare had been so remote; men on horseback looking rather fine ... Stark, unhidden fear was something she had not considered."[15]

Tom, Catrin's brother, joins up because he thinks it his duty; rather like his namesake, Twm, in Kate Roberts' *Feet in Chains*, he also believes "it will all be over by Christmas". Also like Roberts' characters, Tom is moved by the plight of Belgium, "a peaceful little country, not much bigger than Wales".[16] However, like Owen in the earlier novel, Tom's experiences in the War make him suddenly aware of his Welsh identity, one which he has previously scoffed at as an Oxford-educated, sophisticated young man. In a letter to his sister, Tom expresses his homesickness poignantly:

> I intend to come home. And when I do, I shall be like old Prosser, never venturing beyond Erw Fach Bridge. I think a man is essentially the product of the area that begets him. I seem to have forgotten Shrewsbury and Oxford ... When I think of the civilization we're fighting for, I can only think about the patch I know best ... It seemed so strange that in this place, with all hell's forces of destruction let loose about me, I should be concerned with things like the language and culture of our unimportant small country: I suppose we must all fix on something to keep us sane.[17]

Yet another attitude to the war is expressed by a old man who has never left his local 'patch': "The bloody English ... wanted me to fight once; against the Russians, I think, or the Turks. Not I. My family fight against the bloody English, not for them ... My father burnt his ricks in the tithe war, ready to starve rather than pay the tithes ... My grandfather was one of 'Becca's maidens in the hungry forties. They were fighters if you like ..."[18] This construction of Welsh history is one of continual resistance, a warrior-like readiness for war but only on Welsh terms.

James' novel clearly positions itself in relation to a Welsh female tradition of writing about war, primarily with relation to Kate Roberts' *Feet in Chains*, which is constantly echoed and alluded to in the text. In some ways, though, James is re-writing Roberts' account of the family, gender and marriage from a later, feminist point of view. Where Roberts highlights the role of the suffering mother in war and emphasises the cohesiveness of the family and its demand for propriety and duty, James' family is falling apart through adultery and Anglicisation, her female characters challenging their traditional roles and taking the opportunities offered them by the War – ironically – to forge a vocation for themselves.

James' representation of young women temporarily abandoning suffrage is echoed from a much more conservative point of view by the romance writings of the Anglo-Welsh popular novelist, Berta Ruck. Several of the stories in her volume *Khaki and Kisses* (1915) have a female protagonist who was an erstwhile militant suffragist suddenly realising that what she really wants is, in the title words of one of the stories, 'A Master'. In the latter story, Sydney (her ambiguous name apparently suggesting her former androgyny) concludes that "it's taken war, and the sight of man doing a man's old job as a woman's protector, to put all these things in the right places".[19]

As the daughter of a Welsh Indian army officer, Berta Ruck's conservative ideology is perhaps not surprising but it does illustrate the great variety of Welsh women's responses to war, from that of the gung-ho British propagandist like Ruck to that of the pacifist (like the Welsh Jewish novelist, Lily Tobias[20]) and nationalist (like Kate Roberts) who utterly reject its validity. Moreover, some female pacifists also rejected nationalism, as famously illustrated in Virginia Woolf's 1938 dictum "As a woman I have no country. As a woman I want no country. As a woman my country is the whole world".[21] Arguably, however, such an internationalist statement was more difficult to make for Welsh women writers emerging from 'a small country' perceived as vulnerable, rather than a country, like England, which boasted a great Empire.

The argument between the pacifist and the idealist who wants to do his duty is dramatised in another of Siân James' novels, *Love and War* (1997) which is set in a west Wales town during the Second World War. Rhian, a young schoolteacher, has a husband away at war and a lover, Gwynn, who insists on obeying his call-up papers, despite Rhian's impassioned pacifist and nationalist arguments against his doing so. The focus in this novel is very much on the anxieties and trauma of those left behind in rural Wales; James' innovation here is that she mixes tragic material with a great deal of social comedy. Rhian's mother-in-law, for example, is outraged that their local minister is preaching Christianity:

> To hear him carrying on about the Germans being God's children, only led astray, is deeply offensive, don't you think so, Rhian? Gwilym Martin, Horeb, isn't such a milksop, I can tell you. No, Mr Martin gets to the point quick enough, praying for the forces of God to smash the legions of Satan, and no nonsense about forgiveness either. I'd switch to Horeb in a minute, only Bryn's afraid of losing custom in Tabernacle.[22]

Another young teacher at Rhian's school, Miss Mary Powell, Maths, has a fiancé fighting in Burma called Alun Brooke. However, bizarrely, this fiancé turns out to be an elaborate figment of Miss Powell's imagination, much to Rhian's disgust since she has spent many hours empathising with Miss Powell over the fate of this non-existent person. Indeed, 'Alun Brooke' has become more real to Rhian than her almost forgotten husband, Huw; Rhian ponders:

> I wonder what the Head will say when he hears about them? ... Perhaps she'll tell him that Alun was killed in action. It would certainly be a hero's death ... I'm beginning to feel quite unhinged. Why can't I stop thinking about him? I can see his face so clearly; the band of peeling sunburn over his nose and cheeks, his sweat-soaked blond hair curling slightly on his neck even after the severest army haircut ... My hold on reality seems as weak as Mary's. I repeat Huw's army number under my breath! 14405196. Why can't I see his face?[23]

Alun Brooke, the fictional Welsh soldier in Burma, inevitably brings to the reader's mind Alun Lewis, the real Welsh soldier-poet who died in Burma. Siân James appears to be reflecting on the way in which truth and fiction, reality and dream, become intermingled in our memories and reconstructions of war. By the end of the novel, the real fate of Alun Lewis has been displaced onto his doubly-fictional fiancée, Mary Powell, who commits suicide by drowning herself in a river. Despite this death, and that of Gwynn in the war, the final pages of the novel emphasise a sense of survival and endurance; a baby is born and Rhian finds herself, after all, "glad to be alive".²⁴ Nevertheless, the sadness of war remains, expressed in the words of a Welsh folk song:

> *Derfydd aur a derfydd arian, derfydd melfed, derfydd sidan,*
> *Derfydd pob dilledyn hiraeth ond er hyn, ni dderfydd hiraeth.*
> Nothing lasts except grief.²⁵

The rather stark 'translation' of the Welsh song in James' text appears to uphold Rhian's own ardent defence of Wales in her earlier argument with Gwynn about what she sees as "joining the English army":

> He says my concept of Wales is over-romantic, that the Welsh way of life I talk about is no different from the way of life of any poor, radical, non-conformist section of society in any part of Britain.
>
> I say that our language and literature make us a separate nation so that we are set apart from any other section of society. We are a nation with a national culture and if that's an over-romantic idea, I admit to being over-romantic.²⁶

Thus, the sense of survival at the end of James's novel relates not only to the end of the war but also to a sense of national persistence, despite the odds.

Hilda Vaughan's novels reveal an interesting dual sensibility in regard to Wales, Britain and the War. In *Pardon and Peace* (1945) which actually deals directly with both World Wars, Wales is figured as a beautiful, timeless place to which the wounded First World War soldier longs to return in order to heal himself of his physical and psychological wounds. Yet, paradoxically, Mark Osbourne is not a native returning to his homeland but an Englishman who has visited rural Wales only once, fleetingly, before the war. Nevertheless, the memory of Cwm Tawel has sustained him in the trenches and he returns there "to be made whole again".²⁷ The healing is also associated with a woman, Flora, the daughter of Ty-Mawr, who embodies the quiet, unsullied beauty of the valley she inhabits. Nor is this trope of the female as healer rare in women's writing about war; in Rebecca West's well-known novel *The Return of the Soldier* (1918) a very similar trope is used of the damaged returning soldier being healed by a childhood sweetheart. What distinguishes Vaughan's novel, though, is the emphasis upon Welsh difference; it is as if the deracinated, urbane London artist, Mark, needs to re-establish his connection with the world of nature and tradition, now only available in Wales. There is a gesture of appropriation, certainly, with Mark insisting upon his place in a Cwm Tawel which is not too friendly towards strangers but there is no doubt that the novel legitimises this metaphorical planting of the Union Jack in Welsh territory. The consummation of the relationship between Wales and England is delayed – through a somewhat melodramatic but nonetheless fascinating plot – until the Second World War and the scene of the action shifts to London, where Britons, Welsh and English are united in the terrors and suffering of the Blitz, so lately over when Vaughan published the novel. Mark and Flora are reunited and the final vision is one of stoic survival; as Mark observes: "You've come through ... we both have."[28] Nevertheless, the most powerful writing in this novel comes when Vaughan is exploring the psychological scars of war on the individual; as Mark observes: "It is over. But it hasn't done with us yet."[29] He is afflicted with a recurring memory of an experience in the trenches when he is forced to shoot a dying man:

> There it was, struggling in the barbed wire, like a fly in a spider's web, jerking its limbs grotesquely and screaming. He shook, so that he could not steady his pistol. Once, twice, three times, he took aim. And he was horribly lucid, aware of risking his own life to end another's. He felt no pity; only a qualm of loathing. The shot barked. The mangled thing hung limp; and, thank God, silent! ... The churned mire, the weary faces of men ploughing through it, every detail of the battle's ugly havoc, was photographed on his mind. He could never remember, though, whether the man he had shot wore a British or an enemy uniform ... he himself might have been that abject creature. It had been necessary to kill him.[30]

Vaughan's powerful imagining of Mark's terrible experience of war is a bold appropriation of an experience marked out as distinctively male. More recently the acclaimed Resurrection trilogy by the English novelist Pat Barker has gone even further to render the traumatic experiences of male combatants in the First World War in a female writer's distinctive vision.[31] This appropriation is important because it indicates that women writers are in a sense no longer emphasising a distinctively female territory of war experience but rather asserting a common experience of suffering: male and female. As Sharon Ouditt puts it in her study of women writers of the First World War: "Women were not then so concerned to express that imaginary area of their experience which was literally 'no-man's-land', off-limits to men and so outside the dominant culture. Rather, their literature is concerned with women's entry into that exclusive part of the national culture which had previously been forbidden to women [including] military institutions and the martial zone."[32] Ouditt also argues, convincingly, that the shift in collective consciousness effected by the First World War, as outlined by Paul Fussell[33], applies equally to women and is strongly expressed in their war writings.

Women poets, too, have responded movingly to the experiences of war during the twentieth century. Dilys Cadwaladr's powerful 1945 ode '*Bara*' ('Bread') deals in a majestic and epic fashion with the suffering and aftermath of war. Cadwaladr would go on to be one of the few women to win the Crown at the National Eisteddfod with her 1953 poem '*Y Llen*' ('The Veil'). '*Bara*' emphasises physical want and suffering, set in a landscape of post-war devastation:

> *Mae'r cnawd yn pydru ar sgerbydau'r plant,*
> *A bronnau'r gwragedd fel orennau gwyw.*
> *Pa gellwair oerllyd yw murmuron sant?*
> *Heb fara, ar beth y byddwn byw? ...*
>
> *Yr hwn a rydd im faeth a gaiff y galon*
> *Sy'n llusgo yn y llaid pan gerddwyf i;*
> *A chaiff ei thalu'n llog i'r Temtiwr rhadlon*
> *Sy'n gwneud anialwch o'n credoau ni*[34]

(The flesh is rotting on the children's bones,
The women's withered breasts, like fruit, are dead.
There's a grim joke in what the saint intones,
For what are we to live on, without bread? ...

He who gives me food will receive my heart
That's dragging in the dust and craves relief;
The heart that yields to the kind Tempter's art
Who makes a barren waste of our belief.)[35]

A contemporary of Cadwaladr, the English-language Welsh poet Lynette Roberts also attempted the epic mode in some of her most notable poetry of the Second World War. Although the grand sweep

of epic verse has often, if erroneously, been regarded as beyond the
scope of the female poet, it is clear that a number of women poets
of this period felt that the experience of war called for epic expression. Roberts is a bold and experimental war poet, whose major
work is the book-length 'heroic poem', 'Gods with Stainless Ears'.[36]
Although this was not published until 1951, it is a poem which
chronicles, albeit in a fictionalised, surrealist and often hallucinatory
style, some of Lynette Roberts' own experiences during 1941-3 as a
woman left alone by war in a small village in rural Carmarthenshire,
Llanybri. Roberts' editor, Patrick McGuinness, has expressed the
tone of her work very aptly in stating that "her poems reflect the
drudgery, fretfulness and inertia of one woman's life in wartime."[37]
The poem is an extraordinary mixture of humdrum domestic detail
and epic grandiloquence. She has been described as a "naive
modernist" whose work is challenging and innovative but lacks the
characteristic irony of the better-known modernists like Eliot (who
was her editor at Faber in the 1940s and 1950s). Roberts' work has
a distinctive verbal texture; as Tony Conran puts it, she "throw[s] her
language at you like a bombardment."[38]

> Overseas battles in circles of lust:
> Spirit put to no better purpose than
> Grain of sand. Overwhich. Backwards and
> Forwards soldiers ran. Such battles of mule
> Stubbornness; or retreat from vast stone walls,
>
> Brought non-existence of past, present and
> Future 1, 2, 1, 2, 1, 2, left, right, left, right,
> Accumulating into a monotonous pattern
> Of dereliction and gloom. When battles should be
> Fought at Home: as trencher-companions. *He at my side.*[39]

In this section the female speaker laments and longs for her absent
lover who, as a soldier, is engaged in fruitless, circular, barren battles
abroad. The description contrasts with repeated positive evocations of
'Saint Cadoc's estuary,' a bird-loud sanctuary whose ferryman, John
Roberts, is a benign Charon and whose fertile soil, in "striped tidy
plot[s] aproned women work, / Spadeing clay and coal dust into 'pele'
jet".[40] The juxtaposition is clear: the soldiers' circular marching in
foreign fields is pointless, while the women who stay behind, suffering
from *hiraeth* for their men, are engaged in productive work, such as
making coal bricks for the domestic hearth. However, Roberts'
domesticity is not cosy; she emphasises, too, women's suffering – the

loss of a baby in Part IV, which the woman bears alone, "no near doctor for six days".[41] By the last part of the poem, the woman is reunited with her soldier lover and there is a cinematic science-fiction fantasy of escape but eventually they are forced to return, to a bay which has been frozen and tarnished by mechanised war:

> ... Down, gunner and black
> Madonna with heart of tin ...
> ... To the bay known before,
> The warm and stagnant air raising wellshafts
> Of putrid flesh sunk deep in desert sands. Stepped out onto
> Blue blaze of snow. Barbed wire. No man of bone.
> A placard to the right which concerned us:
>
> Mental Home for Poets. He alone on this
> Isotonic plain: against a jingle of Generals
> And Cabinet Directors determined
> a stand. Declared a Faith. Entered 'Foreign
> Field' like a Plantagenet King: his spirit
>
> Gorsefierce: hands like perfect quatrains ...
> Catoptric on waterice he of deep love
> Frees dragon from the glacier glade
> Sights death fading into chilblain ears.[42]

It is difficult to determine the tone of the ending; on the one hand, there is a suggestion of defiant, even nationalistic rebellion in the image of "freeing the dragon" from the ice which entraps it, and the suggestion of death receding into silence perhaps looks towards a tenuous survival, yet the chillingly modernist, technological landscape which has overwhelmed the formerly knowable, communal and natural bay leaves a bitter aftertaste. The narrative of the poem, despite being explained in a prose 'argument' preceding each section, is actually less coherent and less convincing than the poem's overall impressionistic evocation of a west Wales enclave becoming a waste land, which is all the more striking for the strange vocabulary drawn from chemistry, botany, and geology used to create this unnerving, cinematic picture. Nevertheless, Roberts' modernist techniques are no more puzzling or disorientating than those of T.S. Eliot himself in *The Waste Land*. It might even be that Eliot championed Roberts' work because he saw in it a Second World War version of his own anguished, truncated epic of the First World War and its aftermath. Unfortunately, 'Gods with Stainless Ears' – perhaps partly because of the poet's gender and nationality – has suffered critical neglect until recently; it is to be hoped that the recent publication of the *Collected Poems* may lead to a renewed interest in Roberts' work.

Wars are always with us. Although most of the literary responses by Welsh women discussed here are to the First and Second World Wars, other, more recent wars, have also been the subject of Welsh women's writing. Eluned Phillips' poem '*Clymau*' ('Ties'), for example, was the winning poem in the Crown competition of the 1983 National Eisteddfod. It is based on the Falklands War and in two alternating verse sequences parallels events of 1865 when Welsh migrants first sailed to Patagonia and 1982 when Welsh soldiers again found themselves en route to South America, for very different reasons. Welsh people are evicted from their home, Pantglas, in the opening of the poem and decide to sail from Liverpool to Argentina on the ship *Mimosa*; en route, a daughter dies and is buried at sea. Despite their grief, they throw themselves into work in their new land, recreating a new 'Pantglas'. They are seen in heroic terms, like Arthur's knights seeking for the Holy Grail:

> *Ymchwil feunyddiol drwy'r oriau dyfal*
> *Fel marchog Arthur yn ceisio'r Greal,*
> *Nes darganfod ffrwd risial, a synnu*
> *Gweld dŵr yn saethu o lestr yr anial.*[43]

(Daily search through the eager hours
Like an Arthurian knight questing for the Grail,
Until a crystal stream is found, and he wonders
To see water shooting from the barren dish.)

In 1982, a latter-day son of Pantglas joins the British army and is sent to fight in the Falklands. The voyage south of the *Sir Galahad* (with ironic echoes of the pioneering Welsh knights) is compared with the earlier voyage of the *Mimosa*. The ship is hit and explodes, there is mourning for the dead soldier, explicitly likened to the warriors of Catraeth. In the hospital there is a strange meeting between a young man from Buenos Aires and the blinded son of Pantglas; they speak the same language, Welsh: "*dau o'r un tylwyth ŷnt*" ("they are two from the same family").[44]

In a sense this is a television ode which works most vividly when it is describing scenes actually screened at the time of the Falklands War. The description of the *Sir Galahad* is both televisual and has echoes of the Old Testament:

> *Mae* Syr Galahad *fel rhyw anghenfil,*
> *A'i cheg ar angor fel genau morfil.*
> *Sudda'r tanciau yn ufudd i'w chrombil,*
> *A'r gynnau swrth yn wrych ar ei gwegil.*[45]

> (The *Sir Galahad* is like some great behemoth,
> Its mouth wide open like the jaws of a whale.
> The tanks sink obediently into its maw,
> And the sullen guns like a hedge on its back).

Its destruction is a scene which many of us remember – or at least believe we remember – from television news reports of the time:

> Syr Galahad *yn wenfflam.*
> *Y rhuthr i'r dwr mewn bedlam*
> *Rhag gweflau uffern o fflam.*

> *Cacwn o helicoptrau*
> *Yn sugno'r byw i'w boliau*
> *Cyn i lygaid gobaith gau.*[46]

> (The *Sir Galahad* in a sheet of white flame
> The scramble into the water in bedlam
> To escape the hellish lips of flame.

> A swarm of helicopters
> Sucking the living into their bellies
> Before the eyes of hope close forever).

Despite its attack on British imperialism, the poem has a deeply conservative ideology (though this is not unwonted in women's literary responses to war, as we have seen). '*Clymau*' laments the Anglicisation of Wales and the advent of English and European migrants to rural west Wales, representing such migrants in extremely negative terms (whereas the Welsh migrants to Patagonia are unproblematically seen as heroic pioneers). Welshness is viewed as being defined by blood: "*Celtiaid o'r un gwaed ydynt*" ("they are Celts of the same blood"),[47] a notion which today sounds old-fashioned and politically suspect. As a response to war, however, this is a vivid and imaginative poem which shows great technical skill (as the awarding of the Crown to Phillips at the Eisteddfod suggests) but, understandably perhaps, remains rather distant from the experience of war. Nevertheless, the poem is indicative of the way that many of us in the privileged Western world nowadays see images of war – as a kind of televisual hyper-reality, a simulacrum.[48]

Nevertheless, the illusion of closeness which the media can create in presenting us with a barrage of information and images from contemporary wars can also give rise to literary responses of great tenderness and empathy. One example of this is Menna Elfyn's well-known poem, 'Eucalyptus', the title poem of her 1995 collection. The source seems to have been a news report rather than a visual image of the first Gulf War in the early 1990s. A note explains that the poet had heard that the pungent scent of eucalyptus pervaded the streets of Baghdad at the time since, in the absence of electricity, the inhabitants of the city were using eucalyptus oil to cook with and to heat their homes. The poem then is full of images of taste and smell, conjured up by the word 'eucalyptus' and its personal memories. The eucalyptus lozenge which eased the speaker's throat and helped her to breathe in her childhood is now helping – literally – to keep families alive as the bombs burst all around them. The imagery employed is both domestic and sacramental – families gather together at the "*bwrdd bendithiol*" ("table of blessedness").[49] The poem expresses a palpable sense of empathy with people suffering in a war not of their own making, asserting a sense of community across cultures, based on simple physical needs and family ties:

> *Yr olew syml:*
> *Fu'n dal anadl cynhaliaeth*
> *Gan lathru goleuni*
> *Dros fywydau gloywddu.*[50]
>
> (The simple oil
> once kept me breathing,
> now over blackened lives
> shines like light).

Elfyn's linking of the personal and domestic with the global and political might be seen as a similar impulse to that which impelled Lynette Roberts to create her peculiarly hybrid science-fiction Llanybri in 'Gods with Stainless Ears', though the poetic results for Elfyn are certainly more lucid. Nor is this yoking of the personal and the political unusual in modern women's writing, being the fruit of the second wave of the feminist movement which emphasised just such a link. Arguably, though, that insistence on the personal in a time of war, whose tendency is to depersonalise and even dehumanise (soldiers become numbers, not names, for instance – such as Gunner 1620B64, who is Keidrych Rhys in Lynette Roberts' poem), has been a permanent characteristic of women's writing about war and is one of the primary means of their protest against it.

Two brief final examples of this are Joyce Herbert's lyrical elegy 'When I stood there among bullets' and Section 6 of Gillian Clarke's poem sequence 'The King of Britain's Daughter'. Joyce Herbert's poem focuses on the physical suffering of a single individual who is nevertheless representative of the Welsh *gwerin* and of the poetic tradition. It is a tribute to the Welsh-language poet, Hedd Wyn, who won the so-called 'Black Chair' of the 1917 Eisteddfod at Birkenhead in which he never sat, having been killed in action in France. Herbert's poem vividly imagines the long-dead poet's thoughts just before his death on the Somme, his memory taking him back to the sound of the River Prysor near his home in Trawsfynydd:

> The water talks like small bells in summer,
> moving the grasses,
> bending them gently
> as a ewe nudging her lamb.
>
> I see you crossing the broken land
> surely, wet wool against your ear,
> sheepshanks flopping on your shoulder
>
> Carrying the dead
> from the screaming fires of the Somme...[51]

Although this is a moving elegy, a lament, it is also, by its very existence, an assertion of the continuity and survival of a poetic tradition and a sense of place. Interestingly, also, it is the assertion of a continuity which crosses gender and linguistic boundaries.

Gillian Clarke's poem, too, is about the daughter's debt to the father, this time literal rather than poetic. 'The King of Britain's Daughter' is a complex elegy for Clarke's father, which consists of an interweaving of memories of a wartime childhood and the mythological story of Branwen who was exiled, rescued and eventually died of grief. The brief Section 6 exemplifies how skilfully the dual narratives are interwoven and how the news of war is first received and understood by a female child in a west Wales kitchen:

> When the world wobbled
> We heard it on a radio chained
> By its fraying plait of wires
> To the kitchen window-sill

> Between a sheaf of letters,
> Bills and things needing to be done,
> And a jar of marigolds.
> And over its Bakelite crown
> The sea, level as milk.
> The news came out of the sky,
> A mist off the sea,
> An incoming shadow
> Of rain or wings.[52]

Again, this is an example of the mass news media bringing distant wars uncomfortably into the midst of an ordinary domesticity. The portentous news fixes everyone's attention on the physical object of the old-fashioned wireless and the perspective of a child is suggested by the use of the word 'wobbled'. Despite the childlike register, the word is apt and evocative of a world of stability suddenly slipping off its axis, echoed also by the suggestion of the sea as a vessel of milk, which it is vital to keep level to avoid spillage. There is a hint of a pun on spilt milk lurking in the text; the suggestion of childhood transgressions, clumsiness, tears. The miscellaneous objects grouped around the radio speak of a life of work and duty, lightened by the beauty of the natural world. The brittle Bakelite brings a message which will displace and transform this life. The final lines of the passage introduce the echo of the Branwen story: like Branwen's starling bringing the news of her incarceration over the Irish sea, the mysterious waves of sound have brought this message of war; the future is unclear but the shadows suggest impending sorrow and grief. Clarke's poem, brief and simple as it is, reveals how women's response to war has no need to sound the martial strain to create a vivid and poignant impression of its devastating effects on people's lives.

Most critical accounts in English of the literature of war until recent decades have largely excluded women writers.[53] However, since the 1980s there have appeared quite a large number of scholarly works by feminist critics which have sought to redress that neglect and to replace women in the canon of war literature.[54] This recuperation has been supplemented and aided both by the publication of many first-hand accounts of women's war experiences, including two volumes by Welsh women, *Parachutes and Petticoats*[55] in English and *Iancs, Conchis a Spam*[56] in Welsh, and by feminist historians' work in disinterring Welsh women's history during the two world wars.[57] This brief survey of some Welsh women writers' responses to wars in the twentieth century has, I hope, shown that war literature is not an exclusively male domain and that women's war writing is as varied and as thought-provoking as that of their male peers. If modern warfare has effected a shift in human consciousness, as some male critics have claimed, that shift is as perceptible in women's literary work as in men's, for the pity and suffering of war is common to all.

Notes

1. '*Stafell Cynddylan*' ('Cynddylan's Hall') in: ed. Thomas Parry, *TheOxford Book of Welsh Verse*, London: OUP, 1976, p12 and ed. and trans. Tony Conran, *Welsh Verse*. Bridgend: Poetry Wales Press, 1986, p.127.
2. For example, the Glyndŵr rebellion in Allen Raine's novel *Hearts of Wales* (1905); the 1868 tithe wars in Gwyneth Vaughan's novel *Plant y gorthrwm* (1908).
3. Kate Roberts, *Feet in Chains* (trans. John Idris Jones). Ruthin: John Jones Publishing, 1996, p.109.
4. *Ibid.*, p.110.
5. *Ibid.*, p.113.
6. *Ibid.*, p.113.
7. *Ibid.*, pp.119-120.
8. *Ibid.*, p.122.
9. *Ibid.*, p.123.
10. "*[N]id yw'r gorffennol yn bwysig iddynt o gwbl.Y mae'n golygu popeth i mi* …". Letter to Saunders Lewis, 8th March 1961 in: *Annwyl Kate,Annwyl Saunders: Gohebiaeth 1923-1983*. Aberystwyth: Llyfrgell Genedlaethol Cymru, 1992, p.191.
11. *Feet in Chains*, pp.128-129.
12. *Ibid.*, p.132.
13. Siân James, *A Small Country*. Bridgend: Seren, 1989 [1979], pp.131-132.
14. *Ibid.*, p.160.
15. *Ibid.*, p.161.
16. *Ibid.*, p.133.
17. *Ibid.*, p.180.
18. *Ibid.*, p.189.
19. Berta Ruck, 'Wanted – A Master' in *Khaki and Kisses*. London: Hutchinson, 1915, p.210.
20. See her novels *My Mother's House* (1931) and *The Samaritan* (1939).
21. Virginia Woolf, *Three Guineas* in: *A Room of One's Own and Three Guineas* (ed. Michèle Barrett). Harmondsworth: Penguin, 1993, p.234.
22. Siân James, *Love and War*. Bridgend: Seren, 2004, p.22.
23. *Ibid.*, p.82.
24. *Ibid.*, p.217.
25. *Ibid.*, p.210.
26. *Ibid.*, p.85.

27. Hilda Vaughan, *Pardon and Peace*. London: Macmillan, 1945, p.4.
28. *Ibid.*, p.195.
29. *Ibid.*, p.20.
30. *Ibid.*, p.122.
31. Pat Barker, *Regeneration* (1991), *The Eye in the Door* (1993) and *The Ghost Road* (1995) all published by Penguin.
32. Sharon Ouditt, *Fighting Forces, Writing Women*. London: Routledge, 1994, p.14.
33. Paul Fussell, *The Great War and Modern Memory*. London: Oxford University Press, 1975.
34. Dilys Cadwaladr, '*Bara*' in *Welsh Women's Poetry 1460-2001* (eds. Katie Gramich and Catherine Brennan). Dinas Powys: Honno, 2003, p.166.
35. *Ibid.*, p.167 (my translation).
36. Lynette Roberts, 'Gods with Stainless Ears' in *Collected Poems* (ed. Patrick McGuinness). Manchester: Carcanet, 2005, pp.43-78.
37. Patrick McGuinness, lecture on Lynette Roberts delivered at the Association for Welsh Writing annual conference, Gregynog Hall, Powys, April 2005.
38. Tony Conran, 'Lynette Roberts: War Poet' in *The Cost of Strangeness*. Llandysul: Gomer, 1983, p.191.
39. Lynette Roberts, 'Gods with Stainless Ears' Part III in *Collected Poems*, p.59.
40. *Ibid.*, Part I, p.47.
41. *Ibid.*, Part IV, p.61.
42. *Ibid.*, Part V, pp.68-69. "Catoptric" = relating to mirrors or reflections.
43. Eluned Phillips, '*Clymau*' in *Cerddi Glyn-y-Mêl*. Llandysul: Gomer, 1985, p.72 (my translation).
44. *Ibid.*, p.80 (my translation).
45. *Ibid.*, p.76 (my translation).
46. *Ibid.*, p.78 (my translation).
47. *Ibid.*, p.80 (my translation).
48. See: Jean Baudrillard, *The Gulf War did not Take Place* (trans. P. Patton). London: Power, 2004 [original French ed. 1991] and Christopher Norris' persuasive refutation of Baudrillard in *Uncritical Theory: Postmodernism, Intellectuals and the Gulf War*. London: Lawrence & Wishart, 1992.
49. Menna Elfyn, 'Eucalyptus' (trans. Tony Conran) in *Welsh Women's Poetry 1460-2001*, pp.290-291.
50. *Ibid.*, pp.290-291.
51. Joyce Herbert, 'When I stood there among bullets' in *Ibid.* p.196.
52. Gillian Clarke, Section 6 of 'The King of Britain's Daughter' in *Collected Poems*. Manchester: Carcanet, 1997, p.173.
53. Typical examples are Bernard Bergonzi's *Heroes' Twilight: A Study of the Literature of the Great War* (London: Constable, 1965) and the previously mentioned seminal work by Paul Fussell, *The Great War and Modern Memory*.
54. Notable examples include Claire M. Tylee's *The Great War and Women's Consciousness* (London: Macmillan, 1990) and the previously cited

Sharon Ouditt's *Fighting Forces, Writing Women.*

55. eds. Leigh Verrill-Rhys and Deirdre Beddoe, *Parachutes and Petticoats.* Dinas Powys: Honno, 1992.

56. ed. Leigh Verrill-Rhys, *Iancs, Conchis a Spam.* Dinas Powys: Honno, 2002.

57. For example, Deirdre Beddoe, *Out of the Shadows: A History of Women in Twentieth-Century Wales* (Cardiff: University of Wales Press, 2000) and Mari A. Williams, '"Where is Mrs Jones Going?": Women and the Second World War in South Wales'. Aberystwyth: Canolfan Uwchefrydiau Cymreig a Cheltaidd Prifysgol Cymru, 1995.

'The Stones of the Field' and the Power of the Sword: R.S. Thomas as War Poet [1]

M. Wynn Thomas

In 1942, the enterprising and arrestingly exotic M.J. Tambimuttu edited *Poetry in Wartime*, which the publishers, Faber, claimed to be "unique in that it is not an anthology of 'war poems', but a collection [including the work of Brenda Chamberlain, Alun Lewis, Lynette Roberts, Dylan Thomas and Vernon Watkins] of the best poems written since the beginning of war – some of which are also 'war-poems'".[2] The distinction is an important one, pointing up the complexity of the relationship between literature and war, another facet of which is the inevitable inflection of any work produced during wartime by the special conditions that enter, however insensibly or indirectly, into the very marrow of its making. When Dylan Thomas entitles his 1937 poem 'I make this in a warring absence', he is referring primarily to his wish for a 'peace' in his turbulent relationship with his wife Caitlin; "an armistice of a moment, to come out of the images on *her* warpath".[3] But the image is rootedly expressive of the time in which it was written, when memories of the Great War haunted a young generation uneasily eyeing the ever grimmer circumstances that, passing for 'peace' in contemporary Europe, ominously threatened to turn the two decades since 1918 into a mere 'armistice'.

Thomas' poem was included in Keidrych Rhys' groundbreaking 1944 anthology *Modern Welsh Poetry*.[4] Among its thirty-seven mostly young contributors were conscientious objectors like Pennar Davies, Glyn Jones and Roland Mathias; World War One veterans like Wyn Griffith and David Jones; home-front writers like Lynette Roberts, the Argentinian incomer suspiciously eyed as a spy at Llanybri, and Brenda Chamberlain, who from her Llanberis cottage helped with mountain rescue of wrecked aircrew; and serving soldiers such as the reluctant combatant Alun Lewis and the wholly unlikely Vernon Watkins. Several of them were to produce war-related volumes that have been forgotten but would bear revisiting – Brenda Chamberlain's remarkable *The Green Heart* (1958) and Nigel Heseltine's *The Four-Walled Dream* are as undeservedly neglected as the wartime poetry of T. Harri Jones and Harri Webb.[5] And because of the range of its contributors, Rhys' volume itself deserves to be better appreciated as a valuable record, such as perhaps poetry alone could offer, of the otherwise elusive sensibilities and modalities of wartime Wales.

Here, for instance, a survivor of Mametz stands aghast in Wyn Griffith's "farewell to ... all remembering": "If there be time enough before the slaughter / Let us consider our heritage / Of wisdom".[6] A young Nigel Heseltine is devastated by the venerable T. Gwynn Jones' refusal, in August 1939, to countenance the awarding of the main awards at that year's National Eisteddfod in Denbigh: "An old man speaking of poetry / Gave us no crown no chair / No father no mother no voice / For tomorrow // For tomorrow death".[7] And a similar need (sometimes desperate, always urgent) for an adequate, answerable 'voice', a language to make sense of direst experience, is to be felt in most, if not all, of this poetry. It is what prompts Ken Etheridge to fulminate against indulgence in "the lechery / Of much used metaphors", and to plead "Let us be clean in language".[8] And it leads many to reconnect themselves to Wales, either by finding appropriate symbolic language in Welsh myth, or by grounding themselves, Antaeus-like, in Welsh land, in Welsh communities, and within the continuities of Welsh history. As Keidrych Rhys' case demonstrates, mobilisation could result in a newly palpable realisation that "I'm not an Englishman", "My roots lie in another region"; so that, in an intense, reflexive effort of cultural recovery, "I try to remember the things / At home that mean Wales but typical / Isn't translated across / The Channel".[9]

The rural landscape and community life Rhys thus recuperates was at that time being experienced somewhat ambivalently by his wife, Lynette Roberts: "To the village of lace and stone / Came strangers. I was one of these", writes Roberts, implicitly associating herself, after a fashion, with evacuees.[10] She, however, was a refugee of a very different kind, in search of her ancestral roots and attempting, in the process, to recall a Welsh people alienated from their own historical origins to their authentic cultural inheritance. Hers was therefore a wartime enterprise closely paralleling that attempted, through the *Caseg Broadsheets*, by Brenda Chamberlain and Alun Lewis, to whom Roberts addressed her 'Poem from Llanybri', inviting him to visit.[11] The poem itself seeks to re-enact ancient social

customs and poetic conventions, and to discover the kind of English
that alone can vouch for this distinctively Welsh locality, and author-
itatively speak for it. It becomes what Tony Conran would later call
a 'gift poem' – a poem that is offered as a gift, as if it were a
proffered piece, a real substantial token, of the landscape itself: "I
will offer you / A fist full of rock cress fresh from the bank".[12] But it
is her own insuperable alienation from this place that comes through
in 'Lamentation', a poem which, in properly insisting that the
anguish of miscarriage can exceed even that caused by a local air-
raid, is a rare reminder of how 'normal', quotidian life will always
continue to furnish experiences as searing as those that war may
bring. The poems in the collection also remind us of other continuities between pre-war life and wartime experiences. In industrial
south Wales, war followed hard upon the heels of a decade and a half
of economic crisis and social devastation. This is indicated, in Huw
Menai's case, through the juxtaposition of a poem on the terrible
siege of Stalingrad with others on the mental torment of working
underground: "Where shall the eyes a darkness find / That is a
menace to the mind / Save in the coal mine, where one's lamp / Is
smothered oft by afterdamp?"[13]

All the important emergent writers of the time – from Dylan
Thomas to Alun Lewis, and from Emyr Humphreys to Idris Davies
– are included in Rhys' *Modern Welsh Poetry*. And yet it is with a start
that one comes upon R.S. Thomas in this company. Rarely has he
been regarded as a wartime poet, let alone as a 'war poet'. And so to
read two of his poems in this context is to be bewildered, disorien-
tated, discomfited. "Iago Prytherch his name":[14] what on earth is
Thomas' celebrated "ordinary man of the bald Welsh hills" doing in
this company? And who would have expected Thomas' chronically
absconding God to make his absent presence first known here, as
"the voice that lulled / Job's soothing mind to a still calm / Yet tossed
his heart to the racked world?"[15] Could it somehow be, against all
probability, that the early R.S. Thomas, too, was a war poet?

The answer, as we shall see, is yes; and to read a signature poem
of Thomas' such as 'A Peasant' in the context of this collection is
to begin to notice that his early poetry shares several of its central
concerns with the poetry of his 'wartime' generation of (mostly)
young Welsh poets. Writing under duress, they sought for new
forms, new themes, and above all a new language adequate for
expressing their situation. As their Wales became luridly back-lit by
the glare of conflict, they found that everything they had previously unconsciously valued about their country – the land, the

people, the communities – was rendered newly precious, sharply silhouetted by the fires that threatened to consume them. The antiquity of Wales, whether suggested by myth and legend or embodied in the ancientness of rocks and mountains, became for them the warrant of survival; even the devastations pre-war Wales had endured – the dreadful depression years commemorated by Idris Davies and Huw Menai; the decline of Welsh rural and upland communities angrily mourned by R.S. Thomas – were now paradoxically metamorphosed into proofs of invincible endurance. And, with eyes rawly exposed to the ubiquity of violence, these poets could look differently even upon the most conventionally tranquil and reassuring scenes:

> When birds and brittle leaves come down
> When trees and grass freeze out their blood
> And fishes die in floods of rain,
> This is the time for Death.
> A mouse is spiked on blades of grass
> A sparrow swings from the gibbet of a twig.[16]

It is by bearing features such as these in mind that we may best prepare ourselves for understanding important aspects of R.S. Thomas' groundbreaking first collection, *The Stones of the Field* (1946).

There we are stopped in our tracks by passages like this:

> Nor shot, nor shell, but the fused word,
> That rocks the world to its white root,
> Has wrought a chaos in the mind,
> And drained the love from the split heart;
>
> Nor shock, nor shower of the sharp blows,
> That fall alike from life and death,
> But some slow subsidence within,
> That sinks a grave for the sapped faith.[17]

Here, surely, is a poem that – with its self-conscious sonorities, declamatory rhetoric, dramatic off-rhymes and impacted images – could almost pass for one by Dylan Thomas? Or that would not be out of place in *Raiders' Dawn*, that disturbing first volume by Alun Lewis whose language is so fraught with violence and from which several poems were extracted for Rhys' *Modern Welsh Poetry*? And yet, this is 'Propaganda' by R.S. Thomas, one of those short lyrics he effectively disavowed by choosing not to reprint them in his later, mature collection *Song at the Year's Turning*. That these poems have been overlooked by critics is understandable since, by omitting them, Thomas presumably meant to indicate that they were only apprentice pieces and that the early growing points of his distinctive, authentic talent lay elsewhere – in the farmer poems (including those about Prytherch) that were also included in *The Stones of the Field*.

But those discarded early lyrics are not, I feel, entirely without interest or indeed without significance. They seem to bespeak a 'chaos in the mind', a sensibility under stress. And the affinity between 'Propaganda' and certain poems by Dylan Thomas and Alun Lewis is, in my opinion, one that is worth noting – not because of any suggestion of influence but because it dramatically highlights a shared social experience. All three writers were living through a period when, as Yeats put it, 'mere anarchy' had been loosed upon the world, and it was Yeats himself, of course, who showed younger poets in his poetry how to construct a language strong enough to convey the brutalities of breakdown.[18] R.S. Thomas, in his turn, showed he had learnt lessons from the master by writing Yeatsian poems in the early 1940s like the following, 'On a Portrait of Joseph Hone by Augustus John':

> As though the brute eyes had seen
> In the hushed meadows the weasel,
> That would tear the soft down of the throat
> And suck the veins dry
> Of their glittering blood.
>
> And the mouth formed to the cry,
> That gushed from the cleft heart
> And flowed coldly as spring water over
> The stone lips.[19]

It is with a poem like this very much in mind that I would like to suggest that *The Stones of the Field* might usefully be read as war poetry. Obviously I do not mean that the collection directly addresses the subject of war. What I do mean is that the poetry frequently comes from an imagination fearfully alerted by war to the ferocities of existence: "Your love is dead, lady, your love is dead; / Dribbles no sound / From his stopped lips, though swift underground / Spurts his wild hair" ('Madrigal').[20] Indeed, there is a terrible Jacobean relish about such lines, that shows how R.S. Thomas, like Alun Lewis, understood how sexually arousing and sensually heightening the experience of violence and disaster could be.

So much has been written, not least by R.S. Thomas himself, about the move to Manafon that precipitated the Iago Prytherch poems, and a *rite de passage* it clearly was, involving the rude awakening of an innocent, sentimental, cosseted, romantic bourgeois to the harsh and sometimes cruel facts of life on the upland farms. But what the critics seem to have consistently overlooked is one of the reasons for the move, as R.S. Thomas has recalled it in his autobiography *Neb*. He is remembering the period he spent from 1940 to 1942 as a curate at Hanmer, in Flintshire border-country:

By now the war had started in earnest, and although there was not much risk locally, the parish was in the path of the German planes as they aimed at Merseyside. Every night, when the weather permitted, the planes came across on their way in and they soon began to get on the curate's nerves, not so much because of fear but because of despair and hopeless-ness at the thought that they were on their way to drop their evil loads on helpless women and children ... Although Merseyside was about twenty miles away as the crow flies, as he stood at the door with his wife listening to the sound of bombs in the distance and watching the flames lighting the sky, he felt an occasional puff of air going through his hair and lifting his wife's skirt. Sometimes the Germans would drop a few bombs in the area, after seeing a light somewhere perhaps, but without harming anyone, thanks to the open character of the land. One night, he happened to be looking through the window when he heard a bomb screaming on its way down quite near. He waited for the explosion, but nothing happened. The following day it was discovered that the bomb had plummeted to earth a yard or two away from a zinc-roofed cottage, where an old couple was living. They were sleeping soundly at the time, not realising that anything unusual was happening! The curate decided to build a defen-sive wall against the wall of the parsonage opposite the place under the stairs, as a place to shelter in, should more bombs start to fall. One night when he was leaving the church that was next door to the house, he heard a terrible explosion quite near. He ran in and urged his wife to come to shelter under the stairs, and there they were for hours, while the enemy aircraft circled above their heads. They heard after-wards that there were Italians as well as Germans, and that they were having difficulties in trying to get near Merseyside. Several bombs were dropped in the area that night, and the hill-country was set on fire in the neighbourhood of Minera. Seeing the flames, they started to drop bombs there too, and

some shepherd that was living near the moorland got the
fright of his life. The curate so hated to think about the
damage that was occurring almost every night, and so longed
for the hills in the distance (Moel Famau could be seen
clearly enough towards the north-west) that he decided to
learn Welsh, in order to come back to the real Wales.[21]

It took more than forty years for R.S. Thomas to reflect directly on
these events in a poem. It was in *The Echoes Return Slow* (1988) that
he at last confronted feelings whose repressed presence had, it now
seems, covertly influenced the poetry of *The Stones of the Field*:

> In the country house
> doorway the wind that ruffled
> the woman's skirt came
> from no normal direction.
>
> Skies were red where no
> sun had ever risen
> or set. He earned fear,
> the instinctive fear
>
> of the animal that finds
> the foliage about its den
> disarranged and comes to know
> it can never go there again.[22]

The shock-wave from the distant bombs here becomes a very
suggestive trope for the unnatural, for a reversal of the ordinary,
proper direction of things. And it is the same shock wave that shakes
R.S. Thomas to the foundations of his inner being, creating a funda-
mental sense of insecurity and mistrust. It was this 'animal'
experience of 'instinctive fear' that, in actual, historical reality
prompted him to try to make his home safe, as best he could, and to
construct a sanctuary for his wife and himself under the stairs. And
it was also the same fear of the animal, that finds its very den has
been disturbed, that perhaps led him half-admiringly to associate the
Manafon upland farmers with "The land's patience and a tree's /
Knotted endurance".[23] In his wartime poetry he invests Prytherch
and his kind with a power of survival that makes them more reassur-
ingly trustworthy than any "*cwtsh dan stâr*". Moreover, baffled and
pained though R.S. Thomas chronically is by Prytherch's "uncouth
ways", he is also ambiguously attracted to his unselfconsciousness.
And this attraction, usually explained in terms of Thomas' reaction

against his urban bourgeois background, can also be seen in a new light – the light of the Merseyside bombing, as it were – if we remember what Thomas reveals about his wartime self in *The Echoes Return Slow*. The portrait he there paints is of a lonely, isolated figure tormented by the unceasing arguments he was having with himself. He even half-envied the men of action, who had gone to war with promptness and conviction: "yes, action has its compensations. What does one do when one does not believe in action, or in certain kinds of action? Are the brave lacking in imagination? Are the imaginative not brave, or do they find it more difficult to be brave? What does a man do with his silence, his aloneness, but suffer the sapping of unanswerable questions?"[24] Through the 'unimaginative' figure of Prytherch he was able at once to articulate his inner doubts aloud and also to imagine a human existence apparently proof against "the sapping of unanswerable questions". When reading his wartime poems we should, I feel, bear in mind the revealing picture of his wartime self that R.S. Thomas gave us for the first time in *The Echoes Return Slow*: "Casualty of the quarrel with strong men, bandaging himself with Yeats' sentence about the quarrel within, he limped on through an absence of sympathy. His poetry was bitter."[25]

R.S. Thomas' pre-Manafon experience of the bombing of Merseyside obviously underlies the only poem in *The Stones of the Field* that deals directly with the war. 'Homo Sapiens 1941' is a mock-epic study of man the hubristic aviator, the Icarus of modern technological warfare, and it exposes the spurious glamour of the Romantic will-to-power that was prevalent in the aesthetics as well as in the politics of the 1930s:

> Murmuration of engines in the cold caves of air,
> And, daring the starlight above the stiff sea cloud,
> Deadly as a falcon brooding over its prey,
> In a tower of spirit-dazzling and splendid light,
> Pedestrian man holds grimly on his way.
> Legions of winds, ambushed in crystal corries,
> Conspiring to destroy him, and hosts of ice,
> Thronging him close, weigh down his delicate wings;
> But loud as a drum in his ear the hot blood sings,
> And a frenzy of solitude mantles him like a god.[26]

The episode is reminiscent of Satan's sinister flight towards earth in Book II of *Paradise Lost*, when he 'heroically' withstands the buffetings of chaos. But the poem reads primarily as an ironic pastiche of the Romantic modernist style favoured by, say, the Futurist artists and writers. R.S. Thomas' imagination sweeps the sky like a flurry of searchlights as he tries to fix the image of self-intoxicated modern man, caught in all the destructiveness of his mad daring. There are moments of particular resonance. Take that opening line, for instance: "Murmuration of engines in the cold caves of air". Is Thomas recalling and rewriting the famous lines about the First World War in *The Waste Land?* "What is that sound high in the air / Murmur of maternal lamentation".[27] It could be that this distorted echo of Eliot is Thomas' way of introducing into his poem those feelings about the women and children of Merseyside that he mentions in *Neb* – so the murmur of maternal lamentation becomes the dark accompaniment to the murmuration of masculine engines.

Concern with aerial warfare had, of course, been a commonplace of the thirties, greatly exacerbated by the infamous case of Guernica, and 'Homo Sapiens 1941' could profitably be juxtaposed with the Huw Menai poem 'In the Vale of Glamorgan' of around the same period, included in Rhys' *Modern Welsh Poetry*:

> Bird-men, the devil's alloy in their metal,
>   Go roaring Southward while a throstle sings;
> Above, then below the clouds – wonder of wonders!
> The sunset's beauty flashing on their wings.
>
> And I, with humble sparrows in the cornfield,
>   Know less of exultation than of pain
> For thinking that these miracles of conquest
> May not come home again![28]

Very different in their style though these poems are (and for once Menai's reactionary Georgian pastoral seems here to serve a poignantly ironic purpose), they exhibit a shared nexus of edgy feelings – a kind of modern, tortured version of the sublime, where awe at human conquest of the air is accompanied by terror at the consequences.

Because there is no other poem like it in *The Stones of the Field*, 'Homo Sapiens 1941' has tended to be discussed in isolation.[29] I have never seen it referred to in connection with the Iago Prytherch poems, and yet it is with reference to 'Homo Sapiens 1941' that R.S. Thomas' early farmer poems acquire a pointed 'period' meaning that immediately politicises them. To put it simply, Prytherch is the elemental opposite of 'Homo Sapiens 1941' – earth-bound where the latter is air-borne, doggedly ancient where the latter is dangerously modern. The point seems to be underlined by R.S. Thomas when, in *Song at the Year's Turning*, he arranges 'Homo Sapiens 1941' opposite his familiar poem 'A Labourer'.[30] If "legions of winds, ambushed in crystal corries" have conspired to destroy the modern airman, then the question with which 'A Labourer' opens is: "Who can tell his years, for the winds have stretched / So tight the skin on the bare racks of bone / That his face is smooth, inscrutable as stone?"[31] If the airman is mockingly depicted as braving the fury of the skies, then the 'peasant', in Thomas' poem of that name, season after season "Against siege of rain and the wind's attrition, / Preserves his stock, an impregnable fortress / Not to be stormed even in death's confusion. / Remember him, then, for he, too, is a winner of wars".[32] I take that admonition to be more than a casual rhetorical gesture, since the early figure of Prytherch seems to be, in certain of its features, partly the product of a wartime imagination.

The opening poem of *The Stones of the Field* is 'Out of the Hills' where the upland farmer, "Dreams clustering this on his sallow skull, / Dark as curls", comes "ambling with his cattle / From the starved pastures".[33] Thomas follows his progress down into the valley with distinct unease, unwilling to "witness his swift undoing / In the indifferent streets: the sudden disintegration / Of his soul's hardness, traditional discipline / Of flint and frost thawing in ludicrous showers / Of maudlin laughter, the limpid runnels of speech / Sullied and slurred, as the beer-glass chimes the hours". There is obviously a lot that could be said about Thomas' distaste for the corrupting softness of life on the valley bottom, but in the context of this period study it is worth noticing the belief that was current when the poem was written. It was generally accepted at the time that the dwellers in the valleys along the Welsh borders belonged to an entirely different race of people from the farmers who lived in the neighbouring uplands.[34] The former were the English descendants of the foreign invaders from post-Roman times onwards, while the latter were the Welsh remnants of the original pre-Celtic tribes that had retreated into the hills. This belief seemed solidly based on scholarly, 'scientific' evidence. The eminent Professor of Geography at Aberystwyth, H.J. Fleure, had, from the 1920s onwards, been conducting a systematic anthropological study of the different racial elements in the Welsh population. He was able to report in the October 1939 issue of *Wales* that: "The work of measuring the types of Welsh people has been proceeding very rapidly during the last five years and there are now measurements of between 4,000 and 5,000 adult men of ascertained localised ancestries."[35] The reference here is to the measuring of human skulls, a practice undertaken because it was believed that there was a precise correlation between skull size and shape and racial antecedents. In his article, Fleure listed and described six different racial types that could be readily distinguished in the Welsh population. He labelled these from A to F, and then roughly explained which categories predominated in the different areas of Wales. He concluded, for instance, that "Montgomeryshire [where Manafon, of course, was located], Brecknock, and Radnor show increasing proportions of F as one goes towards England and increasing proportions of B as one goes towards the western hills".[36] By F he meant "tall, rather long headed fair men with sharp profiles" who were descended from "the post-Roman invaders of Britain".[37] These, he added, were "the famous or should we now say, thanks to the wild exaggerations of Nazi propaganda, notorious Nordic types". As for B, these were "the little dark Welshmen occurring everywhere, short or medium in height, with oval faces and long, rather than extremely long heads, dark eyes less deeply set than those of A, but sometimes the eye pigment has been almost lost".[38]

To call attention to Fleure's categories is not, for one moment, to suggest that Prytherch is simply a version of his type B, a "little, dark Welshman". But it does seem possible that the idea, which could be extrapolated from such evidence as Fleure offered, that the "aboriginal" Welsh could still be found stubbornly surviving in the western hills above Manafon, proved attractive to an R.S. Thomas who had been so disturbed at Hanmer by modern images of violent invasion. If so, then as the pages of *Wales* during that period show, he was certainly not the only writer to be influenced directly or indirectly by anthropological thinking such as Fleure's. There are two other particularly interesting examples. In the July 1943 issue a Lieutenant J.B. Sidgwick from Leicester, stationed apparently in the Newtown area, just down the road from Manafon, published a poem called 'Welsh Station':

> The hills in this part of the world
> Are hard worked and domestic, harrowed
> And horse drawn to their summits.
> Slick smooth-pastured hill flanks
> Slip into the valleys, usurp the old wild
> Strongholds of the long-headed defenders,
> Saturnine and slight, who burnt their earth
> Before the encroaching east. Barrow
> Is buried now beneath black-suit Sabbaths
> Hard cash, alicks and social pretenders.[39]

The poem concludes on a note of lament for the defeated aboriginal inhabitants, now assimilated into the invading culture: "Rout leaps out of planned retreat – / And liquid vowels, gentle eyes / Merely serve to emphasise / Dolichocephalic defeat." R.S. Thomas was, of course, to press beyond these domesticated hills around Newtown and to find in the harsher upland areas farmers whose faces and accents were still as yet unsubdued by modern civilisation.

Sidgwick was an unknown writer, but John Cowper Powys was not. During the course of an article on 'Wales and America' in the summer 1944 issue of *Wales*, Powys cited Fleure in support of his claim "that there exists in a Wales a deep tradition of pre-historic understanding between the mountains and the people such as is rare on our migratory planet".[40] He went on to elaborate the point, in terms that seem almost to anticipate some of R.S. Thomas' feeling about the 'native' Welsh:

> Geographically and historically – pre-historically too, no doubt! – Wales is the last stronghold of the oldest race in Europe. Here, in the mountain-plateaus and the deep valleys, with the Irish Sea to prevent further escape, migratory invaders have been forced, for some ten thousand years, to amalgamate with aboriginals who, as Professor Fleure hints, go back in long uninterrupted descent to a branch of our Homo Sapiens who succeeded the hardly human Neanderthal. And it may well have been that the difficult and delicate art of sinking into your native soul and your native soil, while wave after wave of warlike invaders pass over you, has in all these thousands of years given to the Welsh their predominant characteristics.

Alerted by this, we can see signs of Fleure's influence everywhere in the piece on 'Welsh Aboriginals' that Powys published in the July 1943 issue of *Wales*. In his own inimitable fashion he there gloried, with eccentric Romantic zeal and panache, in his own "real Aboriginal Welsh blood", which was "true Non-Aryan Berber".[41] He enthusiastically agreed with Dr Iorwerth Peate "that it is the inaccessibility of certain parts of our land that has saved our 'remnant' of Real Welshmen". He further quoted Peate's opinion that the "People of the mountains were the natives; but men of the plains were Romans. *There* you get the story of every new influence in our land":

> *I'r estron, os mynu* [sic]
> *Boed hawl tros y glyn;*
> *I ninnau boed byw*
> *Ar ymyl gwisg Duw*
> *Yn y grug – yn y grug –*

Let the strangers, if so must be
Stake his claim in the valley:
Give us to live our life
Where the Deity garments himself
In the heather – in the heather –[42]

This Welsh folk-rhyme is, of course, the very one quoted by R.S.
Thomas in 'The Depopulation of the Welsh Hill Country' (first
published in *Wales* in 1945), at the end of a passage where he
argues that it is in the hill country that there "beats the old heart of
Wales".[43] To set his poem 'Out of the Hills' in this extensive context
is, then, to understand why that poem ends with Thomas reassuring himself and us that at midnight the farmer will extricate himself
from the clutches of the valleys folk and make his way home. "Be
then his fingerpost / Homeward", the poem urges us: "The earth is
patient; he is not lost."[44] As *The Echoes Return Slow* shows, Thomas'
imagination had become particularly sensitised to ideas of invasion
during his stay at Hanmer. He recalls listening as "All night the
freight trains thundered over the viaduct on their way south. The
English coast was in danger. The tall headlines in the papers
marched grimly into an uncertain future".[45] There may be an ironic
emphasis here on the way the English (as opposed to the Welsh)
react to the threat of invasion. What Thomas later became aware of,
at Manafon, was that the arming of England to repel invasion
meant the 'invasion' of Wales by the 'modernising' required by the
war effort. As he recalls in *The Echoes Return Slow*: "The tractor
invaded the age-old quietness of the land. As the war proceeded,
technology directed its infiltration. The farmer changed his
allegiance from Ceres to Mars, from subsistence to profit. The
priest again questioned his vocation."[46] Invasion also came in a
cruder form – in the form of 'barbarians' from Hackney, evacuees
who were quartered on the vicar and his wife during the latter
stages of the war. Thomas' later testimony was that the women
neglected their children scandalously, preferring to spend most of
their time in the local pubs, when they were not 'flirting' with the
wounded soldiers housed at Gregynog. And this, he adds with
disgust, when their men-folk were "in danger of their lives on the
continent".[47] There are traces – even sources? – here of the misog-
yny that sometimes seems evident in Thomas' later poetry.

It will not do, though, to see Prytherch and his people, full
though they are of "the artistry of [their] dwelling on the bare hill",
simply as the kind of figure of traditional endurance outlasting
cataclysm that we famously get in Hardy's poem 'In Time of The

Breaking of Nations'.[48] Because another of the ways in which the war leaves its mark on the poetry of *The Stones of the Field* is by foregrounding for Thomas the violence that is so troublingly a part of existence itself – whether it be noticed in nature, or in man's dealings with nature. It is a violence that Thomas sometimes sees as inseparable from fertility and sexuality. Notice, for example, the question on which 'A Labourer' ends: "Is there love there, or hope, or any thought / For the frail form broken beneath his tread, / And the sweet pregnancy that yields his bread?"[49] It is in the neglected lyrics, though, rather than in the much more promising and relatively accomplished farmer poems, that one feels exactly how exposed and raw were R.S. Thomas' emotions at this time. The poem he simply called 'Song' can still startle us because it is so uncharacteristic of the R.S. Thomas we know – the poet's mature self. But it is in the very immaturity (in this sense) of the sentiments that the interest of the poem lies.

> We, who are men, how shall we know
> Earth's ecstasy, who feels the plough
> Probing her womb,
> And after, the sweet gestation
> And the year's care for her condition?
> We, who have forgotten, so long ago
> It happened, our own orgasm,
> When the wind mixed with our limbs,
> And the sun had suck at our bosom;
>
> We, who have affected the livery
> Of the times' prudery,
> How shall we quicken again
> To the lust and thrust of the sun
> And the seedling rain?[50]

This enthusiastically primitivistic account of man's intercourse with nature is not entirely convincing – R.S. Thomas is no Stravinsky, and his 'Song' is no orgiastic 'Rite of Spring'. In fact, one seems to sense there's a desperation behind the affirmation – a will to wholeness that is itself a symptom of sickness. And the sickness, judging at least from other poems in the collection, is his dismayed awareness not only of a misfit between man and nature but also of the inherently mis-shapen character of nature itself, the equivocal character of her energies.

This is most simply evident from the two poems R.S. Thomas chose to pair at the precise centre of *The Stones of the Field*. On one page is 'Country Church (Manafon)';[51] on the other is 'Birch Tree',[52] a short poem full of rapturous wonder at the world's power of self-transfiguration:

> When the cloud left you, you smiled and sang
> With day's brightness, O birch tree among
> The envious moors, sullen and frowning;
> Your long veins filled with light,
> And broke in showers on the night,
> Your dark head with silver crowning.[53]

Here the released joy of the birch tree is literally radiant – that is, it radiates outwards until, in darkness, it becomes the light and fire that we know as stars. The image appears to be a spiritual one, since the Virgin Mary is traditionally represented in iconographic tradition as crowned with stars, in accordance with the famous passage from the Book of Revelation – "And there appeared a great wonder in heaven: a woman clothed with the sun, and the moon under her feet, and upon her head a crown of twelve stars" – but fused with this Christian imagery is the older Celtic association of the birch tree with love.[54] As Alwyn and Brinley Rees pointed out long ago in their classic study of *Celtic Heritage*, medieval Welsh love poetry (including that of Dafydd ap Gwilym) is full of "lines associating the birch-tree with love. The lover's bower usually stood beneath a birch-tree or in a birch-bush; wreaths of birch were presented as love-tokens, and in Wales the may-pole was usually a birch-tree".[55] So R.S. Thomas has here combined Christian with pagan elements, to produce what might be loosely called a sacramental image, finding a sacred, celebratory joy in the sensuous and even the sensual life of nature.

But before resting content with such intense lyrical affirmation, we should glance at the qualifying poem with which 'Birch Tree' is, as it were, paired in *The Stones of the Field*. 'Country Church (Manafon)' is obviously as precisely accurate an evocation of that building as the title would suggest. Indeed, in his late autobiography *Neb*, R.S. Thomas described the church in terms strikingly similar to those he had used in his poem forty years before:

> The church stands, built from the river stone,
> Brittle with light, as though a breath could shatter
> Its slender frame, or spill the limpid water,
> Quiet as sunlight, cupped within the bone.

> It stands yet. But though soft flowers break
> In delicate waves round limbs the river fashioned
> With so smooth care, no friendly God has cautioned
> The brimming tides of fescue for its sake.[56]

'No friendly God' – what a fine, minatory title that would make for a study of R.S. Thomas' religious poetry. But the phrase also warns us that in *The Stones of the Field* the natural world is not seen as benignly spiritual in character. If in 'Birch Tree' light comes to triumph over darkness, then in 'Country Church' light makes even 'built' stone 'brittle' – an inspired conjunction of terms that makes one word ('brittle') seem the virtual disarrangement of the other ('built'), so that language itself, in its unsettling pliability, seems to endorse the sense of an unstable universe. Indeed, the quiet, haunting power of this poem derives in good part from what might be called the metaphysics of its sonic patterns. Throughout, moments of confidence instilled in us by concatenations of sounds that link words of solidly like meaning ("stands ... Stone") alternate with unnerving moments when like sounds leave us adrift among unlike meanings: "built ... brittle ... spill ... limpid". In the last stanza an effect of magical idyll, of a suspension of time, is created by the lulling repetition of soft consonants – "soft flowers ... delicate waves ... limbs ... fashioned ... so smooth", only for the very same sounds to lead us unawares into a very different world – of "no friendly God" and of the "brimming tides of fescue". Again, R.S. Thomas highlights this aspect of his wartime experience at Manafon in *The Echoes Return Slow*, when he recalls that "life in the remotest backwater is prompter of a hundred and one questions. As to be alive is to be vulnerable to pain, so it is to be conscious that peace is transitory".[57]

'Peace is transitory': when we bear in mind that this comment on the general nature of life is made in the context of R.S. Thomas' recollections of wartime life in Manafon, we notice how implicit in it is a sense that war, with its pain and violence, exemplifies – in extreme and obscene form – abiding aspects of existence itself. And there are poems in *The Stones of the Field* where R.S. Thomas seems to me to be forcefully reminding himself of that – anxious to lose any lingering Romantic innocence he had about the pastoral life. Take his poem 'Winter Retreat', for example:

> Accustomed to see death like a wild boar
> Running amok, eyes red, great jaws
> Slavering horribly with their mad lust for blood;
> Accustomed to listen to the bewildering uproar

Inseparable from its usual method,
These last stragglers through a world of snow,
Failing to recognize under the glib mask
Of innocent whiteness the traditional foe,
Abandoned themselves with a child's trust to sleep
On its dissembling pillow.[58]

One wonders to what extent the lurid nightscape of burning
Merseyside influenced those opening lines. It is difficult to discon-
nect R.S. Thomas' image of "death like a wild boar" not only from
the legend of the Twrch Trwyth, but also from Alun Lewis' evocation in 'Post-Script: For Gweno', of "the mad tormented valley /
Where blood and hunger rally / And Death the wild beast is
uncaught, untamed". Or the same poet's memory of the invasion of
Greece: "When the raving tusked boar / Gored the sensual
innocent."[59] In other words, even if Thomas was not specifically
thinking of the war in those opening lines, the Behemoth images he
used were very much part of the vocabulary of psychic stress during
the Second World War, as of course they had been during the First
World War.

In so far as it is a collection in which R.S. Thomas, partly
challenged by war, determined to face up undeviatingly to the
harshness of existence, *The Stones of the Field* is also what Whitman
famously called "a language experiment". The poems are the record
of his search for a truthful vocabulary for experience, and he effectively says as much in the final poem in the volume. But before we
consider that, it is worth remembering what Thomas had to say
about language in the essay on Scottish writing that appeared in
Wales the same year that *The Stones of the Field* was published. There
he enviously praised the fierce, uninhabited style of Scots writers
such as Douglas Young: "Scots has ... a braw quality in keeping with
its environment which makes one wonder why in equally stern
surroundings so much modern Welsh writing is jingling and sweet.
There are people living under the harsh crags of Cadair Idris and Yr
Wyddfa, or on the bare gaunt moorlands of central Wales, but their
verse is tame to the point of lifelessness."[60] With those comments in
mind we should be better able to understand the significance of the
closing poem in *The Stones of the Field*:

Do not say, referring to the sun,
"Its journey northward has begun",
As though it were a bird, annually migrating,
That now returns to build in the rich trees

Its nest of golden grass. Do not belie
Its lusty health with words such as imply
A pallid invalid recuperating.
The age demands the facts, therefore be brief –
Others will sense the simile – and say:
"We are turning towards the sun's indifferent ray".[61]

"The age demands the facts" is a phrase that could have served as an epigraph to *The Stones of the Field*. But the poem is very much about the different pictures of the world that lurk behind our 'factual' descriptions of it – because these pictures reveal the faith by which we actually live. In the examples he gives, Thomas brings several buried similes to light only in order to reject them. But he concludes by admitting that we can offer no substantial description of the world that is completely simile-free – in which there is no implied suggestion of what the world is *like*. The real work therefore is the work of finding appropriate similes and viewed in the light of this concluding assertion the whole collection can be seen as an exercise in figurative language. Not only are the poems in *The Stones of the Field* full of similes, they are ostentatiously full of similes, to an extent that almost invites us to see them as poems about similes. This is clear enough in a short poem like 'A Thought for Nietzche' [sic] which is an extended conceit, based on a trope that treats the human body as if it were an acre of ground.[62] Related conceits occur throughout the collection – particularly comparisons, verging on the mythopoeic, between men and trees. And it is not only in the short lyrics that troping is so prominent as virtually to constitute the topic of the poetry.

The farmer-portraits are full of foregrounded figures of speech, as is the long narrative poem 'The Airy Tomb'.[63] And just as, in the final lines of the final poem, the emphasis is on the 'indifference' of nature to the human condition, so throughout the collection the similes tend to work to establish the same harsh truth about the elemental nature of the universe and man's place in it – whether Iago Prytherch is described as penning "a few sheep in a gap of cloud", or a farmer is described (wonderfully) as "Gaitered with mud, lost in his own breath", or a labourer is seen "as his back comes straight / Like an old tree lightened of the snow's weight".[64] In other words, R.S. Thomas' wartime responses to his demanding age was to render life in uncompromising similes that pictured the world not as reliably ordained or managed by a humanity-orientated God, but as provocatively neutral – glorious and harsh in equal measure, and expressing something of divinity in both its aspects. Indeed to re-

read *The Stones of the Field* is to discover how consistent with that
view of a distant God he articulated in his poetry over the last thirty
years of his life is the troubled sense of the divine one gets from this,
his first collection.

And with this in mind, it is easy to understand why R.S. Thomas
took the collection's title from the Book of Job. The phrase "the
stones of the field" occurs during the following passage:

> In famine he shall redeem thee from death: and in war from
> the power of the sword. Thou shalt be hid from the scourge
> of the tongue: neither shalt thou be afraid of destruction
> when it cometh. At destruction and famine thou shalt laugh:
> neither shalt thou be afraid of the beasts of the earth. For
> thou shalt be in league with the stones of the field; and the
> beasts of the field shall be at peace with thee. And thou shalt
> know that thy tabernacle shall be in peace; and thou shalt visit
> thy habitation, and shalt not sin.[65]

Here indeed, one might say, is a vision of a providential God, but
placed in the context of the Book of Job as a whole, these words have
a tragically hollow ring to them. They are not Job's words, but the
words of Eliphar the Temanite, as he rebukes the afflicted,
tormented Job for his loss of faith in the Almighty. But by the end of
the Book of Job it is with this very same Eliphar the Temanite that
God is angry: "for ye have not spoken of me the thing that is right,
as my servant Job hath."[66] By then, Job has been brought to realise
that God is like the mighty ungovernable Leviathan, not to be
measured or constrained by a human being: "Canst thou draw out
leviathan with a hook? Or his tongue with a cord which thou lettest
down?"[67] It is this vision of God that has always been R.S. Thomas'
mastering vision, his answer to the irreducible puzzle of existence as
presented to him in general by the nature of the universe, and in
particular by the cruelties of his demanding age. And it is with the
Job who reaches this understanding that he identifies in *The Stones
of the Field*, as is shown in that poem included by Rhys in *Modern
Welsh Poetry* and aptly entitled 'The Question':

> Who is skilled to read
> The strange epitaph of the salt weed
> Scrawled on our shores? Who can make plain
> The thin, dark characters of rain,
> Or the hushed speech of wind and star
> In the deep-throated fir?

> Was not this the voice that lulled
> Job's seething mind to a still calm,
> Yet tossed his heart to the racked world?[68]

"Then answered the Lord unto Job out of the whirlwind, and said, 'Gird up thy loins now like a man: I will demand of thee, and declare thou unto me. Wilt thou also disannul my judgement? Wilt thou condemn me, that thou mayest be righteous? Hast thou an arm like God? Or canst thou thunder with a voice like him?'"[69] This was the voice that eventually spoke to R.S. Thomas out of that wind of war that lifted his wife's skirts as they stood at the door watching Merseyside burn. It was also the voice that intermittently spoke to him out of the stones of the fields above Manafon. It lulled his seething mind to a still calm; but it also tossed his heart to the racked world. And the poems of *The Stones of the Field* show him to us in this double aspect.

But if these were the longer-term implications of the title *The Stones of the Field*, the short-term message was somewhat different. It was that humankind should seek to renew its ancient peaceful acquaintance with "the stones of the field" and "the beasts of the field" so as to be redeemed "from death ... and from the power of the sword". Born of wartime, every bit as much as those poems Rhys included in *Modern Welsh Poetry*, Thomas' collection remains a singular and compelling record of Wales' complex response to the Second World War.

Notes

1. An earlier, bilingual, version of this essay, in the form of the Arts Council of Wales' Ben Bowen Lecture for 1994, appeared in pamphlet form as *R.S. Thomas: Bardd Rhyfel (R.S. Thomas:War Poet)*. Arts Council of Wales: Gwasg y Castell, Cricieth, 1995. The English text was reprinted as 'R.S. Thomas War Poet' in Tony Brown (ed.), *Welsh Writing in English 2*. Cardiff: New Welsh Review, 1996, pp.82-97.
2. M.J. Tambimuttu (ed.), *Poetry in Wartime*. London: Faber and Faber, 1952, cover blurb.
3. Dylan Thomas, *Collected Poems 1934-53* (eds. Walford Davies and Ralph Maud). London: J.M. Dent & Sons, 1988, p.68, p.216.
4. Keidrych Rhys (ed.), *Modern Welsh Poetry*. London: Faber and Faber, 1944.
5. Brenda Chamberlain, *The Green Heart*. London: Oxford University Press, 1958; Nigel Heseltine, *The Four-Walled Dream*. London: The Fortune Press, 1941.

6. *Modern Welsh Poetry*, p.52.

7. *Ibid.*, p.66.

8. *Ibid.*, p.42.

9. *Ibid.*, pp.112-113.

10. *Ibid.*, p.115.

11. Brenda Chamberlain, *Alun Lewis and the Making of the Caseg Broadsheets*. London: Enitharmon, 1970.

12. *Modern Welsh Poetry*, p.116.

13. *Ibid.*, p.95.

14. *Ibid.*, p.130.

15. *Ibid.*, p.131.

16. *Ibid.*, p.103.

17. R.S. Thomas, *The Stones of the Field*. Carmarthen: The Druid Press Limited, 1946, p.10.

18. W.B. Yeats, 'The Second Coming' in *Collected Poems*. London: Macmillan, 1963, p.211. *The Stones of the Field* contains a poem addressed to Yeats, 'Memories of Yeats whilst Travelling to Holyhead' (p.22).

19. *The Stones of the Field*, p.35.

20. *Ibid.*, p.32.

21. R.S. Thomas, *Neb* (gol. Gwenno Hywyn). Caernarfon: Gwasg Gwynedd, 1985, pp.38-39. (My translation.)

22. R.S. Thomas, *The Echoes Return Slow*. London: Macmillan, 1988, p.19.

23. *The Stones of the Field*, p.27.

24. *The Echoes Return Slow*, p.20.

25. *Ibid.*, p.22.

26. *The Stones of the Field*, p.12.

27. T.S. Eliot, *The Waste Land* (V: 'What the Thunder Said') in *Collected Poems 1909-1962*. London: Faber, 1965 impression, p.77.

28. *Modern Welsh Poetry*, p.94.

29. It is well discussed in Ned Thomas, 'R.S. Thomas: the Question about Technology' in *Planet* 92, pp.54-60.

30. R.S. Thomas, *Song at the Year's Turning*. London: Rupert Hart-Davis, 1955; 1965 reprint, pp.18-19.

31. *The Stones of the Field*, p.8.

32. *Ibid.*, p.14.

33. *Ibid.*, p.33.

34. The belief that the mountains provide the key to the Welsh character is, of course, an old one, and it was reinforced towards the end of the nineteenth century and the beginning of the twentieth century by the work of geographers who emphasised the influence of environment on the development of national character. One writer who was interested in these theories was O.M. Edwards, as has been pointed out in E.G. Millward, 'O.M. Edwards' in Geraint Bowen (gol.), *Y Traddodiad Rhyddiaith yn yr Ugeinfed Ganrif*. Llandysul: Gwasg Gomer, 1976, pp.37-51, especially pp.48-49. Millward adds an appendix (pp.52-53) of Edwards' statements, in both Welsh and

English, on this subject. I am grateful to Professor Dafydd Johnston, University of Wales, Swansea, for drawing this essay to my attention. For discussion of the broader appeal of this concept to writers and artists in the 1930s and 1940s, see: Linda Adams, 'Fieldwork: The Caseg Broadsheets and the Welsh Anthropologist' in Tony Brown (ed.), *Welsh Writing in English: a Yearbook of Critical Essays* 5 (1999), pp.51-85.

35.   H.J. Fleure, 'The Welsh People' in *Wales* 10 (October 1939); reprinted in *Wales: 1-11*. London: Frank Cass and Company, 1969, pp.265-269 (p.269).

36.   *Ibid.*, p.269.

37.   *Ibid.*, p.268.

38.   *Ibid.*, p.267.

39.   J.B. Sidgwick, 'Welsh Station' in *Wales* 1 (July 1943), p.32; subsequently collected in Keidrych Rhys (ed.), *More Poems from the Forces*. London: Routledge, 1943, pp.258-259.

40.   John Cowper Powys, 'Wales and America' in *Wales* 4 (Summer 1944), pp.66-71 (p.69).

41.   John Cowper Powys, 'Welsh Aboriginals (or the Real Welsh)' in *Wales* 1 (July 1943), pp.60-69 (p.61).

42.   *Ibid.*, p.61.

43.   R.S. Thomas, 'The Depopulation of the Welsh Hill Country' in *Wales*; reprinted in Sandra Anstey (ed.), *R.S. Thomas: Selected Prose*. Bridgend: Poetry Wales Press, 1983, pp.19-25 (p.24). Anstey also cites other places where Thomas quotes these lines. For Thomas' other uses of this folk rhyme see Jason Walford Davies, *Gororau'r Iaith: R.S. Thomas a'r Traddodiad Llenyddol Cymraeg*. Caerdydd: Gwasg Prifysgol Cymru, 2003, p.244.

44.   *The Stones of the Field*, p.7.

45.   *The Echoes Return Slow*, p.18.

46.   *Ibid.*, p.28.

47.   *Neb*, p.112.

48.   *The Stones of the Field*, p.29.

49.   *Ibid.*, p.8.

50.   *Ibid.*, p.23.

51.   *Ibid.*, p.24.

52.   *Ibid.*, p.25.

53.   For the echoes of Welsh language literature and tradition in this poem, see Jason Walford Davies, *Gororau'r Iaith*, p.190.

54.   Book of Revelation, 12:i.

55.   Alwyn and Brinley Rees, *Celtic Heritage*. London: Thames and Hudson, 1961, p.287.

56.   *The Stones of the Field*, p.24.

57.   *The Echoes Return Slow*, p.28.

58.   *The Stones of the Field*, p.28.

59.   Alun Lewis, *Raiders' Dawn*. London: Allen and Unwin, 1942; 1946 reprint, p.45.

60.   *Selected Prose*, p.31.

61.   *The Stones of the Field*, p.48.
62.   *Ibid.*, p.13.
63.   *Ibid.*, pp.42-45.
64.   *Ibid.*, p.14, p.20, p.8.
65.   Book of Job, 5:xx-xxiv.
66.   *Ibid.*, 42:i.
67.   *Ibid.*, 41:i.
68.   *The Stones of the Field*, p.15.
69.   Book of Job, 40:vi-ix.

APPENDIX

"Soul-Conscripting War-Mechanic": *Writers and Artists who Objected to War[1]* *– Notes towards Further Writing[2]*

Tony Curtis

It should be noted that in both the major conflicts of the twentieth century there was a significant number of men who for a variety of reasons declared themselves unwilling to bear arms.[3] In the First World War their position was likely to be underpinned by religious commitment; in the Second World War to those religious beliefs were added the rationale that the carnage of the 1914-1918, the sacrifice of a whole generation across the major European nations and their empires, had been made to ensure that there would be no further loss of life through war in that century. The 'war to end all wars' could only be accepted, emotionally, historically and politically if it had indeed brought a lasting peace. The reprisals, tensions, re-arming, reclamation of territories and invasion of lands which characterised the 1920s and 1930s was a clear warning that this would not be the case, but the 'piece of paper' which Chamberlain brought back from Hitler was significant because so many people wanted to believe in its legitimacy; the building of the Maginot Line by France in an astonishingly rigid refusal to believe it could again be out-flanked, was a refusal to revisit the lessons of the Great War and to laterally re-think strategy from them. In Britain, 1,500 men absolutely refused to be party to the war effort; nine men died as a result of the treatment they received as COs in the Great War. No-one could imagine another carnage in that generation. Approximately 40,000 Welshmen had been killed in the First World War; there were to be 15,000 killed in the 1939-45 conflict. In that war, citizens would refuse to volunteer their lives into the hands of imperialistic rulers and a discredited staff officer class. The League of Nations and International Socialism claimed allegiances beyond national boundaries.[4] From the years of the First World War through to the anti-nuclear protests of the 1960s and 1970s and the recent anti-Iraq War campaigns Welsh writers and artists have taken both absolute and specific stands against conflicts. In the figures of R.S. Thomas and Waldo Williams in particular, the conjunction of Welsh nationalism, Christianity and anti-war principles was embodied.

Pacifism in Wales can be traced much further back, to the Quakers and other non-conformists. Henry Richard (1812-1888),[5] born in Cardiganshire, was a Congregational minister in London; later the Liberal member for Merthyr Tydfil, he became the Secretary of the Peace Society in 1848 and was known as 'The Apostle of Peace'.

In the First World War the natural pride and loyalty felt in Wales towards Lloyd George was an unifying principle (particularly from 1915 when he persuaded the Army to form divisions of Welshmen, who were allowed to speak Welsh for the first time without reprimand). There was, however, the continued campaigning of the Fellowship of Reconciliation, the editorials of Thomas Rees of Bangor in the monthly journal *Y Deymas* and the ground-swell of Socialism. One of the Fellowship's founding members, George M. Ll. Davies was elected to Parliament in 1923 as the Christian Pacifist MP for the University of Wales. From its inception Plaid Cymru held to pacifist principles and in the Second World War Saunders Lewis (1893-1985),[6] one of its founders, who had been commissioned in the South Wales Borderers in the First World War, wrote a regular column for *Y Faner*. It was the cause of much controversy for Lewis expressed sympathy for Hitler's position; Lewis' fear that Catholic churches would be destroyed by the Allied bombing campaign seemed to many to be misguided in the wider context of the war and he was reported to the police on several occasions.

The political and social situation in Wales during both wars was, of course, complex. Despite being crucial to the war effort, Welsh miners went on strike in July 1915 and again in May 1917; Lloyd George himself travelled back to Wales to settle things. Also in 1917 the *Merthyr Leader* could proclaim: "There was no place outside of Russia where the Revolution has caused greater joy than in Merthyr Tydfil." Later, the South Wales Miners Federation[7] resolved to contact the German trade union movement to work for peace. Behind the jingoism and flag waving, the class struggle and the power of the chapel communities was very much in evidence.

The poet T.E. Nicholas, known by his bardic name, Niclas y Glais, was born in Pembrokeshire in 1879; he was a preacher, lecturer and dentist. He was a pacifist during the First World War and was imprisoned during the Second World War for his political beliefs. Nicholas exemplifies the complexity of the pacifist position. He was a founder member of the Communist Party of Great Britain and lectured widely on the conflict between labour and international capitalism. He held to the Christian conviction that one's task was to improve man's condition throughout the world. To a sparrow which has flown into his prison cell he says,

> We two could take, amid war's turbulence,
> Communion, though the cell lacks cross and altar.
> The Bread's as holy as it needs to be
> Offering of a heart not under lock and key.

During the Second World War this prolific poet published five collections. An English version of his *Prison Sonnets* was published in 1948.

Gwenallt (David James Jones, 1899-1968) poet and critic, lost his father in an industrial accident and lost his faith too. He became an atheist and Marxist and was imprisoned in Wormwood Scrubs and Dartmoor in the First World War as a CO. A prolific poet, he won the Chair at the National Eisteddfod in 1926. He writes of hearing the news of the Russian Revolution while in prison:

> I remember, in a London prison one night, hearing the cells shake with the triumph of 'The Red Flag' and 'The Internationale'. For news had just reached us of the revolution in Russia: Russia, the land of Tolstoy, Dostoevsky, Lenin.[8]

Siegfried Sassoon (1886–1967), a commissioned officer with the Royal Welsh Fusiliers, was the most publicised objector to the First World War.[9] His objections were those of a decorated war hero, an MC, one of the landed gentry, who, by 1917, characterised the war as profoundly misguided, lacking clear moral intentions and badly executed. His public declaration caused these issues to be raised in Parliament and the national press. He wrote:

> I am making this statement as an act of wilful defiance of military authority, because I believe that the war is being deliberately prolonged by those who have the power to end it.

I am a soldier, convinced that I am acting on behalf of
soldiers. I believe that this war, on which I entered as a war of
defence and liberation, has now become a war of aggression
and conquest. I believe that the purpose for which I and my
fellow soldiers entered upon this war should have been so
clearly stated as to have made it impossible to change them,
and that, had this been done, the objects which actuated us
would now be attainable by negotiation. I have seen and
endured the sufferings of the troops, and I can no longer be
a party to prolong these sufferings for ends which I believe to
be evil and unjust. I am not protesting against the conduct of
the war, but against the political errors and insincerities for
which the fighting men are being sacrificed. On behalf of
those who are suffering now I make this protest against the
deception which is being practiced on them; also I believe
that I may help to destroy the callous complacency with
which the majority of those at home regard the contrivance
of agonies which they do not, and which they have not sufficient imagination to realize.

Sassoon had thrown his Military Cross ribbon into the river Mersey,
but remained loyal to the cause of his 'Flintshire Fusiliers', seeing
them as the true heroes. Most of these men were from "the poorer
classes [who] stood for hours in queues outside food shops" while
"profiteers and officials gorged at the Ritz and the Savoy". His
pacifism was specific, directed at the nature of the conflict on the
Western Front and the disassociation of those Fusiliers in action
from the political and social systems which powered the Army.

In my chapter on the visual arts I refer to the artist John Petts, the
Caseg Broadsheets and his inspiring of Jonah Jones who joined Petts
and Brenda Chamberlain at that press after the war. Jonah Jones
talked of that time when I interviewed him in *Welsh Artists Talking*.[10]
His father had been wounded at Vimy Ridge, possibly when mining
under the German lines: "... he talked very little about it ... All I
knew was he hated it all, and he preached at me, and it was horrible.
So I was a pacifist, that was it." Jonah and John Petts were unarmed
medics in the Parachute Regiment, the 224 Field Parachute Field
ambulance:

> Never carried arms. Only a Red Cross armband in actual
> operations ... half the idiots there were pacifists. Because the
> army had great difficulty finding medical personnel to
> parachute. And these chaps were willing to do that, but not to
> carry arms. Looking back, it seemed a very odd position to take.

Clearly, pacifist sentiments were expressed and acted upon in a number of ways. Eventually, Jonah Jones reached Belsen and from that point began to abandon his pacifist position: "… looking back, I find the position untenable … Really I've come to think it was an untenable thing, but I held it then. It was a hard principle."

Alun Lewis, as Cary Archard contends, had very deep misgivings about army life and his role as a writer. Jonah Jones says: "Alun Lewis himself was a pacifist, who eventually gave way in the face of what was happening, and died at the end of the war in tragic circumstances." Lewis, who may well have taken his own life in Burma, personifies the dilemma of an intelligent, sensitive person forced to act in time of war in a regimented way.

In June 1940 the teacher and writer Roland Mathias appeared before a tribunal for conscientious objectors and was registered for non-combatant duties. He refused, however, to comply with the decision of the tribunal; he appealed, but when that was denied and he failed to report for duty, he was sentenced and served a period of hard labour in prison. In the same year he published his first collection of poems, *Days Enduring* (1942). Mathias had been born in Breconshire in 1915, the son of an army chaplain. He went to Jesus College, Oxford, in 1933, where he took a first in history and wrote poems that would later appear in *Days Enduring*. In 1938, he became a teacher and his second volume of poems, *Break in Harvest*, was published in 1946. Two years later he became headmaster of Pembroke Dock Grammar School where he founded with Raymond Garlick *Dock Leaves* (later *The Anglo-Welsh Review).*

Other teachers lost their jobs for declaring their pacifism. Glyn Jones (1905-95), poet, short-story writer and novelist, whose collection of essays and autobiography *The Dragon has Two Tongues*[11] is a seminal work on Welsh Literature in English, was born and raised in Merthyr Tydfil, into a Welsh-speaking family. His father had served in the British Army in France in the Great War. Jones believed that: "Merthyr in fact had a strong pacifist tradition, a combination of the pacifism of Welsh nonconformity and of left-wing politics." He became a teacher in the slums of Cardiff, where his experience of that society's poverty in the 1920s and 1930s affected him deeply. He was "very greatly influenced by the Depression and left-wing politics, and also by the pacifist debate and the fear of war". Though he was above the age of conscription in 1939, Jones chose to make a stand: he was dismissed from his teaching post when he registered as a conscientious objector; in subsequent posts during the war he felt discriminated against.

When in his poem 'Merthyr' he writes, "Lord, when they kill me let the job be thorough," he is referring to the fear that many COs held that they were regarded as a security risk and would be killed in the event of a German invasion.[12]

Glyn Jones writes of the shock and concern he experienced as a teacher in the Cardiff slums of the 1930s.

> I could not see how war was ever to be reconciled with Christian belief. I felt convinced that pacifism was implicit in Christianity. And how, I asked myself, was the desperate plight of those around me to be improved by war, which was more likely to impoverish them further and even destroy them and their community? I was quite wrong. About a twelvemonth before war broke out I remember sitting by the fire in a large bus garage at the derelict top end of one of the valleys, chatting to a group of unemployed miners. They were cheerful. As we talked one of them got up, went to the work-bench under the window and returned with half a pint of engine oil which he poured on the fire. The flames went up bright and yellow, illuminating the gloomy barn-like garage with their brilliance. This was a celebration. The men, after years of unemployment, had been promised jobs within a matter of days. One, a miner who hadn't worked for fifteen years, was the next day to start in an arms factory.

Attending meetings of the Quakers, Peace Pledge activists and the Fellowship of Reconciliation at their recruitment stall in Cardiff Market, Glyn Jones spent agonised Saturday mornings.

Through his pacifist position, Glyn Jones became a close friend of the artist John Elwyn (1916-1977). Born in Newcastle Emlyn, Elwyn studied at Carmarthen Art School, the West of England College of Art, Bristol, and under Carel Weight at the Royal College of Art (1938-40 and 1946-47). As a conscientious objector, he was directed to land work and food production in the valleys above Neath, and the experiences of those mining communities during the Second World War drove much of his work as an artist through the 1940s, work which often conveyed anguish of the war's suffering. He thus managed to stay active as a artist and he contributed to an exhibition at the National Eisteddfod of Wales in 1942. With his later work, Elwyn's landscapes and scenes of farm and chapel life in Ceredigion have come to represent an Edenic existence in west Wales, Ceredigion in a palette of greens illuminated by sunshine. That peacetime rural pattern of life is a salve to the twisted bones and roots of his wartime surreal visions.

On the 11th September, 1939 Glyn Jones received a letter from Laugharne.[13] Dylan Thomas had been alarmed from the moment Chamberlain made that declaration of war: "I want to get something out of the war, and put very little in (certainly not my one and only body)." The outstanding Welsh writer of his generation, and arguably, of the century, was determined to avoid any direct involvement with the war, to such an extent that he expended huge amounts of time and energy to render himself exempt. He even thought that declaring himself a member of Plaid Cymru might do the trick. To Desmond Hawkins on 14th September he wrote: "The Army Medical Corps is presumably admirable, but I don't want to help – even in a most inefficient way – to patch poor buggers up to send them out again into quick insanity and bullets." To Bert Trick on 29th September: "I am going to register as an objector, but also, because I want to get something out of the mess if possible, I'm trying to get a mild job."

Dylan thought of joining, belatedly, the Peace Pledge Union in order to use that in any forthcoming tribunal. To Glyn Jones again on 14th October he raised the project of a movement of writers such as Jones and Keidrych Rhys, with articles published, "to be called Objections to War". Anything, in fact, to avoid the fate he felt sure awaited him: "Be in the Army & see the next world."[14]

To Rayner Heppenstall on 2nd November he was most fulsome in his justification of his position:

> When you come to talk about one's duty as a writer, then one can only say that his duty is to write. If to undergo contemporary reality to its most extreme is to join in a war – the evil of which is the war itself & not the things it is supposed, wrongly, to be attempting to exterminate – against people you do not know, and probably to be killed or maimed, then one can only say flippantly that the best poems about death were always written when the poets were alive, that Lorca didn't have to be gored before writing a bullsong, that for a writer to undergo the utmost reality of poverty is for him to starve to death and therefore to be, as a writer, useless.

Thomas is caught up in a perception of the coming war in terms of the last war, as were many others. In the event, he was pronounced unfit for active service and worked on propaganda films and for the BBC. Ironically, the poems he wrote in 1944 and 1945, including 'A Refusal to Mourn', 'Ceremony After a Fire Raid' and 'Among Those Killed in the Dawn Raid was a Man Aged a Hundred', were some of the finest written in war-time Britain. His *18 Poems* was re-published in 1942 and a new collection *Deaths and Entrances* appeared in 1946; it secured his reputation. After all, apart from being subjected to a machine gun attack by a crazed officer on leave in New Quay, west Wales, Dylan Thomas had a good war.[15]

Arthur Giardelli (b.1911) had first lived in Wales when his family moved from London to Amroth in Carmarthenshire in 1928. But in 1940 he was evacuated to the Glamorgan valleys as teacher of English and French with Folkestone Grammar School. It was there that he registered as a conscientious objector and, like Glyn Jones, lost his post. During the Second World War he served as a part-time fireman, taught music at Cyfarthfa Grammar School and lectured on the history of European art for the Workers' Educational Association. He also became associated with the Quaker communities in the valleys. He settled eventually in west Wales and through his work in community and university education and his sponsorship of artists such as David Jones and Ceri Richards, Arthur Giardelli made a very valuable contribution to the life of letters and the arts in post-war Wales.

Waldo Williams (1904-1971) was born in Haverfordwest, the son of a schoolteacher. English was the language of his family and it wasn't until he moved to Fynachlog-ddu and attended the local primary school that he learnt Welsh. His parents were staunch chapel-goers; as pacifists, they were strongly opposed to the First World War. He was a conscientious objector in the Second World War, and expressed the horror of war in poems such as '*Y Tangnefeddwyr*' ('The Peacemakers'), which describes "*Abertawe'n fflam*" – Swansea in flames during the Blitz.[16]

Later in life Waldo Williams was imprisoned for his stance against the Korean War, refusing to pay taxes; in 1950 and again in the 1960s, in protest at the British government's policies, in particular the extension of the Army's artillery ranges in the Preseli Hills, he opted to go to court. He was appalled by the development of nuclear weapons and wrote passionately about the bombing of Nagasaki and Hiroshima. Waldo Williams lost possessions and money as a result of his principled action and was to suffer ill health as a result of his prosecution and imprisonment. His most famous poem 'Mewn Dau Gae / In Two Fields' is both a Christian celebration and a pacifist plea.[17]

One of Wales' leading novelists Emyr Humphreys (b.1919) was called up whilst at university at Aberystwyth; he declared that he was a conscientious objector and was directed to farm work in Pembrokeshire. In 1944 he undertook war relief work in the Middle

East and Italy and this continued until 1946 by which time he was working for the UN's Save the Children Fund. His war-time experiences as a non-combatant built on his commitment to the politics and language of Wales acquired at university. His position as a CO was as a direct consequence of his Christianity and a growing sense of Welsh nationalism. His novel *A Toy Epic*[18], written in its first form during that wartime farm work in Pembrokeshire but not published until 1958, portrays the challenges of growing up in Wales in the 1930s with the increasing threat of war. In the closing section from an early version of the novel Humphreys includes a debate on the political situation at the outbreak of war at Aberystwyth University. The central character Michael calls for his fellow students to prioritise Wales:

> A Welshman's first duty is therefore to Wales ... and our birthright is not only a duty, it is also a privilege ...
> The storm which threatens to destroy Welsh civilisation is the storm which threatens to destroy European civilisation as a whole. Remember the story of the drowned land that lies in this bay – the youth of a country are its watchers in the tower, today we sleep while the waters that threaten our land are rising hour by hour. Our duty to humanity as a whole is to guard our section of the wall, for if Wales is annihilated, civilisation in our part of the world will be annihilated too ....

At university Emyr Humphreys learned Welsh and committed himself to Wales, rather than Great Britain. His refusal to fight in the British Army was the logical decision following the argument of his alter ego Michael. It was a position legitimised by the Penyberth direct actions of the Plaid Cymru activists in 1936.[19] During the novel Michael and Iorwerth have a debate about what they will do in the forthcoming war in which British and Welsh loyalties are balanced. Michael says: "Of course I could be a CO on Welsh political grounds. Could do that. But I don't think I will. I'm terribly keen to learn more about discipline and authority. The army would be just the place for that." At the end of the published novel, Michael kneels in church and says: "In the midst of life we are in doubt." Much of Humphreys' work as a novelist is rooted in such questions of faith and action in a precariously Christian post-war world.

In his own life and those of his fictional characters Humphreys epitomises many of the dilemmas facing patriotic Welshmen freshly coming to a commitment to their Wales above other countries. It is significant that this writer, like Jonah Jones and others, opts to commit himself eventually to idealistic work in Europe. They engage with the wider world, but on their own terms. With our knowledge of what ruthless inhumanity the Nazis and the Japanese Imperialist armies were capable the religious and moral debates of the 1930s seem to pale. However, in Wales, as we may see, severe economic suffering, political uncertainties with regard to our country's place in a greater Britain and its exhausted empire, and a long tradition of free thought and independent moral action through nonconformity created a matrix in which many obstacles were perceived to a whole-hearted engagement with the armed struggle against the Axis powers.

Notes

1. From Sassoon's poem 'War Experience', first published in 1933 and collected in *The War Poems*. London: Faber, 1983.
2. This appendix takes the place of a commissioned essay which, for reasons of ill health, could not be delivered. This is, of course, a huge area which could well justify a complete book. The present piece may offer pointers to further reading and consideration.
3. COs who were imprisoned numbered: approximately 6,000.
    Men who resisted military conscription: 6,312.
    Men who appeared before a military court: 5,790.
    Men imprisoned for two years or more: 843.
    Men released from prison on health grounds: 333.
    Men who took work under auspices of the Home Office: 3,612.
    Men who died after being arrested (10 in prison): 69.
    Men who suffered mental ill health after arrest: 39.
    Men who did military service or non-combatant duties after arrest: 349.
    Notes taken from statistics given in *The Tribunal* (8 January 1920) which was published by the No-Conscription Fellowship (NCF).
4. More Welsh COs were recorded in the 1939-45 conflict than the 1914-18 war; more were imprisoned proportionally in the first war. John Davies, *A History of Wales*. London: Penguin, 1990.
5. For more details of the history of pacifism in Wales, see Philip Jenkins, *A History of Modern Wales*. London: Longman, 1992 and John Davies, *A History of Wales*.
6. Bruce Griffiths, *Saunders Lewis*. Cardiff: University of Wales Press, 1989.
7. Roughly the same number of men fought – 250,000 – as were employed in the mining industry.
8. I am grateful to Professor Meic Stephens for his advice regarding this subject. His *New Companion to the Literature of Wales* (Cardiff, UWP, 1998) is the standard reference book.
9. All quotations are from *Memoirs of an Infantry Officer*. London: Faber, 1930 (2000).

10. Bridgend: Seren, 2000.
11. Edited by Tony Brown. Cardiff: University of Wales Press, 2001.
12. I am grateful to Meic Stephens, the executor of the Glyn Jones literary estate, for pointing this out.
13. All quotations are from *The Collected Letters of Dylan Thomas* edited by Paul Ferris. London: Dent, 2000 new edition.
14. Dylan also approached Gwynfor Evans of Plaid: Evans later wrote "I didn't think I ought to help such a fallible and yet unprincipled fellow". Gwynfor Evans was secretary of the *Heddychwyr*, the main pacifist group in Wales. Pen-y-bont is the next farm to Wernellyn, where Gwynfor first lived in Llangadog and where he grew tomatoes. It was known locally as 'Conchies' Corner' because he employed so many of his fellow COs. (Note supplied by Meic Stephens.)
15. Dylan's best friend, poet Vernon Watkins, served as an R.A.F. policeman. In Bletchley Park he met his future wife, Gwen. In 1944, Dylan infamously failed attend their wedding at which he was best man.
16. Two books by Professor Gerwyn Williams of Bangor University relate to the Welsh language literature of the First World War: *Y Rhwyg* (*The Rupture*) (1993) which considers the response of Welsh poets to the conflict and *Tir Neb* (*No-man's Land*) (1996) which deals with prose accounts of the war. In 2005 he published *Tir Newydd* (*New Territory*), a critical study of Welsh literature and the Second World War; in 2006 he published an essay, 'Cofio Rhyfel Anghofiedig' ('Commemorating a Forgotten War') which analyses the range of responses to the 1982 Falklands / Malvinas conflict.
17. See Damion Walford Davies' 'In Two Fields' and the 38th Parallel' in T. Robin Chapman's *The Idiom of Dissent: Protest and Propaganda in Wales*, Llandysul, Gomer Press, 2006. Davies gives a full critique of the poem and examines Archbishop Rowan Williams' translation and its new emphasis on the imagery of war.
18. Edited by M. Wynn Thomas with a full introduction and notes. Bridgend: Seren, 1989.
19. That action was specifically against the Army's plan to demolish a traditional farmhouse in Llyn in order to establish a bombing range. On 9th September 1936, three members of Plaid – Saunders Lewis, Lewis Valentine and D.J. Williams – gave themselves up to the police and stood trial for the act, first at Caernarfon and then, following that jury's reluctance to reach a verdict, at the Old Bailey. They were sentenced to nine months imprisonment. Their action came to represent a serious challenge to the Crown and the Army and to galvanise later coalitions of Christian, Welsh Nationalist and Pacifist activists.
20. For a discussion of more recent pacifist protests by women from Wales see Avril Rolph's chapter 'Greenham and its Legacy – the Women's Peace Movement in Wales in the 1980s' in T. Robin Chapman's book. Rolph deals with Greenham, the Porth movement and the Brawdy and Llanishen protests. She also cites Deidre Beddoe's observation that branches of the Women's International League for Peace and Freedom had existed in Wales from 1915.

Index

Contributors Notes

Cary Archard edited *Poetry Wales* from 1980 to 1986 and founded the publisher, Seren, in 1981. Among his publications are *Alun Lewis: Collected Poems*, *Alun Lewis: Collected Stories*, *Poetry Wales: 25 Years* and *Welsh Retrospective*, a selection of Dannie Abse's poetry.

Duncan Campbell works in electronic publishing in Cambridge, and one day hopes to find the time to finish his book on David Jones. He completed a PhD on the work of Laurence Sterne at the University of Wales, Cardiff, and was formerly commissioning editor at the University of Wales Press.

James A. Davies was born in Llandeilo and brought up in south-east Wales. He is a former member of the Department of English, University of Wales Swansea. He has taught at Cardiff University, and in Texas as a visiting professor. He was Mellon Research Fellow at the University of Texas at Austin. His numerous books and articles on Victorian literature and Welsh Writing in English include *John Forster: A Literary Life* (1983), *The Textual Life of Dickens's Characters* (1989), *Leslie Norris* (1991), and three volumes on Dylan Thomas: *Dylan Thomas's Places* (1987), *A Reference Companion to Dylan Thomas* (1998) and *Dylan Thomas's Swansea, Gower and Laugharne* (2000). Most recently he has expanded and updated *A Swansea Anthology* (1996; 2006). Dr Davies is a Fellow of the Welsh Academy.

Katie Gramich is a Senior Lecturer in English Literature at Cardiff University. She is originally from Rhydlewis in Ceredigion and was educated at the Universities of Wales, London, and Alberta. Her main research interests are in women's writing, the literatures of Wales in both languages, postcolonialism and modernism. She is the general co-editor of the Honno Classics series, which brings books by neglected Welsh women writers back into print. Currently Chair of the Association for Welsh Writing in English, she is also an elected Fellow of the Welsh Academi. Her book, *Twentieth-Century Women's Writing in Wales: Land, Gender, Belonging*, will be published by the University of Wales Press in 2007.

Jeremy Hooker has published ten collections of poetry since 1974 which are represented in a substantial selection, *The Cut of the Light: Poems 1965-2005*, from Enitharmon. His extensive critical writings include *Writers in a Landscape* (1996) and *Imagining Wales: A View of Modern Welsh Writing in English* (2001) both published by University of Wales Press. His edited books include a selection of Edward Thomas' stories (Enitharmon) and a selection of Wilfred Owen's poems and letters (Gregynog Press). His *Welsh Journal* was published by Seren in 2001 and *Upstate: A North American Journal* is due from Shearsman in 2007. His features for BBC Radio 3 include *A Map of David Jones* and *Landscape of Childhood*. He is professor of English at the University of Glamorgan.

Eric Rowan was formerly senior lecturer in Art History at Cardiff College of Art and is now a freelance artist, art historian and lecturer. Author of *Art in Wales, 1850-1980*, University of Wales Press, 1985; *An Elusive Tradition*, UWP, 2002; 'The Visual Arts' in *The Arts in Wales 1950-75* (ed. Meic Stephens), Welsh Arts Council, 1979. He has written art criticism for *The Times*, *Western Mail* and *Studio International* among others and has curated exhibitions for Welsh Arts Council, National Museum of Wales, Museum of Fine Art, Ghent and the Mostyn Gallery, Llandudno. He is a scriptwriter and director of documentary art films for BBC2, BBC Wales and the Arts Council of Great Britain; and a freelance lecturer for the Royal Academy, British Museum and Swan Hellenic among others. He was a member of *56 Group Wales* from 1966 to 1978, and has exhibited paintings in the UK, USA, France, Germany, Holland and Ireland, with works in public and private collections. He now lives in Shropshire.

M. Wynn Thomas is Professor of English and Director of CREW (Centre for Research into the English literature and language of Wales), University of Swansea. A Fellow of the British Academy, of the English Association and of Academi Gymreig and currently Chair of the Welsh Books Council, he has published over twenty books, one of the latest of which is *Transatlantic Connections: Whitman US – Whitman UK*.

Tony Curtis is Professor of Poetry at the University of Glamorgan, where he leads the M. Phil in Creative Writing. He is the author of nine collections of poetry, most recently *Crossing Over* (Seren, 2007), and has edited several anthologies of poetry and prose including the companion to this volume, *After the First Death*. He is also the author of a study of the work of Dannie Abse and editor of the acclaimed critical book, *The Art of Seamus Heaney*. Alongside this literary work Tony Curtis has also been a groundbreaking observer and critic of visual art in Wales, editing two collections of interviews, *Welsh Painters Talking* and *Welsh Artists Talking*.